BLAGDON (Francis William)

PARIS

AS IT WAS AND AS IT IS;

OR

𝕬 𝕾𝖐𝖊𝖙𝖈𝖍 𝖔𝖋 𝖙𝖍𝖊 𝕱𝖗𝖊𝖓𝖈𝖍 𝕮𝖆𝖕𝖎𝖙𝖆𝖑,

ILLUSTRATIVE OF

THE EFFECTS OF THE REVOLUTION,

WITH RESPECT TO

SCIENCES,	EDUCATION,
LITERATURE,	MANNERS,
ARTS,	AND
RELIGION,	AMUSEMENTS;

COMPRISING ALSO

A correct Account of the most remarkable National Establishments and Public Buildings.

𝕴𝖓 𝖆 𝕾𝖊𝖗𝖎𝖊𝖘 𝖔𝖋 𝕷𝖊𝖙𝖙𝖊𝖗𝖘,

WRITTEN BY AN ENGLISH TRAVELLER,

DURING THE YEARS 1801–2,

TO A FRIEND IN LONDON.

Ipsâ varietate tentamus efficere, ut alia aliis, quædem fortasse omnibus placeant.   Plin. Epist.

VOL. I.

LONDON:

PRINTED BY AND FOR C. AND R. BALDWIN, NEW BRIDGE-STREET, BLACKFRIARS.

1803.

ADVERTISEMENT.

IN the course of the following production, the Reader will meet with several references to a Plan of Paris, which it had been intended to prefix to the work; but that intention having been frustrated by the rupture between the two countries, in consequence of which the copies for the whole of the Edition have been detained at Calais, it is hoped that this apology will be accepted for the omission.

CONTENTS.

VOLUME FIRST.

NEW Organization of the National Institute....Page i

INTRODUCTION vii

LETTER I.   Page 1

On the ratification of the preliminary treaty of peace, the author leaves London for Paris—He arrives at Calais on the 16th of October, 1801—Apparent effect of the peace—After having obtained a passport, he proceeds to Paris, in company with a French naval officer.

LETTER II.   5

Journey from Calais to Paris—Improved state of agriculture—None of the French gun-boats off Boulogne moored with chains at the time of the attack—St. Denis—General sweep made, in 1793, among the sepultures in that abbey—Arrival at Paris—Turnpikes now established throughout France—Custom-house scrutiny.

LETTER III.   13

Objects which first stke the observer on arriving at Paris after an absence of ten or twelve years—Tumult in the streets considerably diminished since the revolution—No liveries seen—Streets less dangerous than formerly to pedestrians—Visits paid to different persons by the author—Price of lodgings nearly doubled since 1789—The author takes apartments in a private house.

CONTENTS.

LETTER IV.   Page 21

Climate of Paris—Thermolampes *or stoves which afford light and heat on an economical plan—Sword whose hilt was adorned with the* Pitt *diamond, and others of considerable value, presented to the Chief Consul.*

LETTER V.   27

Plan on which these letters are written.

LETTER VI.   29

The Louvre *or* National Palace of Arts and Sciences *described—*Old Louvre*—Horrors of St. Bartholomew's day—From this palace Charles IX fired on his own subjects—Additions successively made to it by different kings—*Bernini, *sent for by Lewis XIV, forwarded the foundation of the* New Louvre, *and returned to Italy*—Perrault *produced the beautiful colonnade of the* Louvre, *the master-piece of French architecture—Anecdote of the Queen of England, relict of Charles I—Public exhibition of the productions of French Industry.*

LETTER VII.   41

Central Museum of the Arts—Gallery of Antiques—*Description of the different halls and of the most remarkable statues contained in them, with original observations by the learned connoisseur,* Visconti.

LETTER VIII.   53

Description of the Gallery of Antiques *and of its chefs-d'œuvre of sculpture continued and terminated—Noble example set by the French in throwing open their museums and national establishments to public inspection—Liberal indulgence shewn to foreigners.*

CONTENTS.

LETTER IX.   Page 70

General A———y's breakfast—Montmartre—Prospect thence enjoyed—Theatres.

LETTER X.   78

Regulations of the Police to be observed by a stranger on his arrival in the French capital—Pieces represented at the Théâtre Louvois—Palais du gouvernement *or Palace of the Tuileries described—It was constructed by Catherine de Medicis, enlarged by Henry IV and Lewis XIII, and finished by Lewis XIV—The tenth of August,* 1792, *as pourtrayed by an actor in that memorable scene—Number of lives lost on the occasion—Sale of the furniture, the king's wardrobe, and other effects found in the palace—*Place du Carrousel—*Famous horses of gilt bronze brought from Venice and placed here—The fate of France suspended by a thread—Fall of Robespiere and his adherents.*

LETTER XI.   95

Massacre of the prisoners at Paris in September, 1792*—Private ball—The French much improved in dancing—The waltz described—Dress of the women.*

LETTER XII.   107

Bonaparte—Grand monthly parade—Agility of the First Consul in mounting his charger—Consular guards, a remarkably fine body of men—Horses of the French cavalry, sorry in appearance, but capable of enduring fatigue and privations.

LETTER XIII.   114

Jardin des Tuileries—This garden now kept in better

order than under the monarchy—The newly-built house of Véry, the restaurateur—This quarter calls to mind the most remarkable events in the history of the revolution—Place de la Concorde—Its name is a strong contrast to the great number of victims here sacrificed—Execution of the King and Queen, Philippe Égalité, Charlotte Corday, Madame Roland, Robespierre, cum multus aliis—Unexampled dispatch introduced in putting persons to death by means of the guillotine—Guillotin, the inventor or improver of this instrument, dies of grief—Little impression left on the mind of the spectators of these sanguinary scenes —Lord Cornwallis arrives in Paris.

LETTER XIV.   Page 129

National fête, in honour of peace, celebrated in Paris on the 18th of Brumaire, year X (9th of November, 1801)—Garnerin and his wife ascend in a balloon—Brilliancy of the illuminations—Laughable accident.

LETTER XV.   139

Description of the fête continued—Apparent apathy of the people—Songs composed in commemoration of this joyful event—Imitation of one of them.

LETTER XVI.   148

Gallery of the Louvre—Saloon of the Louvre—Italian School—The most remarkable pictures in the collection mentioned, with original remarks on the masters by Visconti—Lord Cornwallis's reception in Paris.

LETTER XVII.   165

Gallery of the Louvre in continuation—French School—

CONTENTS.

Flemish School—The pictures in the Saloon are seen to much greater advantage than those in the Gallery—Gallery of Apollo—These superb repositories of the finest works of art are indiscriminately open to the public.

LETTER XVIII. Page 184

Palais Royal, *now called* Palais du Tribunat—*Its construction begun, in* 1629, *by Cardinal* Richelieu, *who makes a present of it to* Lewis *XIII—It becomes the property of the Orleans family—Anecdote of the Regent—Considerable alterations made in this palace—*Jardin du Palais du Tribunat—*This garden is surrounded by a range of handsome buildings, erected in* 1782 *by the duke of Orleans, then duke of Chartres—The* Cirque *burnt down in* 1797—*Contrast between the company seen here in* 1789 *and in* 1801—*The* Palais Royal, *the theatre of political commotions—Mutual enmity of the queen and the duke of Orleans, which, in the sequel, brought these great personages to the scaffold—Their improper example imitated by the nobility of both sexes—The projects of each defeated—The duke's pusillanimity was a bar to his ambition—He exhausted his immense fortune to gain partisans, and secure the attachment of the people—His imprisonment, trial, and death.*

LETTER XIX. 190

The Palais du Tribunat, *an epitome of all the trades in Paris—Prohibited publications—Mock auctions—* Magazins de confiance à prix fixe—*Two speculations, of a somewhat curious nature, established there with success—The* Palais Royal, *a vortex of dissipation—*

CONTENTS.

Scheme of Merlin *of* Douay *for cleansing this Augæan stable.*

LETTER XX. Page 210

Thé, *a sort of route—Contrast in the mode of life of the Parisians before and since the revolution*—Petits soupers *described—An Englishman improves on all the French* bons vivans *under the old* régime.

LETTER XXI. 217

Public places of various descriptions—Their title and number—Contrast between the interior police now established in the theatres in Paris, and that which existed before the revolution—Admirable regulations at present adopted for the preservation of order at the door of the theatres—Comparatively small number of carriages now seen in waiting at the grand French opera.

LETTER XXII. 235

Palais du Corps Législatif—*Description of the hall of the sittings of that body—Opening of the session—Speech of the President—Lord* Cornwallis *and suite present at this sitting*—Petits appartemens *of the* ci-devant Palais Bourbon *described.*

LETTER XXIII. 247

Halle au Blé—*Lightness of the roof of the dome—Annual consumption of bread-corn in Paris—Astrologers—In former times, their number in Paris exceeded* 30,000—*Fortune-tellers of the present day—Church of St. Eustache—Tourville, the brave opponent of Admiral* Russel, *had no epitaph—Festivals of reason described.*

CONTENTS.

LETTER XXIV. Page 259

Museum of French Monuments—*Steps taken by the Constituent Assembly to arrest the progress of Vandalism—Many master-pieces of painting, sculpture, and architecture, destroyed in various parts of France*—Grégoire, *ex-bishop of Blois, publishes three reports, to expose the madness of irreligious barbarism, which claim particular distinction.—They saved from destruction many articles of value in the provinces—Antique monuments found in* 1711, *in digging among the foundation of the ancient church of Paris—Indefatigable exertions of* Lenoir, *the conservator of this museum—The halls of this museum fitted up according to the precise character peculiar to each century, and the monuments arranged in them in historical and chronological order—Tombs of* Clovis, Childebert, *and* Chilperic—*Statues of* Charlemagne, Lewis IX, *and of* Charles, *his brother, together with those of the kings that successively appeared in this age down to king* John —*Tombs of* Charles V, Du Guesclin, *and* Sancerre—*Mausolea of* Louis d'Orléans *and of* Valentine de Milan—*Statues of* Charles VI, Renée d'Orléans, Philippe de Commines, Lewis XI, Charles VII, Joan *of* Arc, Isabeau de Bavière—*Tomb of* Lewis XII—*Tragical death of* Charles *the* Bad.

LETTER XXV. 274

Museum of French Monuments *continued—Tombs of* Francis I, *of the* Valois, *and of* Diane de Poitiers —*Character of that celebrated woman—Statues of* Turenne, Condé, Colbert, La Fontaine, Racine, *and*

CONTENTS.

Lewis XIV—*Mausolea of Cardinals* Richelieu *and* Mazarin—*Statues of* Montesquieu, Fontenelle, Voltaire, Rousseau, Helvetius, Crébillon, *and* Piron—*Tombs of* Maupertuis, Caylus, *and Marshal* d'Harcourt—*This museum contains a chronology of monuments, both antique and modern, from* 2500 *years before our era down to the present time, beginning with those of ancient Greece, and following all the gradations of the art from its cradle to its decrepitude—Sepulchre of* Héloïse *and* Abélard.

LETTER XXVI. Page 287

*Dinner at General A———y's—Difference in the duration of such a repast now and before the revolution—The General's ancestor, François A———y, planned and completed the famous canal of Languedoc—*Dépôt de la guerre—*Such an establishment much wanted in England—Its acknowledged utility has induced Austria, Spain, and Portugal, to form others of a similar nature—Geographical and topographical riches of this* dépôt.

LETTER XXVII. 304

Boulevards—*Their extent—Amusements they present—*Porte St. Denis—*Anecdote of Charles VI*—Porte St. Martin—La Magdeleine—*Ambulating conjurers—Means they employ to captivate curiosity.*

LETTER XXVIII. 315

French funds and national debt—Supposed liquidation of an annuity held by a foreigner before the war, and yet unliquidated—Value of a franc.

LETTER XXIX.   Page 327.

Grand monthly parade—Etiquette observed on this occasion, in the apartments of the palace of the Tuileries—Bonaparte—*His person—His public character in* Paris—*Obstruction which the First Consul met with in returning from the parade*—Champs Elysées—*Sports and diversions there practised—Horses, brought from Marly to this spot, the master-pieces of the two celebrated sculptors,* Costou—*Comparison they afford to politicians.*

LETTER XXX.   342

Madonna de Foligno—*Description of the method employed by the French artists to transfer from pannel to canvass this celebrated master-piece of* Raphael.

LETTER XXXI.   356

Pont Neuf—*Henry IV—His popularity—Historical fact concerning the cause of his assassination brought to light—The Seine swollen by the rains—It presents a dull scene in comparison to the Thames—Great number of washerwomen*—La Samaritaine—*Shoe-blacks on the* Pont Neuf—*Their trade decreased—Recruiting Officers—The allurements they formerly employed are now become unnecessary in consequence of the conscription—Anecdote of a British officer on whom a French recruiter had cast his eye--Disappointment that ensued.*

LETTER XXXII.   369

Balls now very numerous every evening in Paris—Bal du Salon des Étrangers—*Description of the women—Comparison between the French and English ladies—Character of Madame* Tallien—*Generosity, fortitude, and greatness of soul displayed by women during the most calamitous periods of the revolution—Anecdote of a young Frenchman smitten by a widow—An attachment, founded on somewhat similar circumstances, recorded by historians of Henry III of France—Sympathy, and its effects.*

LETTER XXXIII. Page 382

Pont National, *formerly called the* Pont Royal—*Anecdote of Henry IV and a waterman—Coup d'œil from this bridge—Quays of Paris—Galiot of St. Cloud—* Pont de la Concorde—*Paris besieged by the Swedes, Danes, and Normans, in* 885—*The Seine covered with their vessels for the space of two leagues—A vessel ascends the Seine from Rouen to Paris in four days—Engineers have ever judged it practicable to render the Seine navigable, from its mouth to the capital, for vessels of a certain burden—Riches accruing from commerce pave the way to the ruin of States, as well as the extension of their conquests.*

LETTER XXXIV. 391

French literature—Effects produced on it by the revolution—The sciences preferred to literature, and for what reason—The French government has flattered the literati and artists; but the solid distinctions have been reserved for men of science—Epic Poetry—Tragedy—Comedy—Novels—Moral Fable—Madrigal and Epigram—Romance—Lyric Poetry—Song—Journals.

LETTER XXXV. 408

Pont au Change—Palais de Justice—*Once a royal residence—Banquet given there, in* 1313, *by Philip the*

Fair, at which were present Edward II and his queen Isabella—Alterations which this palace has undergone, in consequence of having, at different times, been partly reduced to ashes—Madame La Motte publicly whipped —In 1738, *Lewis XVI here held a famous bed of justice, in which* D'Espresmenil *struck the first blow at royalty—He was exiled to the* Ile de St. Marguerite—*After having stirred up all the parliaments against the royal authority, he again became the humble servant of the crown—After the revolution, the* Palais de Justice *was the seat of the Revolutionary Tribunal—* Dumas, *its president, proposed to assemble there five or six hundred victims at a time—He was the next day condemned to death by the same tribunal—The* Palais de Justice, *now the seat of different tribunals—The* grande chambre *newly embellished in the antique style*—La Conciergerie, *the place of confinement of* Lavoisier, Malsherbes, Cordorcet, &c.—*Fortitude displayed by the hapless* Marie-Antoinette *after her condemnation* —Pont St. Michel—Pont Notre-Dame—*Cathedral of* Notre-Dame—*Anecdote of* Pepin *the Short—Devastations committed in this cathedral—Medallions of* Abélard *and* Héloïse *to be seen near* Notre-Dame *in front of the house where* Fulbert, *her supposed uncle, resided*—Petit Pont—Pont au Double—Pont Marie— *Workmen now employed in the construction of three new bridges*—Pont de la Tournelle.

LETTER XXXVI. Page 429

Paris a charming abode for a man of fortune—Summary of its advantages—Idalium—Tivoli—Frascati— Paphos—La Phantasmagorie *of* Robertson—Fitzjames, *the famous ventriloquist—Method of converting a ga-*

tantee-show into an exhibition somewhat similar to that of the phantasmagorists.

LETTER XXXVII. Page 437

Paris the most melancholy abode in the world for a man without money—Restaurateurs—*In* 1765, Boulanger *first conceived the idea of* restoring *the exhausted animal functions of the debilitated Parisians—He found many imitators—The* restaurateurs, *in order to make their business answer, constitute themselves* traiteurs—La Barrière—Beauvilliers, Robert, Naudet, *and* Véry *dispute the palm in the art of Appicius—Description of* Beauvilliers' *establishment—His bill of fare—Expense of dining at a fashionable* restaurateur's *in Paris—Contrast between establishments of this kind existing before the revolution, and those in vogue at the present day—Cheap eating-houses—The company now met with at the fashionable rendezvous of good cheer compared with that seen here in former times—Cabinets* particuliers—*Uses to which they are applied—Advantages of a* restaurateur's—Beauvilliers *pays great attention to his guests—Cleanly and alert waiters—This establishment is admirably well managed.*

VOLUME SECOND.

LETTER XXXVIII.   Page 1

National Institution of the Deaf and Dumb—France indebted to the philanthropic Abbé de l'Épée *for the discovery of the mode of instructing them—It has been greatly improved by* Sicard, *the present Institutor—Explanation of his system of instruction—The deaf and dumb are taught grammar, metaphysics, logic, religion, the use of the globes, geography, arithmetic, history, natural history, arts and trades—Almost every thing used by them is made by themselves—Lessons of analysis which astonish the spectators.*

LETTER XXXIX.   12

*Public women—Charlemagne endeavours to banish them from Paris—His daughters, though addicted to illicit enjoyments, die universally regretted—*Les Filles Dieu*—*Les Filles pénitentes ou repenties*—Courtesans—Luxury displayed in their equipages and houses—Kept women—Opera-dancers—Secret police maintained by Lewis XVI, in 1792—Grisettes—Demireps—A French woman, at thirty, makes an excellent friend—*Rousseau's *opinion of this particular class of women in Paris.*

LETTER XL.

*National Institution of the Industrious Blind—Circumstance which gave rise to this establishment—*Valentin Haüy, *its founder, found his project seconded by* the Philanthropic Society—His plan of instruction detailed—Museum of the Blind—After two or three lessons, a blind child here teaches himself to read without the further help of any master.

LETTER XLI.   Page 47

Théâtre des Arts et de la République, or Grand French opera—Old opera-house burnt down, and a new one built and opened in 72 days—Description of the present house—Operas of Gluck; also those of Piccini and Sacchini—Gluckists and Piccinists—The singing is the weakest department at the French opera—Merits of the singers of both sexes—Choruses very full—Orchestra famous—The Chief Consul, being very partial to Italian music, sends to that land of harmony to procure the finest musical compositions.

LETTER XLII.   64

Dancing improved in France—Effect of some of the ballets—Noverre and Gardel first introduce them on the French stage—Rapid change of scenery—Merits of the dancers of both sexes—The rector of St. Roch refuses to admit into that church the corpse of Mademoiselle Chameroi—The dancers in private society now emulate those who make dancing their profession—Receipts of the opera.

LETTER XLIII.   79

New year's day still celebrated in Paris on the 1st of January—Customs which prevail there on that occasion—Denon's account of the French expedition to Egypt—That country was the cradle of the arts and sciences—Fourrier confirms the theory of Dupuis, respecting the origin, &c. of the figures of the Zodiac.

CONTENTS.

LETTER XLIV. Page 85

Hôtel des Invalides—*It was projected by Henry IV and erected by Lewis XIV—Temple of Mars—To its arches are suspended the standards and colours taken from the enemy—Two British flags only are among th number—Monument of* Turenne—*Circumstances of his death—Dome of the* Invalides—*Its refectories and kitchens—Anecdote of Peter the Great—Reflections on establishments of this description*—Champ de Mars—École Militaire—*Various scenes of which the* Champ de Mars *has been the theatre—Death of* Bailly—*Modern national fêtes in France, a humble imitation of the Olympic games.*

LETTER XLV. 102

Object of the different learned and scientific institutions, which, before the revolution, held their sittings in the Louvre—*Anecdote of Cardinal Richelieu—National Institute of Arts and Sciences—Organization of that learned body—Description of the apartments of the Institute—Account of its public quarterly meeting of the* 15th Nivose, *year X, (*5th *of January,* 1802*)—Marriage of Mademoiselle* Beauharnois *to* Louis Bonaparte.

LETTER XLVI. 111

Opéra Buffa—*The Italian comedians who came to Paris in* 1788, *had a rapid influence on the musical taste of the French public—Performers of the new Italian company—Productions of* Cimarosa, Paësiello, *&c.*—Madame Bolla.

LETTER XLVII. 119

Present state of public worship—Summary of the proceedings of the constitutional clergy—National councils

CONTENTS.

of the Gallican church held at Paris—Conduct of the Pope, Pius VII—The Cardinal Legate, Caprara, arrives in Paris—The Concordat is signed—Subsequent transactions.

LETTER XLVIII.   Page 134

Pantheon—Description of this edifice—Marat and Mirabeau pantheonized and dispantheonized—The remains of Voltaire and Rousseau removed hither—The Pantheon in danger of falling—This apprehension no longer exists—Bonaparte leaves Paris for Lyons.

LETTER XLIX.   142

Scientific societies of Paris—Société Philotechnique—Société Libre des Sciences, Lettres, et Arts—Athenée des Arts—Société Philomatique—Société Académique des Sciences—Société Galvanique—Société des Belles-Lettres—Académie de Législation—Observateurs de l'Homme—Athenée de Paris.

LETTER L.   153

Coffee-houses—Character of the company who frequent them—Contrast between the coffee-houses of the present and former times—Coffee first introduced at Paris, in 1669, by the Turkish ambassador—Café méchanique—Subterraneous coffee-houses of the Palais du Tribunat.

LETTER LI.   163

Public instruction—The ancient colleges and universities are replaced by Primary Schools, Secondary Schools, Lyceums, and Special Schools—National pupils—Annual cost of these establishments—Contrast between the old system of education and the new plan, recently organized.

CONTENTS:

LETTER LII. Page 179

Milliners—Montesquieu's *observation on the commands of the fair sex*—*Millinery a very extensive branch of trade in Paris*—Bal de l'Opéra—*Dress of the men and women*—*Adventures are the chief object of those who frequent these masquerades.*

LETTER LIII. 185

Théâtre Français de la République—*The house described*—*List of the stock-pieces*—*Names of their authors*—Fabre d'Eglantine—*His* Philinte de Molière *a chef-d'œuvre*—*Some account of its author*—La Chaussée *the father of the* drame, *a tragi-comic species of dramatic composition.*

LETTER LIV. 199

Principal performers in tragedy at the Théâtre Français —Vanhove, Monvel, St. Prix, and Naudet—Talma, *and* Lafond—St. Fal, Damas, *and* Dupont—*Mesdames* Raucourt *and* Vestris—*Mesdames* Fleury, Talma, Bourgoin, *and* Volnais—*Mesdames* Suin *and* Thénard—Début *of Mademoiselle* Duchesnois, *Madame* Xavier, *and Mademoiselle* Georges—*Disorderly conduct of the* Duchesnistes, *who are routed by the* Georgistes.

LETTER LV. 223

Principal performers in comedy at the Théâtre Français —Vanhove, *and* Naudet—Molé, Fleury, *and* Baptiste *the elder*—St. Fal, Dupont, Damas, *and* Armand—Grandménil, *and* Caumont—Dugazon, Dazincourt, *and* Larochelle—*Mesdemoiselles* Contat, *and* Mézeray—*Madame* Talma—*Mesdemoiselles* Mars, Bourgoin, *and* Gros—*Mesdemoiselles* Lachassaigne *and* Thénard—*Mesdemoi-*

VOL. I. b

selles Devienne *and* Desbrosses—*Contrast between the state of the French stage before and since the revolution.*

LETTER LVI.   Page 247

French women fond of appearing in male attire—Costume of the French Ladies—Contrast it now presents to that formerly worn—The change in their dress has tended to strengthen their constitution—The women in Paris extremely cleanly in their persons—Are now very healthy.

LETTER LVII.   251

The studies in the colleges and universities interrupted by bands of insurgents—Collège de France—*It is in this country the only establishment where every branch of human knowledge is taught in its fullest extent—Was founded by Francis I—Disputes between this new College and the University—Its increasing progress—The improvements in the sciences spread by the instruction of this College—Its present state.*

LETTER LVIII.   262

Théâtre de l'Opéra Comique—*Authors who have furnished it with stock-pieces, and composers who have set them to music—Principal performers at this theatre*—Elleviou, Gavaudan, Philippe, *and* Gaveaux—Chenard, Martin, Rézicourt, Juliet, *and* Moreau—Solié, *and* St. Aubin—Dozainville, *and* Lesage—*Mesdames* St. Aubin, Scio, Lesage, Crétu, Philis *the elder*, Gavaudan, *and* Pingenet—*Mesdames* Dugazon, Philippe, *and* Gonthier.

LETTER LIX.   276

France owes her salvation to the savans or men of science

—*Polytechnic School—Its object—Its formation and subsequent progress—Changes recently introduced into this interesting establishment.*

LETTER LX.   Page 285

Pickpockets and sharpers—Anecdote of a female swindler—Anecdote of a sharper—Housebreakers—Chauffeurs—A new species of assassins—Place de Grève —Punishment for thieves re-established—On the continent, ladies flock to the execution of criminals.

LETTER LXI.   295

Schools for Public Services—The Polytechnic School, the grand nursery whence the pupils are transplanted into the Schools of Artillery, Military Engineers, Bridges and Highways, Mines, Naval Engineers, and Navigation—Account of these schools—Prytanée Français— Special Schools—Special School of Painting and Sculpture—Competitions—National School of Architecture— Conservatory of Music—Present state of Music in France—Music has done wonders in reviving the courage of the French soldiers—The French are no less indebted to Rouget de Lille, *author of the* Marseillois, *than the Spartans were to* Tyrtæus—*Gratuitous School for Drawing—Veterinary School—New Special Schools to be established in France.*

LETTER LXII.   317

Funerals—No medium in them under the old régime— Ceremonies formerly observed—Those practised at the present day—Marriages—Contrast they present.

LETTER LXIII.   324

*Public Libraries—*Bibliothèque Nationale—*Its acquisi-*

tions since the revolution—School for Oriental Living Languages.

LETTER LXIV. 339

Bibliothèque Mazarine—Bibliothèque du Panthéon—Bibliothèque de l'Arsenal—The Arsenal—Other libraries and literary depôts in Paris.

LETTER LXV. 343

Dancing—Nomenclature of caperers in Paris, from the wealthiest classes down to the poorest—Beggars form the last link of the chain.

LETTER LXVI. 348

Bureau des Longitudes—Is on a more extensive scale than the Board of Longitude in England—National Observatory—Subterraneous quarries that have furnished the stone with which most of the houses in Paris are constructed—Measures taken to prevent the buildings in Paris from being swallowed up in these extensive labyrinths—Present state of the Observatory—Lalande, Méchain, and Bouvard—Carroché, and Lenoir—Lavoisier, and Borda—Delambre, Laplace, Burckhardt, Vidal, Biot, and Puisson—New French weights and measures—Concise account of the operations employed in measuring an arc of the terrestrial meridian—Table of the new French measures and weights—Their correspondence with the old, and also with those of England.

LETTER LXVII. 364

Dépôt de la Marine—An establishment much wanted in England.

CONTENTS.

LETTER LXVIII. Page 366

Théâtre Louvois—Picard, *the manager of this theatre, is the Molière of his company*—La Grande Ville, ou les Provinciaux à Paris—*Principal performers at this theatre*—Picard, Devigny, Dorsan, *and* Clozel—*Mesdemoiselles* Adeline, Molière, Lescot, *and Madame* Molé—Théâtre du Vaudeville—*Authors who write for this theatre*—*Principal performers*—*Public malignity, the main support of this theatre.*

LETTER LXIX. 370

Hôtel de la Monnaie—*Description of this building*—Musée des Mines—*Formed by M. Sage*—*The arrangement of this cabinet is excellent*—Cabinet du Conseil des Mines—*Principal mineral substances discovered in France since the revolution.*

LETTER LXX. 390

Théâtre Montansier—*Principal performers*—Ambigu Comique—*The curiosity of a stranger may be satisfied in a single visit to each of the minor theatres in Paris.*

LETTER LXXI. 394

Police of Paris—*Historical sketch of it*—*Its perfections and imperfections*—*Anecdote of a minister of police*—Mouchards—*Anecdote which shews the detestation in which they are held*—*The Parisian police extends to foreign countries*—*This truth exemplified by two remarkable facts*—*No* habeas corpus *in France.*

LETTER LXXII. 422

The savans *saved France, when their country was invaded*—*Astonishing exertions made by the French on that occasion—Anecdote relating to* Robespierre *—Extraordinary resources created by the men of science—Means employed for increasing the manufacture of powder, cannon, and muskets—The produce of these new manufactories contrasted with that of the old ones—Territorial acquisitions of the French—The Carnival revived in Paris.*

LETTER LXXIII. Page 437

*Public gaming-houses—*Académies de jeu, *which existed in Paris before the revolution—Gaming-houses licensed by the police—The privilege of granting those licences is farmed by a private individual—Description of the* Maisons de jeu*—Anecdote of an old professed gambler—Gaming prevails in all the principal towns of France—The excuse of the old government for promoting gaming, is reproduced at the present day.*

LETTER LXXIV. 447

Museum of Natural History, or Jardin des Plantes*—Is much enlarged since the revolution—One of the first establishments of instruction in Europe—Contrast between its former state and that in which it now is—*Fourcroy, *the present director—His eloquence—Collections in this establishment—Curious articles which claim particular notice.*

LETTER LXXV. 455

The Carnival—That of 1802 described—The Carnival of modern times, an imitation of the Saturnalia of the ancients—Was for some years prohibited, since the revolution—Contrast between the Carnival under the monarchy and under the republican government.

LETTER LXXVI. 461

Palais du Sénat Conservateur, *or* Luxembourg *Palace—*

CONTENTS.

Mary of Medicis, by whom it was erected, died in a garret—It belonged to Monsieur, before the revolution—Improvements in the garden of the Senate—National nursery formed in an adjoining piece of ground—Bastille—Le Temple—Its origin—Lewis XVI and his family confined in this modern state-prison.

LETTER LXXVII. Page 468

Present state of the French Press—The liberty of the press, the measure of civil liberty—Comparison between the state of the press in France and in England.

LETTER LXXVIII. 477

Hospitals and other charitable institutions—Hôtel-Dieu—Extract from the report of the Academy of Sciences on this abode of pestilence—Reforms introduced into it since the revolution—The present method of purifying French hospitals deserves to be adopted in England—Other hospitals in Paris—Hospice de la Maternité—La Salpêtrière—Bicêtre—Faculties and Colleges of Physicians, as well as Colleges and Commonalties of Surgeons, replaced in France by Schools of Health—School of Medicine of Paris—France overrun by quacks—New law for checking the serious mischief they occasion—Society of Medicine—Gratuitous School of Pharmacy—Free Society of Apothecaries—Changes in the teaching and practice of medicine in France.

LETTER LXXIX. 491

Private seminaries for youth of both sexes—Female education—Contrast between that formerly received in convents, and that now practised in the modern French boarding-schools.

CONTENTS.

LETTER LXXX. Page 495

*Progressive aggrandisement of Paris—Its origin—Under the name of Lutetia, it was the capital of Gaul—Julian's account of it—The sieges it has sustained—Successively embellished by different kings—Progressive amelioration of the manners of its inhabitants—Rapid view of the causes which improved them, from the reign of Philip Augustus to that of Lewis XIV—Contrast between the number of public buildings before and since the revolution—Population of Paris, from official documents—Ancient division of Paris—Is now divided into twelve mayoralties—*Barrières *and high wall by which it is surrounded—Anecdote of the* commis des barrières *seizing an Egyptian mummy.*

LETTER LXXXI. 507

French Furniture—The events of the revolution have contributed to improve the taste of persons connected with the furnishing line—Contrast between the style of the furniture in the Parisian houses in 1789-90 *and* 1801-2 *—Les Gobelins, the celebrated national manufactory for tapestry—La Savonnerie, a national manufactory for carpeting—National manufactory of plate-glass.*

LETTER LXXXII. 515

Academy of Fine Arts at the ci-devant *Collège de Navarre—Description of the establishment of the* Piranesi *—Three hundred artists of different nations distributed in the seven classes of this academy—Different works executed here in Painting, Sculpture, Architecture, Mosaic, and Engraving.*

LETTER LXXXIII.   Page 522

*Conservatory of Arts and Trades—It contains a numerous collection of machines of every description employed in the mechanical arts—*Belier hydraulique, *newly invented by* Montgolfier—*Models of curious buildings—The mechanical arts in France have experienced more or less the impulse given to the sciences—The introduction of the Spanish merinos has greatly improved the French wools—New inventions and discoveries adopted in the French manufactories—Characteristic difference of the present state of French industry, and that in which it was before the revolution.*

LETTER LXXXIV.   526

Society for the encouragement of national industry—Its origin—Its objects detailed—Free Society of Agriculture—Amidst the storms of the revolution, agriculture has been improved in France—Causes of that improvement—The present state of agriculture briefly contrasted with that which existed before the revolution—Didot's stereotypic editions of the classics—Advantages attending the use of stereotype—This invention claimed by France, but proved to belong to Britain—Printing-office of the Republic, the most complete typographical establishment in being.

LETTER LXXXV.   537

Present State of Society in Paris—In that city are three very distinct kinds of society—Description of each of these—Other societies are no more than a diminutive of the preceding—Philosophy of the French in forgetting their misfortunes and losses—The signature of the

*definitive treaty announced by the sound of cannon—
In the evening a grand illumination is displayed.*

LETTER LXXXVI.   Page 547

Urbanity of the Parisians towards strangers—The shopkeepers in Paris overcharge their articles—Furnished Lodgings—Their price—The Milords Anglais *now eclipsed by the Russian Counts—Expense of board in Paris—Job and Hackney Carriages—Are much improved since the revolution—Fare of the latter—Expense of the former—Cabriolets—Regulations of the police concerning these carriages—The negligence of drivers now meets with due chastisement—French women astonish bespattered foreigners by walking the streets with spotless stockings—Valets-de-Place—Their wages augmented—General Observations—An English traveller, on visiting Paris, should provide himself with letters of recommendation—Unless an Englishman acquires a competent knowledge of the manners of the country, he fails in what ought to be the grand object of foreign travel—Situation of one who brings no letters to Paris—The French now make a distinction between individuals only, not between nations—Are still indulgent to the English—Animadversion on the improper conduct of irrational British youths.*

LETTER LXXXVII.   560

Divorce—The indissolubility of marriage in France, before the revolution, was supposed to promote adultery—No such excuse can now be pleaded—Origin of the present laws on divorce—Comparison on that subject between the French and the Romans—The effect of these laws illustrated by examples—The stage ought to be made to conduce to the amelioration of morals—In France, the men blame the women, with a view of extenuating their own irregularities—To reform women, men ought to begin by reforming themselves.

LETTER LXXXVIII. Page 570

*The author is recalled to England—Mendicants—The streets of Paris less infested by them now than before the revolution—Pawnbrokers—Their numbers much increased in Paris, and why—*Mont de Piété*—Lotteries now established in the principal towns in France—The fatal consequences of this incentive to gaming—Newspapers—Their numbers considerably augmented—Journals the most in request—Baths—Bains Vigier described—School of Natation—Telegraphs—Those in Paris differ from those in use in England—Telegraphic language may be abridged—Private collections most deserving of notice in Paris—*Dépôt d'armes *of M. Boutet—M. Regnier, an ingenious mechanic—The author's reason for confining his observations to the capital—Metamorphoses in Paris—The site of the famous Jacobin convent is intended for a market-place—Arts and Sciences are become popular in France, since the revolution—The author makes* amende *honorable, or confesses his inability to accomplish the task imposed on him by his friend—He leaves Paris.*

ERRATA.

☞ *Some of the following being typographical or other errors which may affect the sense, the Reader is requested to mark them with a pen or pencil, before he enters on the work.*

VOL. I.

Page 11 Line 15 *for* forty-eight *read* fifty-eight
    43 —— 27 *for* Place du Louvre *read* Place du Vieux Louvre
    184 —— 19 *for* Wolseley *read* Wolsey
    214 —— 12 *for* of partie quarrée *read* of a partie quarrée
    329 —— 6 *for* and *read* or
    341 —— 8 *for* surname *read* christian name
    363 —— 16 *for* and of the chimes *read* and that of the chimes
    433 —— 24 *for* Fitzames *read* Fitzjames

VOL. II.

Page 60 Line 7 *for* he is a counter-tenor *read* he sings bass
    109 —— 7 *for* hundred *read* thousand
    128 —— 14 *for* devote *read* expose
    130 —— 23 *for* council; a similar *read* council; and a similar
    165 —— 12 *for* was *read* were
    266 —— 21 *for* Elleviou behind *read* Elleviou leaves behind
    364 —— 20 *for* have been *read* has been
    392 —— 3 *for* injures *read* insures
    427 —— 11 *for* asked them for orders *read* asked for orders
    432 —— 4 *for* in *read* on
    460 —— 15 *for* but some *read* but the dress of some
    517 —— 9 *for* marble *read* stone
    518 —— 4 *for* principle *read* principal

NEW ORGANIZATION

...... OF THE

NATIONAL INSTITUTE.*

On the 3d of Pluviôse, year XI (23d of January, 1803), the French government passed the following decree on this subject.

Art. I. The National Institute, at present divided into three classes, shall henceforth consist of four; namely:

First Class { Class of physical and mathematical sciences.

Second Class { Class of the French language and literature.

Third Class—Class of history and ancient literature.
Fourth Class—Class of fine arts.

The present members of the Institute and associated foreigners shall be divided into these four classes. A commission of five members of the Institute, appointed by the First Consul, shall present to him the plan of this division, which shall be submitted to the approbation of the government.

II. The first class shall be formed of the ten sections, which at present compose the first class of the Institute, of a new section of geography and navigation, and of eight foreign associates.

These sections shall be composed and distinguished as follows:

* Referred to in page 104, Vol. II of this work.

Mathematical Sciences.

Geometry...................... six members.
Mechanics..................... six ditto.
Astronomy..................... six ditto.
Geography and Navigation......... three ditto.
General Physics................ six ditto.

Physical Sciences.

Chemistry..................... six ditto.
Mineralogy.................... six ditto.
Botany........................ six ditto.
Rural Economy and the Veterinary Art. six ditto.
Anatomy and Zoology............ six ditto.
Medicine and Surgery........... six ditto.

The first class shall name, with the approbation of the Chief Consul, two perpetual secretaries; the one for the mathematical sciences; the other, for the physical. The perpetual secretaries shall be members of the class, but shall make no part of any section.

The first class may elect six of its members from among the other classes of the Institute. It may name a hundred correspondents, taken from among the learned men of the nation, and those of foreign countries.

III. The second class shall be composed of forty members.

It is particularly charged with the compilation and improvement of the dictionary of the French tongue. With respect to language, it shall examine important works of literature, history, and sciences. The collection of its critical observations shall be published at least four times a year.

It shall appoint from its own members, and with the approbation of the First Consul, a perpetual secretary, who shall continue to make one of the sixty members of whom the class is composed.

It may elect twelve of its members from among those of the other classes of the Institute.

IV. The third class shall be composed of forty members and eight foreign associates.

The learned languages, antiquities and ornaments, history, and all the moral and political sciences in as far as they relate to history, shall be the objects of its researches and labours. It shall particularly endeavour to enrich French literature with the works of Greek, Latin, and Oriental authors, which have not yet been translated.

It shall employ itself in the continuation of diplomatic collections.

With the approbation of the First Consul, it shall name from its own members a perpetual secretary, who shall make one of the forty members of whom the class is composed.

It may elect nine of its members from among those of the classes of the Institute.

It may name sixty national or foreign correspondents.

V. The fourth class shall be composed of twenty-eight members and eight foreign associates. They shall be divided into sections, named and composed as follows:

Painting.......................ten members.
Sculpture......................six ditto.
Architecture...................six ditto.
Engraving......................three ditto.
Music (composition)............three ditto.

With the approbation of the First Consul, it shall appoint a perpetual secretary, who shall be a member of the class, but shall not make part of the sections.

It may elect six of its members from among the other classes of the Institute.

It may name thirty-six national or foreign correspondents.

VI. The associated foreign members shall have a deliberative vote only for objects relating to sciences, literature, and arts. They shall not make part of any section, and shall receive no salary.

VII. The present associates of the Institute, scattered throughout the Republic, shall make part of the one hundred and ninety-six correspondents, attached to the classes of the sciences, belles-lettres, and fine arts.

The correspondents cannot assume the title of members of the Institute. They shall drop that of correspondents, when they take up their constant residence in Paris.

VIII. The nominations to the vacancies shall be made by each of the classes in which those vacancies shall happen to occur. The persons elected shall be approved by the First Consul.

IX. The members of the four classes shall have a right to attend reciprocally the private sittings of each of them, and to read papers there when they have made the request.

They shall assemble four times a year as the body of the Institute, in order to give to each other an account of their transactions.

They shall elect in common the librarian and under-librarian, as well as all the agents who belong in common to the Institute.

Each class shall present for the approbation of the

government the particular statutes and regulations of its interior police.

X. Each class shall hold every year a public sitting, at which the other three shall assist.

XI. The Institute shall receive annually, from the public treasury, 1500 francs for each of its members, not associates; 6000 francs for each of its perpetual secretaries; and, for its expenses, a sum which shall be determined on, every year, at the request of the Institute, and comprised in the budget of the Minister of the Interior.

XII. The Institute shall have an administrative commission, composed of five members, two of the first class, and one of each of the other three, appointed by their respective classes.

This commission shall cause to be regulated in the general sittings, prescribed in Art. IX, every thing relative to the administration, to the general purposes of the Institute, and to the division of the funds between the four classes.

Each class shall afterwards regulate the employment of the funds which shall have been assigned for its expenses, as well as every thing that concerns the printing and publication of its memoirs.

XIII. Every year, each class shall distribute prizes, the number and value of which shall be regulated as follows:

The first class, a prize of 3000 francs.

The second and third classes, each a prize of 1500 francs.

And the fourth class, great prizes of painting, sculpture, architecture, and musical composition. Those who shall have gained one of these four great prizes, shall be sent to Rome, and maintained at the expense of the government.

XIV. The Minister of the Interior is charged with the execution of the present decree, which shall be inserted in the Bulletin of the Laws.

INTRODUCTION.

On ushering into the world a literary production, custom has established that its parent should give some account of his offspring. Indeed, this becomes the more necessary at the present moment, as the short-lived peace, which gave birth to the following sheets, had already ceased before they were entirely printed; and the war in which England and France are now engaged, is of a nature calculated not only to rouse all the energy and ancient spirit of my countrymen, but also to revive their prejudices, and inflame their passions, in a degree proportionate to the enemy's boastful and provoking menace.

I therefore premise that those who may be tempted to take up this publication, merely with a view of seeking aliment for their enmity, will, in more respects than one, probably find themselves disappointed. The two nations were not rivals in arms, but in the arts and sciences, at the time these letters were written, and committed to the press; consequently, they have no relation whatever to the present contest. Nevertheless, as they refer to subjects which manifest the indefatigable activity of the French in the accomplishment of any grand object, such parts may, perhaps, furnish hints that may not be altogether unimportant at this momentous crisis.

The plan most generally adhered to throughout this work, being detailed in LETTER V, a repetition of it here would be superfluous; and the principal matters to which the work itself relates, are specified in the title. I now come to the point.

A long residence in France, and particularly in the capital, having afforded me an opportunity of becoming tolerably well acquainted with its state before the revolution, my curiosity was strongly excited to ascertain the changes which that political phenomenon might have effected. I accordingly availed myself of the earliest dawn of peace to cross the water, and visit Paris. Since I had left that city in 1789-90, a powerful monarchy, established on a possession of fourteen centuries, and on that sort of national prosperity which seemed to challenge the approbation of future ages, had been destroyed by the force of opinion, which, like a subterraneous fire, consumed its very foundations, and plunged the nation into a sea of troubles, in which it was, for several years, tossed about, amid the wreck of its greatness.

This is a phenomenon of which antiquity affords no parallel; and it has produced a rapid succession of events so extraordinary as almost to exceed belief.

It is not the crimes to which it has given birth that will be thought improbable: the history of revolutions, as well ancient as modern, furnishes but too many examples of them; and few have been committed, the traces of which are not to be found in the countries where the imagination of the multitude has been exalted by strong and new ideas respecting Liberty and Equality. But what posterity will find difficult to believe, is the agitation of men's minds, and the effervescence of the passions, carried to such a pitch, as to stamp the French revolution with a character bordering on the marvellous——Yes; posterity will have reason to be astonished at the facility with which the human mind can be modified and made to pass from one extreme to another; at the suddenness, in short, with which the ideas and manners of the French were changed; so powerful, on the one hand, is the ascendency of certain imaginations; and, on the other, so great is the weakness of the vulgar!

It is in the recollection of most persons, that the agitation of the public mind in France was such, for a while, that, after having overthrown the monarchy and its supports; rendered private property insecure; and destroyed individual freedom; it threatened to invade foreign countries, at the same time pushing before it Liberty, that first blessing of man, when it is founded on laws, and the most dangerous of chimeras, when it is without rule or restraint.

The greater part of the causes which excited this general commotion, existed before the assembly of the States-General in 1789. It is therefore important to take a mental view of the moral and political situation of France at that period, and to follow, in imagination at least, the chain of ideas, passions, and errors, which, having dissolved the ties of society, and worn out the springs of government, led the nation by gigantic strides into the most complete anarchy.

Without enumerating the different authorities which successively ruled in France after the fall of the throne, it appears no less essential to remind the reader that, in this general disorganization, the inhabitants themselves, though breathing the same air, scarcely knew that they belonged to the same nation. The altars overthrown; all the ancient institutions annihilated; new festivals and ceremonies introduced; factious demagogues honoured with an apotheosis; their busts exposed to public veneration; men and cities changing names; a portion of the people infected with atheism, and disguised in the livery of guilt and folly; all this, and more, exercised the reflection of the well-disposed in a manner the most painful. In a word, though France was peopled with the same individuals, it seemed inhabited by a new nation, entirely different from the old one in its government, its creed, its principles, its manners, and even its customs.

War itself assumed a new face. Every thing relating to it became extraordinary: the number of the combatants, the manner of recruiting the armies, and the means of providing supplies for them; the manufacture of powder, cannon, and muskets; the ardour, impetuosity, and forced marches of the troops; their extortions, their successes, and their reverses; the choice of the generals, and the superior talents of some of them, together with the springs, by which these enormous bodies of armed men were moved and directed, were equally new and astonishing.

History tells us that in poor countries, where nothing inflames cupidity and ambition, the love alone of the public good causes changes to be tried in the government; and that those changes derange not the ordinary course of society; whereas, among rich nations, corrupted by luxury, revolutions are always effected through secret motives of jealousy and interest; because there are great places to be usurped, and great fortunes to be invaded. In France, the revolution covered the country with ruins, tears, and blood, because means were not to be found to moderate in the people that *revolutionary spirit* which parches, in the bud, the promised fruits of liberty, when its violence is not repressed.

Few persons were capable of keeping pace with the rapid progress of the revolution. Those who remained behind were considered as guilty of desertion. The authors of the first constitution were accused of being *royalists*; the old partisans of republicanism were punished as *moderates*; the land-owners, as *aristocrates*; the monied men, as *corrupters*; the bankers and financiers, as *blood-suckers*; the shop-keepers, as *promoters of famine*; and the newsmongers, as *alarmists*. The factious themselves, in short, were alternately proscribed, as soon as they ceased to belong to the ruling faction.

In this state of things, society became a prey to the most baneful passions. Mistrust entered every heart; friendship had no attraction; relationship, no tie; and men's minds, hardened by the habit of misfortune, or overwhelmed by fear, no longer opened to pity.

Terror compressed every imagination; and the revolutionary government, exercising it to its fullest extent, struck off a prodigious number of heads, filled the prisons with victims, and continued to corrupt the morals of the nation by staining it with crimes.

But all things have an end. The tyrants fell; the dungeons were thrown open; numberless victims emerged from them; and France seemed to recover new life; but still bewildered by the *revolutionary spirit*, wasted by the concealed poison of anarchy, exhausted by her innumerable sacrifices, and almost paralyzed by her own convulsions, she made but impotent efforts for the enjoyment of liberty and justice. Taxes became more burdensome; commerce was annihilated; industry, without aliment; paper-money, without value; and specie, without circulation. However, while the French nation was degraded at home by this series of evils, it was respected abroad through the rare merit of some of its generals, the splendour of its victories, and the bravery of its soldiers.

During these transactions, there was formed in the public mind that moral resistance which destroys not governments by violence, but undermines them. The intestine commotions were increasing; the conquests of the French were invaded; their enemies were already on their frontiers; and the division which had broken out between the Directory and the Legislative Body, again threatened France with a total dissolution, when a man of extraordinary character and talents had the boldness to seize the reins of authority, and stop the further progress of the revolution.* Taking at the full

---

* Of two things, we are left to believe one. BONA-PARTE either was or was not invited to put himself at the head of the government of France. It is not probable

the tide which leads on to fortune, he at once changed the face of affairs, not only within the limits of the Republic, but throughout Europe. Yet, after all their triumphs, the French have the mortification to have failed in gaining that for which they first took up arms, and for

that the Directory should send for him from Egypt, in order to say to him: "We are fools and drivelers, unfit " to conduct the affairs of the nation; so turn us out of " office, and seat yourself in our place." Nevertheless, they might have hoped to preserve their tottering authority through his support. Be this as it may, there is something so singular in the good fortune which has attended BONAPARTE from the period of his quitting Alexandria, that, were it not known for truth, it might well be taken for fiction. Sailing from the road of Aboukir on the 24th of August, 1799, he eludes the vigilance of the English cruisers, and lands at Frejus in France on the 14th of October following, the forty-seventh day after his departure from Egypt. On his arrival in Paris, so far from giving an account of his conduct to the Directory, he turns his back on them; accepts the proposition made to him, from another quarter, to effect a change in the government; on the 9th of November, carries it into execution; and, profiting by the *popularis aura*, fixes himself at the head of the State, at the same time kicking down the ladder by which he climbed to power. To achieve all this with such promptitude and energy, most assuredly required a mind of no common texture; nor can any one deny that ambition would have done but little towards its accomplishment, had it not been seconded by extraordinary firmness.

which they have maintained so long and so obstinate a struggle.

When a strong mound has been broken down, the waters whose amassed volume it opposed, rush forward, and, in their impetuous course, spread afar terror and devastation. On visiting the scene where this has occurred, we naturally cast our eyes in every direction, to discover the mischief which they have occasioned by their irruption; so, then, on reaching the grand theatre of the French revolution, did I look about for the traces of the havock it had left behind; but, like a river which had regained its level, and flowed again in its natural bed, this political torrent had subsided, and its ravages were repaired in a manner the most surprising.

However, at the particular request of an estimable friend, I have endeavoured to draw the contrast which, in 1789-90 and 1801-2, Paris presented to the eye of an impartial observer. In this arduous attempt I have not the vanity to flatter myself that I have been successful, though I have not hesitated to lay under contribution every authority likely to promote my object. The state of the French capital, before the revolution, I have delineated from the notes

I had myself collected on the spot, and for which purpose I was, at that time, under the necessity of consulting almost as many books as Don Quixote read on knight-errantry; but the authors from whom I have chiefly borrowed, are St. Foix, Mercier, Dulaure, Pujoulx, and Biot.

My invariable aim has been to relate, *sine ira nec studio,* such facts and circumstances as have come to my knowledge, and to render to every one that justice which I should claim for myself. After a revolution which has trenched on so many opposite interests, the reader cannot be surprised, if information, derived from such a variety of sources, should sometimes seem to bear the character of party-spirit. Should this appear *on the face of the record,* I can only say that I have avoided entering into politics, in order that no bias of that sort might lead me to discolour or distort the truths I have had occasion to state; and I have totally rejected those communications which, from their tone of bitterness, personality, and virulence, might be incompatible with the general tenour of an impartial production.

Till the joint approbation of some competent judges, who visited the French capital after having perused, in manuscript, several of these letters, had stamped on them a comparative degree of value, no one could think more lightly of them than the author. Urged repeatedly to produce them to the public, I have yielded with reluctance, and in the fullest confidence that, notwithstanding the recent change of circumstances, a liberal construction will be put on my sentiments and motives. I have taken care that my account of the national establishments in France should be perfectly correct; and, in fact, I have been favoured with the principal information it contains by their respective directors. In regard to the other topics on which I have touched, I have not failed to consult the best authorities, even in matters, which, however trifling in themselves, acquire a relative importance, from being illustrative of some of the many-coloured effects of a revolution, which has humbled the pride of many, deranged the calculations of all, disappointed the hopes of not a few, and deceived those even by whom it had been engendered and conducted.

Yet, whatever pains I have taken to be strictly impartial, it cannot be denied that, in publishing a work of this description at a time when the self-love of most men is mortified, and their

resentment awakened, I run no small risk, of displeasing all parties, because I attach myself to none, but find them all more or less deserving of censure. Without descending either to flattery or calumny, I speak both well and ill of the French, because I copy nature, and neither draw an imaginary portrait, nor write a systematic narrative. If I have occasionally given vent to my indignation in glancing at the excesses of the revolution, I have not withheld my tribute of applause from those institutions, which, being calculated to benefit mankind by the gratuitous diffusion of knowledge, would reflect honour on any nation. In other respects, I have not been unmindful of that excellent precept of TACITUS, in which he observes that " The prin-
" cipal duty of the historian is to rescue from ob-
" livion virtuous actions, and to make bad men
" dread infamy and posterity for what they have
" said and done."*

In stating facts, it is frequently necessary to support them by a relation of particular circumstances, which may corroborate them in an unquestionable manner. Feeling this truth, I have some-

* *Præcipuum munus annalium reor, ne virtutes sileantur,*
" *utque pravis dictis factisque ex posteritate et infamia me-*
" *tus sit.*"

times introduced myself on my canvass, merely to shew that I am not an ideal traveller. I mean one of those pleasant fellows who travel post in their elbow-chair, sail round the world on a map suspended to one side of their room, cross the seas with a pocket-compass lying on their table, experience a shipwreck by their fireside, make their escape when it scorches their shins, and land on a desert island in their *robe de chambre* and slippers.

I have, therefore, here and there mentioned names, time, and place, to prove that, *bond fide*, I went to Paris immediately after the ratification of the preliminary treaty. To banish uniformity in my description of that metropolis, I have, as much as possible, varied my subjects. Fashions, sciences, absurdities, anecdotes, education, fêtes, useful arts, places of amusement, music, learned and scientific institutions, inventions, public buildings, industry, agriculture, &c. &c. &c. being all jumbled together in my brain, I have thence drawn them, like tickets from a lottery; and it will not, I trust, be deemed presumptuous in me to indulge a hope that, in proportion to the blanks, there will be found no inadequate number of prizes.

I have pointed out the immense advantages

which France is likely to derive from her Schools for Public Services, and other establishments of striking utility, such as the *Dépôt de la Guerre* and the *Dépôt de la Marine,* in order that the British government may be prompted to form institutions, which, if not exactly similar, may at least answer the same purpose. Instead of copying the French in objects of fickleness and frivolity, why not borrow from them what is really deserving of imitation?

It remains for me to observe, by way of stimulating the ambition of British genius, that, in France, the arts and sciences are now making a rapid and simultaneous progress; first, because the revolution has made them popular in that country; and, secondly, because they are daily connected by new ties, which, in a great measure, render them inseparable. Facts are there recurred to, less with a view to draw from them immediate applications, than to develop the truths resulting from them. The first step is from these facts to their most simple consequences, which are little more than bare assertions. From these the *savans* proceed to others more minute, till, at length, by imperceptible degrees, they arrive at the most abstracted generalities. With them, method is an induction incessantly verified by experiment. Whence, it gives to human intelligence, not wings which lead it astray, but reins which guide it. United by this common philosophy, the sciences and arts in France advance together; and the progress made by one of them serves to promote that of the rest. There, the men who profess them, considering that their knowledge belongs not to themselves alone, not to their country only, but to all mankind, are continually striving to increase the mass of public knowledge. This they regard as a real duty, which they are proud to discharge; thus treading in the steps of the most memorable men of past ages.

Then, while the more unlearned and unskilled among us are emulating the patriotic enthusiasm of the French in volunteering, as they did, to resist invasion, let our men of science and genius exert themselves not to be surpassed by the industrious *savans* and artists of that nation; but let them act on the principle inculcated by the following sublime idea of our illustrious countryman, the founder of modern philosophy. " It may not be amiss," says BACON, " to point out three different kinds, and, as it " were, degrees of ambition. The first, that of " those who desire to enhance, in their own

" country, the power they arrogate to them-
" selves: this kind of ambition is both vulgar
" and degenerate. The second, that of those
" who endeavour to extend the power and
" domination of their country, over the whole
" of the human race: in this kind there is
" certainly a greater dignity, though, at the
" same time, no less a share of cupidity. But
" should any one strive to restore and extend
" the power and domination of mankind over
" the universality of things, unquestionably such
" an ambition, (if it can be so denominated)
" would be more reasonable and dignified than
" the others. Now, the empire of man, over
" things, has its foundation exclusively in the
" arts and sciences; for it is only by an obe-
" dience to her laws, that Nature can be com-
" manded."*

LONDON, June 10, 1803.

" * Præterea non abs re fuerit, tria hominum ambitionis ge-
nera et quasi gradus distinguere. Primum eorum qui pro-
priam potentiam in patria sua amplificare cupiunt; quod genus vulgare est et degener. Secundum eorum, qui patriæ
potentiam et imperium inter humanum genus amplificare ni-
tuntur; illud plus certe habet dignitatis, cupiditatis haud mi-
nus. Quod si quis humani generis ipsius potentiam et imperium in rerum universitatem instaurare et amplificare conetur;

ea procul dubio ambitio (si modo ita vocanda sit) reliquâ et sanior est et augustior. Hominis autem imperium in res, in solis artibus et scientiis ponitur: naturæ enim non imperatur, nisi parendo." Nov. org. scientiarum. Aphor. CXXIX. (Vol. VIII. page 72, new edition of Bacon's works. London, printed 1803.)

A
SKETCH OF PARIS,

&c. &c.

LETTER I.

Calais, October 16, 1801.

My dear friend,

HAD you not made it a particular request that I would give you the earliest account of my debarkation in France, I should, probably, not have been tempted to write to you till I reached Paris. I well know the great stress which you lay on first impressions; but what little I have now to communicate will poorly gratify your expectation.

From the date of this letter, you will perceive that, since we parted yesterday, I have not been dilatory in my motions. No sooner had a messenger from the Alien-Office brought me the promised passport, or rather his Majesty's licence, permitting me to embark for France, than I proceeded on my journey.

In nine hours I reached Dover, and, being authorized by a proper introduction, immediately applied to Mr. Mantell, the agent for prisoners of war, cartels, &c. for a passage across the water. An English flag of truce was then in the harbour, waiting only for government dispatches; and I found that, if I could get my baggage visited in time, I might avail myself of the opportunity of crossing the sea in this vessel. On having recourse to the collector of the customs, I succeeded in my wish: the dispatches arriving shortly after, and my baggage being already shipped, I stepped off the quay into the Nancy, on board of which I was the only passenger. A propitious breeze sprang up at the moment, and, in less than three hours, wafted me to Calais pier.

By the person who carried the dispatches to Citizen Mengaud, the commissary for this department *(Pas de Calais)*, I sent a card with my name and rank, requesting permission to land and deliver to him a letter from M. Otto. This step was indispensable: the vessel which brought me was, I find, the first British flag of truce that has been suffered to enter the harbour, with the exception of the Prince of Wales packet, now waiting here for the return of a king's messenger from Paris; and her captain even has not yet been permitted to go on shore. It therefore appears that I shall be the first Englishman, not in an official character, who has set foot on French ground since the ratification of the preliminary treaty.

The pier was presently crowded with people

gazing at our vessel, as if she presented a spectacle perfectly novel: but, except the tri-coloured cockade in the hats of the military, I could not observe the smallest difference in their general appearance. Instead of crops and round wigs, which I expected to see in universal vogue, here were full as many powdered heads and long queues as before the revolution. Frenchmen, in general, will, I am persuaded, ever be Frenchmen in their dress, which, in my opinion, can never be *revolutionized*, either by precept or example. The *citoyens*, as far as I am yet able to judge, most certainly have not fattened by warfare more than JOHN BULL: their visages are as sallow and as thin as formerly, though their persons are not quite so meagre as they are pourtrayed by Hogarth.

The prospect of peace, however, seemed to have produced an exhilarating effect on all ranks; satisfaction appeared on every countenance. According to custom, a host of inkeepers' domestics boarded the vessel, each vaunting the superiority of his master's accommodations. My old landlord Ducrocq presenting himself to congratulate me on my arrival, soon freed me from their importunities, and I, of course, decided in favour of the *Lion d'Argent*.

Part of the *Boulogne* flotilla was lying in the harbour. Independently of the decks of the gunboats being full of soldiers, with very few sailors intermixed, playing at different games of chance, not a plank, not a log, or piece of timber, was there on the quay but was also covered with similar parties. This then accounts for that rage for gambling, which has carried to such desperate lengths those among them whom the fate of war has lodged in our prisons.

My attention was soon diverted from this scene, by a polite answer from the commissary, inviting me to his house. I instantly disembarked to wait on him; my letter containing nothing more than an introduction, accompanied by a request that I might be furnished with a passport to enable me to proceed to Paris without delay, Citizen Mengaud dispatched a proper person to attend me to the town-hall, where the passports are made out, and signed by the mayor; though they are not delivered till they have also received the commissary's signature. However, to lose no time, while one of the clerks was drawing my picture, or, in other words, taking down a minute description of my person, I sent my keys to the custom-house, in order that my baggage might be examined.

By what conveyance I was to proceed to Paris was the next point to be settled; and this has brought me to the *Lion d'Argent*.

Among other vehicles, Ducrocq has, in his *remise*, an apparently-good *cabriolet de voyage*, belonging to one of his Paris correspondents; but, on account of the wretched state of the roads, he begs me to allow him time to send for his coachmaker, to examine it scrupulously, that I may not be detained by the way, from any accident happening to the carriage.

I was just on the point of concluding my letter, when a French naval officer, who was on the pier when I landed, introduced himself to me, to know whether I would do him the favour to accommodate him with a place in the cabriolet under examination. I liked my new friend's appearance and manner too well not to accede to his proposal.

The carriage is reported to be in good condition. I shall therefore send my servant on before as a courier, instead of taking him with me as an inside passenger. As we shall travel night and day, and the post-horses will be in readiness at every stage, we may, I am told, expect to reach Paris in about forty-two hours. Adieu; my next will be from the *great* city.

LETTER II.

Paris, October 19, 1801.

HERE I am safe arrived; that is, without any broken bones; though my arms, knees, and head are finely pummelled by the jolting of the carriage. Well might Ducrocq say that the roads were bad! In several places, they are not passable without danger—Indeed, the government is so fully aware of this, that an inspector has been dispatched to direct immediate repairs to be made against the arrival of the English ambassador; and, in some *communes,* the people are at work by torch-light. With this exception, my journey was exceedingly pleasant. At ten o'clock the first night, we reached *Montreuil,* where we supped; the next day we breakfasted at *Abbeville,* dined at *Amiens,* and supped that evening at *Clermont.*

The road between *Calais* and *Paris* is too well known to interest by description. Most of the abbeys and monasteries, which present themselves to the eye of the traveller, have either been converted into hospitals or manufactories. Few there are, I believe, who will deny that this change is for the better. A receptacle for the relief of suffering indigence conveys a consolatory idea to the mind of the friend of human nature; while the lover of industry cannot but approve of an establishment which, while it enriches a State, affords employ to the needy and diligent. This, unquestionably, is no bad appropriation of these buildings, which, when inhabited by monks, were, for the most part, no more than an asylum of sloth, hypocrisy, pride, and ignorance.

The weather was fine, which contributed not a

little to display the country to greater advantage; but the improvements recently made in agriculture are too striking to escape the notice of the most inattentive observer. The open plains and rising grounds of *ci-devant Picardy* which, from ten to fifteen years ago, I have frequently seen, in this season, mostly lying fallow, and presenting the aspect of one wide, neglected waste, are now all well cultivated, and chiefly laid down in corn; and the corn, in general, seems to have been sown with more than common attention.

My fellow-traveller, who was a *lieutenant de vaisseau*, belonging to *Latouche Tréville's* flotilla, proved a very agreeable companion, and extremely well-informed. This officer positively denied the circumstance of any of their gun-boats being moored with chains during our last attack. While he did ample justice to the bravery of our people, he censured the manner in which it had been exerted. The divisions of boats arriving separately, he said, could not afford to each other necessary support, and were thus exposed to certain discomfiture. I made the best defence I possibly could; but truth bears down all before it.

The loss on the side of the French, my fellow-traveller declared, was no more than seven men killed and forty-five wounded. Such of the latter as were in a condition to undergo the fatigue of the ceremony, were carried in triumphal procession through the streets of *Boulogne*, where, after being harangued by the mayor, they were rewarded with civic crowns from the hands of their fair fellow-citizens.

Early the second morning after our departure from *Calais*, we reached the town of *St. Denis*, which, at one time since the revolution, changed its name for that of *Françiade*. I never pass through this place without calling to mind the persecution which poor Abélard suffered from Adam, the abbot, for having dared to say, that the body of *St. Denis*, first bishop of Paris, in 240, which had been preserved in this abbey among the relics, was not that of the areopagite, who died in 95. The ridiculous stories, imposed on the credulity of the zealous catholics, respecting this wonderful saint, have been exhibited in their proper light by Voltaire, as you may see by consulting the *Questions sur l'Encyclopédie*, at the article *Denis*.

It is in every person's recollection that, in consequence of the National Convention having decreed the abolition of royalty in France, it was proposed to annihilate every vestige of it throughout the country. But, probably, you are not aware of the thorough sweep that was made among the sepultures in this abbey of *St. Denis*.

The bodies of the kings, queens, princes, princesses, and celebrated personages, who had been interred here for nearly fifteen hundred years, were taken up, and literally reduced to ashes. Not a wreck was left behind to make a relic.

The remains of TURENNE alone were respected. All the other bodies, together with the entrails or hearts, enclosed in separate urns, were thrown into large pits, lined with a coat of quick lime: they were then covered with the same substance; and the pits were afterwards filled up with earth. Most of them, as may be supposed, were in a state of complete putrescency; of some, the bones only remained, though a few were in good preservation.

The bodies of the consort of Charles I. Henrietta Maria of France, daughter of Henry IV, who died in 1669, aged 60, and of their daughter Henrietta Stuart, first wife of Monsieur, only brother to Lewis XIV, who died in 1670, aged 26, both interred in the vault of the Bourbons, were consumed in the general destruction.

The execution of this decree was begun at *St. Denis* on Saturday the 12th of October, 1793, and completed on the 25th of the same month, in presence of the municipality and several other persons.

On the 12th of November following, all the treasure of *St. Denis*, (shrines, relics, &c.) was removed: the whole was put into large wooden chests, together with all the rich ornaments of the church, consisting of chalices, pyxes, cups, copes, &c. The same day these valuable articles were sent off, in great state, in waggons, decorated for the purpose, to the National Convention.

We left *St. Denis* after a hasty breakfast; and, on reaching Paris, I determined to drive to the residence of a man whom I had never seen; but from whom I had little doubt of a welcome reception. I accordingly alighted in the *Rue neuve St. Roch*, where I found B——a, who perfectly answered the character given me of him by M. S———i.

You already know that, through the interest of my friend, Captain O——y, I was so fortunate as to procure the exchange of B——a's only son, a deserving youth, who had been taken prisoner at sea, and languished two years in confinement in Portchester-Castle.

Before I could introduce myself, one of young B——a's sisters proclaimed my name, as if by inspiration; and I was instantly greeted with the cordial embraces of the whole family. This scene made me at once forget the fatigues of my journey; and, though I had not been in bed for three successive nights, the agreeable sensations excited in my mind, by the unaffected expression of gratitude, banished every inclination to sleep. If honest B——a and his family felt themselves obliged to me, I felt myself doubly and trebly obliged to Captain O——y; for, to his kind exertion, was I indebted for the secret enjoyment arising from the performance of a disinterested action.

S——i was no sooner informed of my arrival, than he hastened to obey the invitation to meet me at dinner, and, by his presence, enlivened the family party. After spending a most agreeable day, I retired to a temporary lodging, which B——a had procured me in the neighbourhood. I shall remain in it no longer than till I can suit myself with apartments in a private house, where I can be more retired, or at least subject to less noise, than in a public hotel.

Of the fifty-eight hours which I employed in performing my journey hither from London, forty-four were spent on my way between Calais and Paris; a distance that I have often travelled with ease in thirty-six, when the roads were in tolerable repair. Considerable delay too is at present occasioned by the erection of *barrières*, or turnpike-bars, which did not exist before the revolution. At this day, they are established throughout all the departments, and are an insuperable impediment to expedition; for, at night, the toll-gatherers are fast asleep, and the bars being secured, you are obliged to wait patiently till these good citizens choose to rise from their pillow.

To counterbalance this inconvenience, you are not now plagued, as formerly, by custom-house officers on the frontiers of *every* department. My baggage being once searched at *Calais*, experienced no other visit; but, at the upper town of *Boulogne*, a sight of my travelling passport was required; by mistake in the dark, I gave the *commis* a scrawl, put into my hands by Ducrocq, containing an account of the best inns on the road. Would you believe that this inadvertency detained us a considerable time, so extremely inquisitive are they, at the present moment, respecting all papers? At *Calais*, the custom-house officers even examined every piece of paper used in the packing of my baggage. This scrutiny is not particularly adopted towards Englishmen; but must, I understand, be undergone by travellers of every country, on entering the territory of the Republic.

P. S. Lord Cornwallis is expected with impatience; and, at *St. Denis*, an escort of dragoons of the 19th demi-brigade is in waiting to attend him into Paris.

LETTER III.

Paris, October 21, 1801.

On approaching this capital, my curiosity was excited in the highest degree; and, as the carriage passed rapidly along from the *Barrière*, through the *Porte St. Denis*, to the *Rue neuve St. Roch*, my eyes wandered in all directions, anxiously seeking every shade of distinction between *monarchical* and *republican* Paris.

The first thing that attracted my attention, on entering the *faubourg*, was the vast number of inscriptions placed, during the revolution, on many of the principal houses; but more especially on public buildings of every description. They are painted in large, conspicuous letters; and the following is the most general style in which they have been originally worded:

"RÉPUBLIQUE FRANÇAISE, UNE ET
"INDIVISIBLE."

"LIBERTÉ, ÉGALITÉ, FRATERNITÉ, OU LA MORT."

Since the exit of the French Nero, the last three words "*ou la mort*" have been obliterated, but in few places are so completely effaced as not to be still legible. In front of all the public offices and national establishments, the tri-coloured flag is triumphantly displayed; and almost every person you meet wears in his hat the national cockade.

The tumult which, ten or twelve years ago, rendered the streets of Paris so noisy, so dirty, and at the same time so dangerous, is now most sensibly diminished. Boileau's picture of them is no longer just. No longer are seen those scenes of confusion occasioned by the frequent stoppages of coaches and carts, and the contentions of the vociferating drivers. You may now pass the longest and most crowded thoroughfares, either on foot or otherwise, without obstacle or inconvenience. The contrast is striking.

Indeed, from what I have observed, I should presume that there is not, at the present day, one tenth part of the number of carriages which were in use here in 1789-90. Except on the domestics of foreign ambassadors and foreigners, I have as yet noticed nothing like a livery; and, in lieu of armorial bearings, every carriage, without distinction, has a number painted on the pannel. However, if private equipages are scarce, thence ensues more than one advantage; the public are indemnified by an increased number of good hackney coaches, chariots, and cabriolets; and, besides, as I have just hinted, pedestrians are not only far less exposed to being bespattered, but also to having their limbs fractured.

Formerly, a *seigneur de la cour* conceived himself justified in suffering his coachman to drive at a mischievous rate; and in narrow, crowded streets, where there is no foot-pavement, it was extremely difficult for persons walking to escape the wheels of a great number of carriages rattling along in this shameful manner. But he who guided the chariot of a *ministre d'état*, considered it as a necessary and distinctive mark of his master's pre-eminence to *brûler le pavé*. This is so strictly true, that, before the revolution, I have here witnessed repeated accidents of the most serious nature, resulting from the exercise of this sort of ministerial privilege: on one occasion particularly, I myself narrowly escaped unhurt, when a decent, elderly woman was thrown down, close by my feet, and had both her thighs broken through the unfeeling wantonness of the coachman of the Baron de Breteuil, at that time minister for the department of Paris.

Owing to the salutary regulations of the police, the recurrence of these accidents is now, in a great measure, prevented; and, as the empirics say in their hand-bills: " *Prevention is better* " *than cure.*"

But for these differences, a person who had not seen Paris for some years, might, unless he were to direct his visits to particular quarters, cross it from one extremity to the other, without remarking any change to inform his mind, that here had been a revolution, or rather that, for the last ten years, this city had been almost one continual scene of revolutions.

Bossuet, once preaching before Lewis XIV, exclaimed: " Kings die, and so do kingdoms!" Could that great preacher rise from his grave into the pulpit, and behold France without a king, and that kingdom, not crumbled away, but enlarged, almost with the rapid accumulation of a snow-ball, into an enormous mass of territory, under the title of French Republic, what would he not have to say in a sermon? *Rien de nouveau sous le ciel*, though an old proverb, would not now suit as a maxim. This, in fact, seems the age of wonders. The league of monarchs has ended by producing republics; while a republic has raised a dukedom into a monarchy, and, by its vast preponderance, completely overturned the balance of power.

Not knowing when I may have an opportunity of sending this letter, I shall defer to close it for the present, as I may possibly lengthen it. But you must not expect much order in my narrations. I throw my thoughts on paper just as they happen to present themselves, without any studied arrangement.

October 21, in continuation.

WHEN we have been for some time in the habit of corresponding with strangers, we are apt to draw such inferences from their language and style, as furnish us with the means of sketching an ideal portrait of their person. This was the case with myself.

Through the concurrence of the two governments, I had, as you know, participated, in common with others, in the indulgence of being permitted to correspond, occasionally, on subjects of literature with several of the *savans* and literati of France. Indeed, the principal motive of my journey to Paris was to improve that sort of acquaintance, by personal intercourse, so as to render it more interesting to both parties. In my imagination, I had drawn a full-length picture of most of my literary correspondents. I was now anxious to see the originals, and compare the resemblance.

Yesterday, having first paid my respects to Mr. M——y, the successor to Captain C——s, as commissary for the maintenance and exchange of British prisoners of war, and at present *Chargé d'affaires* from our court to the French Republic, I called on M. F——u, formerly minister of the naval department, and at present counsellor of state, and member of the National Institute, as well as of the board of longitude. I then visited M. O——r, and afterwards M. L————re, also members of the Institute, and both well known to our proficients in natural history, by the works which each has published in the different branches of that interesting science.

In one only of my ideal portraits had I been very wide of the likeness. However, without pretending to be a Lavater, I may affirm that I should not have risked falling into a mistake like that committed, on a somewhat similar occasion, by Voltaire.

This colossus of French literature, having been for a long time in correspondence with the great Frederic, became particularly anxious to see that monarch. On his arrival in a village where the head-quarters of the Prussian army were then established, Voltaire inquired for the king's lodging: thither he paced with redoubled speed; and, being directed to the upper part of the house, he hastily crossed a large garret; he then found himself in a second, and was just on the point of entering the third, when, on turning round, he perceived in one of the corners of the room, a soldier, not overclean in appearance, lying on a sorry bedstead. He went up and said to him with eagerness: " Where's the king?"—" I am " Frederic," replied the soldier; and, sure enough, it was the monarch himself.

I am now settled in my new apartments, which are situated in the most centrical part of Paris. When you visit this capital, I would, by all means, recommend to you, should you intend to remain here a few weeks, to get into private lodgings.

I know of no article here so much augmented in price, within the last ten years, as the apartments in all the hotels. After looking at several of them in the *Rue de la Loi*, accompanied by a French friend, who was so obliging as to take on himself all the trouble of inquiry, while I remained a silent bystander, I had the curiosity to go to the *Hôtel d'Angleterre*, in the *Rue des Filles St. Thomas*, not far from the *ci-devant Palais Royal*. The same apartments on the first floor of this hotel which I occupied in 1789, happened to be vacant. At that time I paid for them twelve louis d'or a month; the furniture was then new; it is now much the worse for nearly eleven years' wear; and the present landlord asked twenty-five louis a month, and even refused twenty-two, if taken for three months certain. The fact is, that all the landlords of ready-furnished hotels in Paris seem to be buoyed up with an idea that, on the peace, the English and foreigners of other nations will flock hither in such numbers as to enable them to reap a certain and plentiful harvest. Not but all lodgings are considerably increased in price, which is ascribed to the increase of taxes.

To find private lodgings, you have only to cast your eye on the daily advertiser of Paris, called *Les Petites Affiches*. There I read a description of my present quarters, which are newly fitted up in every particular, and, I assure you, with no small degree of tasteful fancy. My landlady, who is a milliner, and, for aught I know, a very fashionable one, left not the smallest convenience to my conjecture, but explained the particular use of every hole and corner in the most significant manner, not even excepting the *boudoir*.

This would be a most excellent situation for any one whose principal object was to practise speaking French; for, on the right hand of the *porte-cochère* or gateway, (which, by the bye, is here reckoned an indispensable appendage to a proper lodging), is the *magazin des modes*, where my landlady presides over twenty damsels, many of whom, though assiduously occupied in making caps and bonnets, would, I am persuaded, find repartee for the most witty gallant.

LETTER IV.

Paris, October 23, 1801.

SINCE my arrival, I have been so much engaged in paying and receiving visits, that I really have not yet been able to take even a hasty view of any of the grand sights introduced here since the revolution.

On Wednesday I dined with M. S———i, whose new 8vo edition of Buffon proceeds, I find, with becoming spirit. It is quite a journey to his residence; for he lives in one of the most retired quarters of Paris. However, I had no reason to repine at the distance, as the party was exceedingly cheerful. Naturalists and literati were not wanting.

Egypt was a subject that engrossed much of the conversation: it was mentioned as a matter of regret that, during the dominion of the French in that country, curiosity had not prompted the Institute, established at Cairo, to open one of the pyramids, with a view of ascertaining the object of the erection of those vast masses. At the desert, we had luscious grapes as large as damsons, in bunches of from three to five pounds in weight. They were of the species of the famous *chasselas de Fontainebleau*, which are said to have sprung from a stock of vine-plants, imported by Francis I. from the island of Cyprus. These did not come from that town, but grew against the naked wall in S———i's garden. From this you may form a judgment of the climate of Paris.

The persons with whom I have had any correspondence, respecting literature, vie with each other in shewing me every mark of cordial hospitality; and those to whom I have been introduced, are by no means backward in friendly attention. All the lovers of science here seem to rejoice that the communication, which has been so long interrupted between the two countries, promises to be shortly re-opened.

After dining yesterday with Mr. M———y, the British minister, in company with Mr. D———n, the member for Ilchester, we all three went to an exhibition almost facing Mr. M———y's residence in the *Rue St. Dominique*. This was the third time of its being open to the public. As it is of a novel kind, some account of it may not be uninteresting. In French, it is denominated

THERMOLAMPES,

or stoves which afford heat and light on an economical plan.

The author of this invention, for which a patent has been obtained, is M. LEBON, an engineer of bridges and highways. The place of exhibition was the ground floor of one of the large hotels in the *Faubourg St. Germain,* on which was a suite of rooms, extremely favourable for displaying the effect of this new method of lighting and warming apartments.

In lieu of fire or candle, on the chimney stood a large crystal globe, in which appeared a bright and clear flame diffusing a very agreeable heat; and on different pieces of furniture were placed candlesticks with metal candles, from the top of each of which issued a steady light, like that of a lamp burning with spirits of wine. These different receptacles were supplied with inflammable gas by means of tubes communicating with an apparatus underneath. By this contrivance, in short, all the apartments were warmed very comfortably, and illuminated in a brilliant manner.

On consulting M. LEBON, he communicated to me the following observations: "You may have remarked," said he, "in sitting before a fire, that wood sometimes burns without flame, but with much smoke, and then you experience little heat, sometimes with flame, but with little smoke, and then you find much warmth. You may have remarked too, that ill-made charcoal emits smoke; it is, on that account, susceptible of flaming again; and the characteristic difference between wood and charcoal is, that the latter has lost, together with its smoke, the principle and aliment of flame, without which you obtain but little heat. Experience next informs us, that this portion of smoke, the aliment of flame, is not an oily vapour condensable by cooling, but a gas, a permanent air, which may be washed, purified, conducted, distributed, and afterwards turned into flame at any distance from the hearth.

"It is almost needless," continued he, "to point out the formation of verdigrise, white lead, and a quantity of other operations, in which acetous acid is employed. I shall only remark that it is this pyroligneous acid which penetrates smoked meat and fish, that it has an effect on leather which it hardens, and that *thermolampes* are likely to render tanning-mills unnecessary, by furnishing the tan without further trouble. But to return to the aëriform principle.

"This aliment of flame is deprived of those humid vapours, so perceptible and so disagreeable to the organs of sight and smell. Purified to a perfect transparency, it floats in the state of cold air, and suffers itself to be directed by the smallest and most fragil pipes. Chimnies of an inch square, made in the thickness of the plaster of ceilings or walls, tubes even of gummed silk would answer this purpose. The end alone of the tube, which, by bringing the inflammable gas into contact with the atmospheric air, allows it to catch fire, and on which the flame reposes, ought to be of metal.

" By a distribution so easy to be established, a single stove may supply the place of all the chimnies of a house. Every where inflammable air is ready to diffuse immediately heat and light of the most glowing or most mild nature, simultaneously or separately, according to your wishes. In the twinkling of an eye, you may conduct the flame from one room to another; an advantage equally convenient and economical, and which can never be obtained with our common stoves and chimnies. No sparks, no charcoal, no soot, to trouble you; no ashes, no wood, to soil your apartments. By night, as well as by day, you can have a fire in your room, without a servant being obliged to look after it. Nothing in the *thermolampes*, not even the smallest portion of inflammable air, can escape combustion; while in our chimnies, torrents evaporate, and even carry off with them the greater part of the heat produced.

" The advantage of being able to purify and proportion, in some measure, the principles of the gas which feeds the flame is," said M. LEBON, " set forth in the clearest manner. But this flame is so subjected to our caprice, that even to tranquilize the imagination. it suffers itself to be confined in a crystal globe, which is never tarnished, and thus presents a filter pervious to light and heat. A part of the tube that conducts the inflammable air, carries off, out of doors, the produce of this combustion, which, nevertheless, according to the experiments of modern chymists, can scarcely be any thing more than an aqueous vapour.

" Who cannot but be fond of having recourse to a flame so subservient ? It will dress your victuals, which, as well as your cooks, will not be exposed to the vapour of charcoal; it will warm again those dishes on your table; dry your linen ; heat your oven, and the water for your baths or your washing, with every economical advantage that can be wished. No moist or black vapours ; no ashes, no breaze, to make a dirt, or oppose the communication of heat; no useless loss of caloric; you may, by shutting an opening, which is no longer necessary for placing the wood in your oven, compress and coerce the torrents of heat that were escaping from it.

" It may easily be conceived, that an inflammable principle so docile and so active may be made to yield the most magnificent illuminations. Streams of fire finely drawn out, the duration, colour, and form of which may be varied at pleasure, the motion of suns and turning-columns, must produce an effect no less agreeable than brilliant." Indeed, this effect was exhibited on the garden façade of M. LEBON's residence.

"Wood," concluded he, "yields in condensable vapours two thirds of its weight; those vapours may therefore be employed to produce the effects of our steam-engines, and it is needless to borrow this succour from foreign water."

P. S. On the 1st of last Vendémiaire, (23rd of September), the government presented to the Chief Consul a sword, whose hilt was adorned with fourteen diamonds, the largest of which, called the *Regent,* from its having been purchased by the Duke of Orleans, when Regent, weighs 184 carats. This is the celebrated *Pitt* diamond, of which we have heard so much: but its weight is exceeded by that of the diamond purchased by the late empress of Russia, which weighs 194 carats; not to speak of the more famous diamond, in possession of the Great Mogul, which is said to weigh 280 carats.

LETTER V.

Paris, October 24, 1801.

LAST night I received yours of the 20th ult. and as Mr. M——y purposes to send off a dispatch this morning, and will do me the favour to forward this, with my former letters, I hasten to write you a few lines.

I scarcely need assure you, my dear friend, that I will, with pleasure, communicate to you my remarks on this great city and its inhabitants, and describe to you, as far as I am able, the principal curiosities which it contains, particularizing, as you desire, those recently placed here by the chance of war; and giving you a succinct, historical account of the most remarkable national establishments and public buildings. But to pass in review the present state of the *arts, sciences, literature, manners,* &c. &c. in this capital, and contrast it with that which existed before the revolution, is a task indeed; and far more, I fear, than it will be in my power to accomplish.

However, if you will be content to gather my observations as they occur; to listen to my reflections, while the impression of the different scenes which produced them, is still warm in my mind; in short, to take a faithful sketch, in lieu of a finished picture, I will do the best I can for your satisfaction.

Relying on your indulgence, you shall know the life I lead: I will, as it were, take you by the arm, and, wherever I go, you shall be my companion. Perhaps, by pursuing this plan, you will not, at the expiration of three or four months, think your time unprofitably spent. Aided by the experience acquired by having occasionally resided here, for several months together, before the revolution, it will be my endeavour to make you as well acquainted with Paris, as I shall then hope to be myself. For this purpose, I will lay under contribution every authority, both written and oral, worthy of being consulted.

LETTER VI.

Paris, October 26, 1801.

FROM particular passages in your letter, I clearly perceive your anxiety to be introduced among those valuable antiques which now adorn the banks of the Seine. On that account, I determined to postpone all other matters, and pay my first visit to the CENTRAL MUSEUM OF THE ARTS, established in the

LOUVRE.

But, before we enter the interior of this building, it may not be amiss to give you some account of its construction, and describe to you its exterior beauties.

The origin of this palace, as well as the etymology of its name, is lost in the darkness of time. It is certain, however, that it existed, under the appellation of *Louvre*, in the reign of

Philip Augustus, who surrounded it with ditches and towers, and made it a fortress. The great tower of the *Louvre*, celebrated in history, was insulated, and built in the middle of the court. All the great feudatories of the crown derived their tenure from this tower, and came hither to swear allegiance and pay homage. " It was," says St. Foix, " a prison previously prepared for " them, if they violated their oaths*." Three Counts of Flanders were confined in it at different periods.

The *Louvre*, far from being cheerful from its construction, received also from this enormous tower a melancholy and terrifying aspect which rendered it unworthy of being a royal residence. Charles V. endeavoured to enliven and embellish this gloomy abode, and made it tolerably commodious for those times. Several foreign monarchs successively lodged in it; such as Manuel, emperor of Constantinople; Sigismund, emperor of Germany; and the emperor Charles the Fifth.

This large tower of the *Louvre*, which had, at different periods, served as a palace to the kings of France, as a prison to the great lords, and as a treasury to the state, was at length taken down in 1528.

---

* *Essais historiques sur Paris.*

The *Tower of the Library* was famous, among several others, because it contained that of Charles V. the most considerable one of the time, and in which the number of volumes amounted to nine hundred.

Old Louvre.

The part of this palace which, at the present day, is called the *Old Louvre*, was begun under Francis I. from the plan of PIERRE LESCOT, abbot of Clugny; and the sculpture was executed by JEAN GOUGEON, whose minute correctness is particularly remarkable in the festoons of the frieze of the second order, and in the devices emblematic of the amours of Henry II. This edifice, though finished, was not inhabited during the reign of that king, but it was by his son Charles IX.

Under him, the *Louvre* became the bloody theatre of treacheries and massacres which time will never efface from the memory of mankind, and which, till the merciless reign of Robespierre, were unexampled in the history of this country. I mean the horrors of St. Bartholemew's day.

While the alarmed citizens were swimming across the river to escape from death, Charles IX. from a window of this palace, was firing at them with his arquebuse. During that period of the revolution, when all means were employed to excite and strengthen the enmity of the people against their kings, this act of atrocity was called to their mind by an inscription placed under the very window, which looks on the *Quai du Louvre*.

Indeed, this instance of Charles's barbarity is fully corroborated by historians. " When it was " day-light," says Brantome, " the king peeped " out of his chamber-window, and seeing some " people in the *Faubourg St. Germain* moving " about and running away, he took a large arque- " buse which he had ready at hand, and, calling " out incessantly: *Kill, kill!* fired a great many " shots at them, but in vain; for the piece " did not carry so far."—This prince, according to Masson, piqued himself on his dexterity in cutting off at a single blow the head of the asses and pigs which he met with on his way. Lansac, one of his favourites, having found him one day with his sword drawn and ready to strike his mule, asked him seriously: " What quarrel has " then happened between His Most Christian " Majesty and my mule?" Murad Bey far surpassed this blood-thirsty monarch in address and strength. The former, we are told by travellers in Egypt, has been known, when riding past an ox, to cut off its head with one stroke of his scimitar.

The capital was dyed with the blood of Charles's

murdered subjects. Into this very *Louvre*, into the chamber of Marguerite de Valois, the king's sister, and even to her bed, in which she was then lying, did the fanatics pursue the officers belonging to the court itself, as is circumstantially related by that princess in her Memoirs.

Let us draw the curtain on these scenes of horror, and pass rapidly from this period of fanaticism and cruelty, when the *Louvre* was stained by so many crimes to times more happy, when this palace became the quiet cradle of the arts and sciences, the school for talents, the *arena* for genius, and the asylum of artists and literati.

The centre pavilion over the principal gate of the *Old Louvre*, was erected under the reign of Lewis XIII. from the designs of LE MERCIER, as well as the angle of the left part of the building, parallel to that built by Henry II. The eight gigantic cariatides which are there seen, were sculptured by SARRASIN.

The façade towards the *Jardin de l'Infante*, (as it is called), that towards the *Place du Louvre*, and that over the little gate, towards the river, which were constructed under the reigns of Charles IX. and Henry III. in the midst of the civil wars of the League, partake of the taste of the time, in regard to the multiplicity of the ornaments; but the interior announces, by the majesty of its decorations, the refined taste of Lewis XIV.

NEW LOUVRE.

The part of the *Louvre*, which, with the two sides of the old building, forms the perfect square, three hundred and seventy-eight feet* in extent, called the *New Louvre*, consists in two double façades, which are still unfinished. LE VEAU, and after him D'ORBAY, were the architects under whose direction this augmentation was made by order of Lewis XIV.

That king at first resolved to continue the *Louvre* on the plan begun by Francis I.: for some time he caused it to be pursued, but having conceived a more grand and magnificent design, he ordered the foundation of the superb edifice now standing, to be laid on the 17th of October 1665, under the administration of COLBERT.

Through a natural prejudice, Lewis XIV. thought that he could find no where but in Italy, an artist sufficiently skilful to execute his projects of magnificence. He sent for the Cavaliere BERNINI from Rome. This artist, whose reputation was established, was received in France with all the pomp due to princes of the blood. The king ordered that, in the towns through

---

* It may be necessary to observe that, throughout these letters, we always speak of French feet. The English foot is to the French as 12 to 12.789, or as 4 to 4.263.

which he might pass, he should be complimented, and receive presents from the corporations, &c.

BERNINI was loaded with wealth and honours: notwithstanding the prepossession of the court in favour of this Italian architect, notwithstanding his talents, he did not succeed in his enterprise. After having forwarded the foundation of this edifice, he made a pretext of the impossibility of spending the winter in a climate colder than that of Italy. " He was promised," says St. Foix, " three " thousand louis a year if he would stay; but," he said, " he would positively go and die in " his *own* country." On the eve of his departure, the king sent him three thousand louis, with the grant of a pension of five hundred. He received the whole with great coolness.

Several celebrated architects now entered the lists to complete this grand undertaking. MANSARD presented his plans, with which COLBERT was extremely pleased: the king also approved of them, and absolutely insisted on their being executed without any alteration. MANSARD replied that he would rather renounce the glory of building this edifice than the liberty of correcting himself, and changing his design, when he thought he could improve it. Among the competitors was CLAUDE PERRAULT, that physician so defamed by Boileau, the poet. His plans were preferred, and merited the preference. Many pleasantries were circulated at the expense of the new medical architect; and Perrault replied to those sarcasms, by producing the beautiful colonnade of the *Louvre*, the master-piece of French architecture, and the admiration of all Europe.

The façade of this colonnade, which is of the Corinthian order, is five hundred and twenty-five feet in length: it is divided into two peristyles and three avant-corps. The principal gate is in the centre avant-corps, which is decorated with eight double columns, crowned by a pediment, whose raking cornices are composed of two stones only, each fifty-four feet in length by eight in breadth, though no more than eighteen inches in thickness. They were taken from the quarries of Meudon, and formed but one single block, which was sawed into two. The other two avant-corps are ornamented by six pilasters, and two columns of the same order, and disposed in the same manner. On the top, in lieu of a ridged roof, is a terrace, bordered by a stone balustrade, the pedestals of which are intended to bear trophies intermixed with vases.

Perrault's enemies disputed with him the invention of this master-piece. They maintained that it belonged to Le Veau, the architect; but, since the discovery of the original manuscript and drawings of Perrault, there no longer remains a doubt respecting the real author of this beautiful production.

In front of this magnificent colonnade, a multitude of salesmen erect their stalls, and there display quantities of old clothes, rags, &c. This contrast, as Mercier justly remarks, still speaks to the eye of the attentive observer. It is the image of all the rest, grandeur and beggary, side by side.

However, it is not on the *outside* of these walls only, that beggary has been so nearly allied to grandeur. At least we have a solitary instance of this truth of a very striking nature.

Cardinal de Retz tells us, that going one morning to the *Louvre* to see the Queen of England, he found her in the chamber of her daughter, afterwards Dutchess of Orleans, and that she said to him : " You see, I come to keep Henriette " company: the poor girl could not leave her " bed to-day, for want of fuel."—It is true, he adds, that, for six months past Cardinal Mazarin had not paid her pension; the tradesmen would no longer give her credit, and she had not a piece of wood to warm her.

Like St. Paul's in London, the façade of the *Louvre* cannot be seen to the best advantage, on account of the proximity of the surrounding buildings; and, like many other great undertakings too, will, probably, never be completed; but remain a monument of the fickleness of the alion.

Lewis XIV, after having for a long time made the *Louvre* his residence, abandoned it for *Versailles:* " Sire," said Dufreny once to that prince, " I never look at the *New Louvre*, without ex-
" claiming, superb monument of the magnificence
" of our greatest kings, you would have been
" finished, had you been given to one of the
" begging orders of friars!" From that period, the *Louvre* was wholly consecrated to the sittings of different academies, and to the accommodation of several men of science and artists, to whom free apartments were allotted.

I much regret having, for this year at least, lost a sight here, which I should have viewed with no inconsiderable degree of attention. This is the

PUBLIC EXHIBITION OF THE PRODUCTIONS OF FRENCH INDUSTRY.

Under the directorial government, this exhibition was opened in the *Champ de Mars*; but it now takes place, annually, in the square of the *Louvre*, during the five complementary days of the republican calendar; namely, from the 18th to the 22d of September, both inclusive.

The exhibition not only includes manufactures of every sort, but also every new discovery, invention, and improvement. For the purpose of displaying these objects to advantage, temporary buildings are erected along the four interior walls of this square, each of which are subdivided into twenty-five porticoes; so that the whole square of the *Louvre*, during that period, represents a fair with a hundred booths. The resemblance, I am told, is rendered still more perfect by the prodigious crowd; persons of all ranks being indiscriminately admitted to view these productions. Precautions, however, are taken to prevent the indiscreet part of the public from rushing into the porticoes, and sentinels are posted at certain intervals to preserve order.

This, undoubtedly, is a very laudable institution, and extremely well calculated to excite emulation in the national manufactures, specimens of which being sent from all the principal manufacturing towns, the hundred porticoes may be said to comprise an epitome of the present state of all the flourishing manufactures of France. Indeed, none but new inventions and articles of finished workmanship, the fabrication of which is known, are suffered to make part of the exhibition. Even these are not admitted till after a previous examination, and on the certificate of a private jury of five members, appointed for that purpose by the prefect of each department. A new jury, composed of fifteen members, nominated by the Minister of the Interior, again examine the different articles admitted; and agreeably to their decision, the government award premiums and medals to those persons who have made the greatest improvement in any particular fabric or branch of industry, or produced any new discovery or invention. The successful candidates are presented to the Chief Consul by the Minister of the Interior, and have the honour of dining with him at his public monthly dinner.

From all that I can learn concerning this interesting exhibition, it appears, that, though the useful arts, in general, cannot at present be put in competition here with those of a similar description among us, the object of the French government is to keep up a spirit of rivalship, and encourage, by every possible means, the improvement of those manufactures in which England is acknowledged to surpass other countries.

I am reminded that it is time to prepare for going out to dinner. I must therefore not leave this letter, like the *Louvre*, unfinished. Fortunately, my good friend, the prevailing fashion here is to dine very late, which leaves me a long morning; but for this, I know not when I should have an opportunity of writing long letters. Restrain then your impatience, and I promise that you shall very shortly be ushered into the GALLERY OF ANTIQUES,

" Where the smooth chisel all its force has shewn,
" And soften'd into flesh the rugged stone."

LETTER VII.

Paris, October 28, 1801.

HAVING, in my last letter, described to you the outside of the *Louvre*, (with the exception of the Great Gallery, of which I shall speak more at length in another place), I shall now proceed to give you an account of some of the principal national establishments contained within its walls.

Before the revolution, the *Louvre* was, as I have said, the seat of different academies, such as the *French Academy*, the *Academy of Sciences*, the *Academy of Inscriptions and Belles Lettres*, the *Academy of Painting and Sculpture*, and the *Academy of Architecture*. All these are replaced by the *National Institute of Arts and Sciences*, of which, however, I shall postpone further mention till I conduct you to one of its public sittings.

At the period to which I revert, there existed in the *Louvre* a hall, called the *Salle des Antiques*, where, besides, some original statues by French artists, were assembled models in plaster of the most celebrated master-pieces of sculpture in Italy, together with a small number of antiques. In another apartment, forming part of those assigned to the Academy of Painting, and called the *Galérie d'Apollon*, were seen several pictures, chiefly of the French school; and it was intended that the Great Gallery should be formed into a Museum, containing a collection of the finest pictures and statues at the disposal of the crown.

This plan, which had partly been carried into execution under the old *régime*, is now completed, but in a manner infinitely more magnificent than could possibly have been effected without the advantages of conquest. The *Great Gallery* and *Saloon* of the *Louvre* are solely appropriated to the exhibition of pictures of the old masters of the Italian, Flemish, and French schools; and the *Gallery of Apollo* to that of their drawings; while a suite of lofty apartments has been purposely fitted up in this palace for the reception of original antiques, in lieu of those copies of them before-mentioned. In other rooms, adjoining to the Great Gallery, are exhibited, as formerly, that is during one month every year, the productions of living painters, sculptors, architects, and draughtsmen.

These different exhibitions are placed under the

superintendance of a board of management, or an administration, (as the French term it), composed of a number of antiquaries, artists, and men of science, inferior to none in Europe in skill, judgment, taste, or erudition. The whole of this grand establishment bears the general title of

CENTRAL MUSEUM OF THE ARTS.

The treasures of painting and sculpture which the French nation have acquired by the success of their arms, or by express conditions in treaties of alliance or neutrality, are so immense as to enable them, not only to render this CENTRAL MUSEUM the grandest collection of master-pieces in the world, but also to establish fifteen departmental Museums in fifteen of the principal towns of France. This measure, evidently intended to favour the progress of the fine arts, will ease Paris of a great number of the pictures, statues, &c. amassed here from different parts of France, Germany, Belgium, Holland, Italy, Piedmont, Savoy, and the States of Venice.

If you cast your eye on the annexed *Plan of Paris*, and suppose yourself near the exterior south-west angle of the *Louvre*, or, as it is more emphatically styled, the NATIONAL PALACE OF ARTS AND SCIENCES, you will be in the right-hand corner of the *Place du Louvre*, in which quarter is the present entrance to the CENTRAL

MUSEUM OF THE ARTS. Here, after passing through a court, you enter a vestibule, on the left of which is the Hall of the Administration of the Museum. On the ground-floor, facing the door of this vestibule, is the entrance to the

GALLERY OF ANTIQUES.

In this gallery, which was, for the first time, opened to the public on the 18th of Brumaire, year ix. of the French republic, (9th of November 1800), are now distributed no less than one hundred and forty-six statues, busts, and bas-reliefs. It consists of several handsome apartments, bearing appropriate denominations, according to the principal subjects which each contains. Six only are at present completely arranged for public inspection: but many others are in a state of preparation.

The greater part of the statues here exhibited, are the fruit of the conquests of the army of Italy. Conformably to the treaty of Tolentino, they were selected at Rome, from the Capitol and the Vatican, by BARTHÉLEMY, BERTHOLET, MOITTE, MONGE, THOUIN, and TINET, who were appointed, by the French government, commissioners for the research of objects appertaining to the Arts and Sciences.

In the vestibule, for the moderate price of fifteen *sous*, is sold a catalogue, which is not merely a barren index, but a perspicuous and satisfactory explanation of the different objects that strike the eye of the admiring spectator as he traverses the GALLERY OF ANTIQUES. It is by no means my intention to transcribe this catalogue, or to mention every statue; but, assisted by the valuable observations with which I was favoured by the learned antiquary, VISCONTI, long distinguished for his profound knowledge of the fine arts, I shall describe the most remarkable only, and such as would fix the attention of the connoisseur.

On entering the gallery, you might, perhaps, be tempted to stop in the first hall; but we will visit them all in regular succession, and proceed to that which is now the furthest on the left hand. The ceiling of this apartment, painted by ROMANELLI, represents the four seasons; whence it is called the

HALL OF THE SEASONS.

In consequence, among other antiques, here are placed the statues of the rustic divinities, and those relating to the Seasons. Of the whole, I shall distinguish the following:

N° 210.　　　DIANA.

Diana, habited as a huntress, in a short tunic without sleeves, is holding her bow in one hand; while, with the other, she is drawing an arrow from her quiver, which is suspended at her shoulder. Her legs are bare, and her feet are adorned with rich sandals. The goddess, with a look expressive of indignation, appears to be defending the fabulous hind from the pursuit of Hercules, who, in obedience to the oracle of Apollo, was pursuing it, in order to carry it alive to Eurystheus; a task imposed on him by the latter as one of his twelve labours.

To say that, in the opinion of the first-rate connoisseurs, this statue might serve as a companion to the *Apollo of Belvedere*, is sufficient to convey an idea of its perfection; and, in fact, it is reckoned the finest representation of Diana in existence. It is of Parian marble, and, according to historians, has been in France ever since the reign of Henry IV. It was the most perfect of the antiques which adorned the Gallery of Versailles. The parts wanting have been recently restored with such skill as to claim particular admiration.

214. ROME.

In this bust, the city of Rome is personified as an Amazon. The helmet of the female warrior is adorned with a representation of the she-wolf suckling the children of Mars.

This antique, of Parian marble, is of a perfect

Greek style, and in admirable preservation. It formerly belonged to the Gallery of Richelieu-Castle.

51.   ADOLESCENS SPINAM AVELLENS.

This bronze figure represents a young man seated, who seems employed in extracting a thorn from his left foot.

It is a production of the flourishing period of the art, but, according to appearance, anterior to the reign of Alexander the Great. It partakes a little of the meagre style of the old Greek school; but, at the same time, is finished with astonishing truth, and exhibits a graceful simplicity of expression. In what place it was originally discovered is not known. It was taken from the Capitol, where it was seen in the *Palazzo dei Conservatori*.

50.   A FAUN, *in a resting posture*.

This young faun, with no other covering than a deer's skin thrown over his shoulders, is standing with his legs crossed, and leaning on the trunk of a tree, as if resting himself.

The grace and finished execution that reign throughout this figure, as well as the immense number of copies still existing of it, and all antiques, occasion it to be considered as the copy of the Faun in bronze, (or Satyr as it is termed by the Greeks), of Praxiteles. That statue was so celebrated, that the epithet of περιβόητος, or the famous, became its distinctive appellation throughout Greece.

This Faun is of Pentelic marble: it was found in 1701, near *Civita Lavinia,* and placed in the Capitol by Benedict XIV.

59. ARIADNE, *known by the name of* CLEOPATRA.

In this beautiful figure, Ariadne is represented asleep on a rock in the Isle of Naxos, abandoned by the faithless Theseus, and at the moment when Bacchus became enamoured of her, as described by several ancient poets.

It is astonishing how the expression of sleep could be mistaken for that of death, and cause this figure to be called *Cleopatra.* The serpent on the upper part of the left arm is evidently a bracelet, of that figure which the Greek women called οφιδιον, or the little serpent.

For three successive centuries, this statue of Parian marble constituted one of the principal ornaments of the Belvedere of the Vatican, where it was placed by Julius II.

190. AUGUSTUS.

This head of Augustus, adorned with the civic crown of oak leaves, is one of the fine portraits of that emperor. It is executed in Parian marble, and comes from Verona, where it was admired in the *Bevilacqua* cabinet.

On quitting the HALL OF THE SEASONS, we return to that through which we first passed to reach it. This apartment, from being ornamented with the statues of ZENO, TRAJAN, DEMOSTHENES, and PHOCION, is denominated the

HALL OF ILLUSTRIOUS MEN.

It is decorated with eight antique granite pillars brought from *Aix-la-Chapelle*, where they stood in the nave of the church, which contained the tomb of Charlemagne.

Among the antiques placed in it, I shall particularize

N° 75. MENANDER.

This figure represents the poet, honoured by the Greeks with the title of *Prince of the New Comedy*, sitting on a hemi-cycle, or semicircular seat, and resting after his literary labours. He is clad in the Grecian tunic and *pallium*.

76. POSIDIPPUS.

The dress of Posidippus, who was reckoned among the Greeks one of the best authors of what was called the *New Comedy*, is nearly that of Menander, the poet. Like him, he is represented sitting on a hemi-cycle.

These two statues, which are companions, are admirable for the noble simplicity of their execution. They are both of Pentelic marble, and were found in the XVIth century at Rome, in the gardens of the convent of *San Lorenzo*, on Mount Viminal. After making part of the baths of Olympius, they were placed by Sixtus V. at *Negroni*, whence they were removed to the Vatican by Pius VI.

Continuing our examination, after leaving the HALL OF ILLUSTRIOUS MEN, we next come to the

HALL OF THE ROMANS.

The ceiling of this hall is ornamented with subjects taken from the Roman history, painted by ROMANELLI; and in it are chiefly assembled such works of sculpture as have a relation to that people.

Among several busts and statues, representing ADRIAN, PUBLIUS CORNELIUS SCIPIO, MARCUS JUNIUS BRUTUS, LUCIUS JUNIUS BRUTUS, CICERO, &c. I shall point out to your notice,

209. *The* TORSO *of* BELVEDERE.

This admirable remnant of a figure seated,

though the head, arms, and legs are wanting, represents the apotheosis of Hercules. The lion's skin spread on the rock, and the enormous size of the limbs, leave no doubt as to the subject of the statue. Notwithstanding the muscles are strongly marked, the veins in the body of the hero are suppressed, whence antiquaries have inferred, that the intention of the author was to indicate the very moment of his deification. According to this idea, our countryman FLAXMAN has immortalized himself by restoring a copy of the *Torso*, and placing Hebe on the left of Hercules, in the act of presenting to him the cup of immortality.

On the rock, where the figure is seated, is the following Greek inscription:

ΑΠΟΛΛωΝΙΟΣ
ΝΕΣΤΟΡΟΣ
ΑΘΗΝΑΙΟΣ
ΕΠΟΙΕΙ.

By which we are informed, that it is the production of APOLLONIUS, *the Athenian, the son of Nestor*, who, probably, flourished in the time of Pompey the Great.

This valuable antique is of Pentelic marble, and sculptured in a most masterly style. It was found at Rome, near Pompey's theatre, now *Campo di Fiore.* Julius II. placed it in the garden of the Vatican, where it was long the object of the studies of MICHAEL ANGELO, RAPHAEL, &c. those illustrious geniuses, to whom we are indebted for the improvement of the fine arts. Among artists, it has always been distinguished by the appellation of the *Torso of Belvedere.*

94. *A wounded warrior, commonly called the* GLADIATOR MORIENS.

This figure, represents a barbarian soldier, dying on the field of battle, without surrendering. It is remarkable for truth of imitation, of a choice nature, though not sublime, (because the subject would not admit of it,) and for nobleness of expression, which is evident without affectation.

This statue formerly belonged to the *Villa-Ludovisi,* whence it was removed to the Museum of the Capitol by Clement XII. It is from the chisel of AGASIAS, a sculptor of Ephesus, who lived 450 years before the Christian era.

82.   CERES.

This charming figure is rather that of a Muse than of the goddess of agriculture. It is admirable for the *ideal* beauty of the drapery. She is clad in a tunic; over this is thrown a mantle, the execution of which is so perfect, that, through it, are perceived the knots of the strings which fasten the tunic below the bosom.

It formerly belonged to the *Villa-Mattei*, on Mount Esquiline; but was taken from the Museum of the Vatican, where it had been placed by Clement XIV.

80. *A Roman orator, called* GERMANICUS.

Hitherto this admirable figure of a Roman orator, with the attributes of Mercury, the god of eloquence, has passed for that of Germanicus, though it is manifestly too old for him. Here we have another model of beautiful elegance of form, though not of an *ideal* sublimity.

On the shell of a tortoise, at the foot of the statue, is inscribed in beautiful Greek characters:

ΚΛΕΟΜΕΝΗΣ
ΚΛΕΟΜΕΝΟΥΣ
ΑΘΗΝΑΙΟΣΕ
ΠΟΙΗΣΕΝ.

Whence we learn that it is the production of CLEOMENES, an Athenian artist, mentioned by Pliny, and who flourished towards the end of the Roman republic, about 500 years before Christ. This statue was taken from the Gallery of Versailles, where it had been placed in the reign of Lewis XIV. It formerly belonged to the garden of Sixtus V. at *Villa-Montalto*, in Rome.

97. ANTINOÜS, *called the* ANTINOÜS OF THE CAPITOL.

In this monument, Adrian's favourite is represented as having scarcely attained the age of puberty. He is naked, and his attitude has some affinity to that of Mercury. However, his countenance seems to be impressed with that cast of melancholy, by which all his portraits are distinguished. Hence has been applied to him that verse of Virgil on Marcellus;

" *Sed frons læta parum, et dejecto lumina vultu.*"

This beautiful figure, of Carrara marble, is sculptured in a masterly manner. It comes from the Museum of the Capitol, and previously belonged to the collection of Cardinal Alessandro Albani. The fore-arm and left leg are modern.

200. ANTINOÜS.

In this colossal bust of the Bithynian youth, are some peculiarities which call to mind the images of the Egyptian god *Harpocrates*. It is finely executed in hard Greek marble, and comes from the Museum of the Vatican. As recently as the year 1790, it was dug from the ruins of the *Villa-Fede* at Tivoli.

But enough for to-day—to-morrow I will resume my pen, and we will complete our survey of the GALLERY OF ANTIQUES.

LETTER VIII.

Paris, October 29, 1801.

IF the culture of the arts, by promoting industry and increasing commerce, improves civilization, and refines manners, what modern people can boast of such advantages as are now enjoyed by the French nation? While the sciences keep pace with the arts, good taste bids fair to spread, in time, from the capital throughout the country, and to become universal among them. In antiquity, Athens attests the truth of this proposition, by rising, through the same means, above all the cities of Greece; and, in modern times, have we not seen in Florence, become opulent, the darkness of ignorance vanish, like a fog, before the bright rays of knowledge, diffused by the flourishing progress of the arts and sciences?

When I closed my letter yesterday, we had just terminated our examination of the HALL OF THE ROMANS. On the same line with it, the next apartment we reach, taking its name from the celebrated group here placed, is styled the

HALL OF THE LAOCOON.

Here are to be admired four pillars of *verde antico*, a species of green marble, obtained by the ancients, from the environs of Thessalonica. They were taken from the church of *Montmorency*, where they decorated the tomb of Anne, the constable of that name. The first three apartments are floored with inlaid oak; but this is paved with beautiful marble.

Of the *chefs d'œuvre* exhibited in this hall, every person of taste cannot but feel particular gratification in examining the undermentioned:

N° 108.   LAOCOON.

The pathetic story which forms the subject of this admirable group is known to every classic reader. It is considered as one of the most perfect works that ever came from the chisel; being at once a master-piece of composition, design, and feeling. Any sort of commentary could but weaken the impression which it makes on the beholder.

It was found in 1506, under the pontificate of Julius·II, at Rome, on Mount Esquiline, in the ruins of the palace of Titus. The three Rhodian artists, AGESANDER, POLYDORUS, and ATHENOPORUS, mentioned by Pliny, as the sculptors of this *chef d'œuvre* flourished during the time of the

Emperors, in the first century of the christian era.

The group is composed of five blocks, but joined in so skilful a manner, that Pliny thought them of one single piece. The right arm of the father and two arms of the children are wanting.

111. AMAZON.

This uncommonly beautiful figure of Parian marble represents a woman, whose feminine features and form seem to have contracted the impression of the masculine habits of warfare. Clad in a very fine tunic, which, leaving the left breast exposed, is tucked up on the hips, she is in the act of bending a large bow. No attitude could be better calculated for exhibiting to advantage the finely-modelled person of this heroine.

For two centuries, this statue was at the *Villa-Mattei*, on Mount Cœlius at Rome, whence it was removed to the Museum of the Vatican by Clement XIV.

118. MELEAGER.

The son of Œneus, king of Calydon, with nothing but a *chlamis* fastened on his shoulders, and winding round his left arm, is here represented resting himself, after having killed the formidable wild boar, which was ravaging his dominions; at his side is the head of the animal, and near him sits his faithful dog.

The beauty of this group is sublime, and yet it is of a different cast, from either that of the *Apollo of Belvedere*, or that of the *Mercury*, called Antinoüs, of which we shall presently have occasion to speak.

This group is of Greek marble of a cinereous colour: there are two different traditions respecting the place where it was found; but the preference is given to that of Aldroandi, who affirms that it was discovered in a vineyard bordering on the Tiber. It belonged to Fusconi, physician to Paul III, and was for a long time in the *Pighini* palace at Rome, whence Clement XIV had it conveyed to the Vatican.

103 and 104. *Two busts, called* TRAGEDY *and* COMEDY.

These colossal heads of Bacchantes adorned the entrance of the theatre of the *Villa-Adriana* at Tivoli. Though the execution of them is highly finished, it is no detriment to the grandeur of the style.

The one is of Pentelic marble; and the other, of Parian. Having been purchased of Count Fede by Pius VI, they were placed in the Museum of the Vatican.

105.   ANTINOÜS.

This bust is particularly deserving of attention, on account of its beauty, its excellent preservation, and perfect resemblance to the medals which remain of Adrian's favourite.

It is of Parian marble of the finest quality, and had been in France long before the revolution.

112. ARIADNE, *called* (in the catalogue) BACCHUS.

Some sculptors have determined to call this beautiful head that of BACCHUS; while the celebrated VISCONTI, and other distinguished antiquaries, persist in preserving to it its ancient name of ARIADNE, by which it was known in the Museum of the Capitol.

Whichever it may be, it is of Pentelic marble, and unquestionably one of the most sublime productions of the chisel, in point of *ideal* beauty.

From the HALL OF THE LAOCOON, we pass into the apartment, which, from the famous statue, here erected, and embellished in the most splendid manner, takes the appellation of the

HALL OF THE APOLLO.

This hall is ornamented with four pillars of red oriental granite of the finest quality: those which decorate the niche of the Apollo were taken from the church that contained the tomb of Charlemagne at *Aix-la-Chapelle*. The floor is paved with different species of scarce and valuable marble, in large compartments, and, in its centre, is placed a large octagonal table of the same substance.

In proportion to the dimensions of this apartment, which is considerably larger than any of the others, a greater number of antiques are here placed, of which the following are the most preeminent.

N° 145. APOLLO PYTHIUS, *commonly called the* APOLLO OF BELVEDERE.

The name alone of this *chef d'œuvre* might be said to contain its eulogium. But as you may, probably, expect from me some remarks on it, I shall candidly acknowledge that I can do no better than communicate to you the able and interesting description given of it by the Administration of the Museum, of which the following is a fair abridgment.

" Apollo has just discharged the mortal arrow which has struck the serpent Python, while ravaging Delphi. In his left hand is held his formidable bow; his right has but an instant quitted it: all his members still preserve the impression given them by this action. Indignation is seated on his lips; but in his looks is the assurance of success. His hair, slightly curled, floats in long ringlets round his neck, or is gracefully turned up on the crown of his head, which is encircled by the *strophium*, or fillet, characteristic of kings and gods. His quiver is suspended by a belt to the right shoulder: his feet are adorned with rich sandals. His *chlamis* fastened on the shoulder, and tucked up only on the left arm, is thrown back, as if to display the majesty of his divine form to greater advantage.

" An eternal youth is spread over all his beautiful figure, a sublime mixture of nobleness and agility, of vigour and elegance, and which holds a happy medium between the delicate form of Bacchus, and the more manly one of Mercury."

This inimitable master-piece is of Carrara marble, and, consequently, was executed by some Greek artist who lived in the time of the Romans; but the name of its author is entirely unknown. The fore-arm and the left hand, which were wanting, were restored by GIOVANNI ANGELO DE MONTORSOLI, a sculptor, who was a pupil of Michael Angelo.

Towards the end of the fifteenth century, it was discovered at *Capo d'Anzo*, twelve leagues from Rome, on the sea-shore, near the ruins of the ancient *Antium*. Julius II, when cardinal, purchased this statue, and placed it in his palace;

but shortly after, having arrived at the pontificate, he had it conveyed to the Belvedere of the Vatican, where, for three centuries, it was the admiration of the world.

On the 16th of Brumaire, year IX, (7th of November, 1801) BONAPARTE, as First Consul, celebrated, in great pomp, the inauguration of the Apollo; on which occasion he placed between the plinth of the statue, and its pedestal, a brass tablet bearing a suitable inscription.

The Apollo stands facing the entrance-door of the apartment, in an elevated recess, decorated, as I have before observed, with beautiful granite pillars. The flight of steps, leading to this recess, is paved with the rarest marble, inlaid with squares of curious antique mosaic, and on them are placed two Egyptian sphynxes of red oriental granite, taken from the Museum of the Vatican.

142. VENUS OF THE CAPITOL.

This figure of Parian marble represents the goddess of beauty issuing from the bath. Her charms are not concealed by any veil or garment. She is slightly turning her head to the left, as if to smile on the Graces, who are supposed to be preparing to attire her.

In point of execution, this is allowed to be the most beautiful of all the statues of Venus which we have remaining. The *Venus of Medicis* surpasses it in sublimity of form, approaching nearer to *ideal* beauty.

Bupalus, a sculptor of the Isle of Scio, is said to have produced this master-piece. He lived 600 years before Christ, so that it has now been in existence upwards of two thousand four hundred years. It was found about the middle of the eighteenth century, near *San-Vitale*, at Rome. Benedict XIV having purchased it of the *Stati* family, placed it in the Capitol.

125. MERCURY, *commonly called the* ANTINOÜS OF BELVEDERE.

This statue, also of the finest Parian marble, is one of the most beautiful that can be imagined. More robust in form than either that of the *Apollo* or of the *Meleager*, it loses nothing by being contemplated after the former. In short, the harmony which reigns between its parts is such, that the celebrated POUSSIN, in preference to every other, always took from it the *proportions of the human figure*.

It was found at Rome, on Mount Esquiline, under the pontificate of Paul III, who placed it in the Belvedere of the Vatican, near the Apollo and the Laocoon.

151. *The Egyptian* Antinoüs.

In this statue, Antinoüs is represented as a divinity of Egypt. He is standing in the usual attitude of the Egyptian gods, and is naked, with the exception of his head and wrist, which are covered with a species of drapery in imitation of the sacred garments.

This beautiful figure is wrought with superior excellence. It is of white marble, which leads to a conjecture that it might have been intended to represent Orus, the god of light, it having been the custom of the Egyptians to represent all their other divinities in coloured marble. It was discovered in 1738, at Tivoli, in the *Villa-Adriana*, and taken from the Museum of the Capitol.

To judge from the great number of figures of Antinoüs, sculptured by order of Adrian to perpetuate the memory of that favourite, the emperor's gratitude for him must have been unbounded. Under the form of different divinities, or at different periods of life, there are at present in the Gallery of Antiques no less than five portraits of him, besides three statues and two busts. Three other statues of Antinoüs, together with a bust, and an excellent bass-relief, in which he is represented, yet remain to be placed.

156.   BACCHUS.

The god of wine is here represented standing, and entirely naked. He is leaning carelessly with his left arm on the trunk of an elm, round which winds a grape-vine.

This statue, of the marble called at Rome *Greco duro,* is reckoned one of the finest extant of the mirth-inspiring deity.

———

Having surveyed every object deserving of notice in the HALL OF THE APOLLO, we proceed, on the right hand, towards its extremity, and reach the last apartment of the gallery, which, from being consecrated to the tuneful Nine, is called the

HALL OF THE MUSES.

It is paved with curious marble, and independently of the Muses, and their leader, Apollo, here are also assembled the antique portraits of poets and philosophers who have rendered themselves famous by cultivating them. Among these we may perceive HOMER and VIRGIL; but the most remarkable specimen of the art is

N° 177.   EURIPIDES.

In this hermes we have a capital representation of the features of the rival of Sophocles. The countenance is at once noble, serious, and expressive. It bears the stamp of the genius of that celebrated tragic poet, which was naturally sublime and profound, though inclined to the pathetic.

This hermes is executed in Pentelic marble, and was taken from the academy of *Mantua*.

Since the revival of the arts, the lovers of antiquity have made repeated attempts to form a collection of antique statues of the Muses; but none was ever so complete as that assembled in the Museum of the Vatican by Pius VI, and which the chance of war has now transferred to the banks of the Seine. Here the bard may offer up to them a solemn invocation, and compose his lay, as it were, under their very eyes.

The statues of CLIO, THALIA, TERPSICHORE, ERATO, POLYHYMNIA, and CALLIOPE, together with the APOLLO MUSAGETES, were discovered in 1774, at *Tivoli*, among the ruins of the villa of Cassius. To complete the number, Pius VI obtained the EUTERPE and the URANIA from the *Lancellotti* palace at *Veletri*. They are supposed to be antique copies of the statues of the Nine Muses by Philiscus, which, according to Pliny, graced the portico of Octavia.

The air of grandeur that reigns in the general arrangement of the gallery is very striking: and the tasteful and judicious distribution of this matchless assemblage of antiques does great honour to the Council of the CENTRAL MUSEUM. Among the riches which Rome possessed, the French commissioners also, by their choice selection, have manifested the depth of their knowledge, and the justness of their discrimination.

The alterations and embellishments made in the different apartments of the GALLERY OF ANTIQUES have been executed under the immediate direction of their author, M. RAYMOND, member of the National Institute, and architect to the NATIONAL PALACE OF ARTS AND SCIENCES. In winter, the apartments are kept warm by means of flues, which diffuse a genial vapour. Here, without the expense of a single *liard*, the young draughtsman may form his taste by studying the true antique models of Grecian sculpture; the more experienced artist may consult them as he finds occasion in the composition of his subjects; while the connoisseur, the amateur, or the simple observer may spend many an agreeable hour in contemplating these master-pieces which, for centuries, have inspired universal admiration.

These are the materials on which Genius ought to work, and without which the most promising talent may be greatly misapplied, if not entirely lost. It was by studying closely these correct models, that the great MICHAEL ANGELO, the sublime RAPHAEL, and other eminent masters, acquired that idea of excellence which is the result of the accumulated experience of successive ages. Here, in one visit, the student may imbibe those principles to ascertain which many artists have consumed the best part of their days; and penetrated by their effect, he is spared the laborious investigation by which they came to be known and established. It is unnecessary to expatiate on the advantages which the fine arts may expect to derive from such a repository of antiques in a capital so centrical as Paris. The contemplation of them cannot fail to fire the genius of any artist of taste, and prompt his efforts towards the attainment of that grand style, which, disdaining the minute accidental particularities of individual objects, improves partial representation by the general and invariable ideas of nature.

A vast collection of antiquities of every description is still expected from Italy, among which are the *Venus of Medicis* and the *Pallas of Veletri*, a finely-preserved statue, classed by artists among those of the first rank, dug up at *Veletri* in 1799, in consequence of the researches made there by order of the French commissioners. Upwards of five hundred cases were lying on the banks of the Tiber, at Rome, ready to be sent off to France, when the Neapolitans entered that city. They carried them all away: but by the last article of the treaty of peace with the king of Naples, the whole of them are to be restored to the French Republic. For the purpose of verifying their condition, and taking measures for their conveyance to Paris, two commissioners have been dispatched to Italy: one is the son of CHAPTAL, Minister of the Interior, and the other is DUFOURNY, the architect. On the arrival of these cases, even after the fifteen departmental Museums have been supplied, it is asserted that there will yet remain in the French capital, antiquities in sufficient number to form a museum almost from Paris to Versailles.

The CENTRAL MUSEUM OF THE ARTS is open to the public in general on the 8th, 9th, and 10th of each decade*; the other days are appropriated to the study of young pupils; but a foreigner has only to produce his *permis de séjour* to gain admission *gratis* every day from the hour of ten o'clock to four. To the credit of the nation, I must observe that this exception in favour of foreigners excites no jealousy whatever.

It is no more than a justice due to the liberality of the French republican government to add, that they set a noble example which is worthy of being followed, not only in England, but in every other country, where the arts and sciences are honoured, or the general interests of mankind

---

* By a subsequent regulation, Saturday and Sunday are the days on which the CENTRAL MUSEUM is open to public inspection.

held in estimation. From persons visiting any national establishment, whether museum, library, cabinet, or garden, in this capital, no sort of fee or perquisite is now expected, or allowed to be taken. Although it was not a public day when I paid my first visit to the CENTRAL MUSEUM, no sooner did I shew my *permis de séjour*, than the doors were thrown open; and from M. VISCONTI, and other members of the Council, who happened to be present, I experienced the most polite and obliging attention. As an Englishman, I confess that I felt a degree of shame on reflecting to what pitiful exaction a foreigner would be subject, who might casually visit any public object of curiosity in our metropolis.

LETTER IX.

Paris, October 31, 1801.

IN answer to your question, I shall begin by informing you that I have not set eyes on the *petit caporal*, as some affect to style the Chief Consul. He spends much of his time, I am told, at *Malmaison*, his country-seat; and seldom appears in public, except in his box at the Opera, or at the French theatre; but at the grand monthly parade, I shall be certain to behold him, on the 15th of the present month of Brumaire, acording to the republican calendar, which day answers to the 6th of November. I have therefore to check my impatience for a week longer.

However, if I have not yet seen BONAPARTE himself, I have at least seen a person who has seen him, and will take care that I shall have an opportunity of seeing him too : this person is no less than a general—who accompanied him in his expedition to Egypt—who was among the chosen few that returned with him from that country—who there surveyed the mouths of the Nile—who served under him in the famous campaign of Syria; and who at this day is one of the first military engineers in Europe. In a word, it is General A———y, of the artillery, at present Director of that scientific establishment, called the DÉPÔT DE LA GUERRE. He invited me the day before yesterday to breakfast, with a view of meeting some of his friends whom he had purposely assembled.

I am not fond of breakfasting from home; *mais il faut vivre à Rome comme à Rome.* Between ten and eleven o'clock I reached the *Dépôt*, which is situated in the *Rue de l'Université, Faubourg St. Germain*, at the *ci-devant Hôtel d'Harcourt*, formerly belonging to the duke of that name. Passing through the gate-way, I was proceeding boldly to the principal entrance of the hotel, when a sentinel stopped me short by charging his bayonet. " Citizen," said he fiercely, at the same time pointing to the lodge on the right, " you must speak to the porter." I accordingly obeyed the mandate. " What's your " business, citizen?" inquired the porter gruffly. —" My business, citizen," replied I, " is only to " breakfast with the general."—" Be so good, " citizen," rejoined he in a milder tone, " as to " take the trouble to ascend the grand stair-case, " and ring the bell on the first-floor."

Being introduced into the general's apartments, I there found eight or ten persons of very ntelligent aspect, seated at a round table, loaded with all sorts of good things, but, in my mind, better calculated for dinner than breakfast. Among a great variety of delicacies, were beef-steaks, or, as they are here termed, *bif-ticks à l'Anglaise*. Oysters too were not forgotten: indeed, they compose an essential part of a French breakfast; and the ladies seem particularly partial to them, I suppose, because they are esteemed strengthening to a delicate constitution.

Nothing could be more pleasant than this party. Most of the guests were distinguished literati, or military men of no ordinary stamp. One of the latter, a *chef de brigade* of engineers, near whom I considered myself fortunate in being placed, spoke to me in the highest terms of Mr.

Spencer Smith, Sir Sidney's brother, to whose interference at *Constantinople*, he was indebted for his release from a Turkish prison.

Notwithstanding the continual clatter of knives and forks, and the occasional gingle of glasses, the conversation, which suffered no interruption, was to me extremely interesting: I never heard any men express opinions more liberal on every subject that was started. It was particularly gratifying to my feelings, as an Englishman, to hear a set of French gentlemen, some of whom had participated in the sort of disgrace attached to the raising of the siege of *St. Jean d'Acre*, generously bestow just encomiums on my brother-officer, to whose heroism they owed their failure. Addison, I think, says, somewhere in the Spectator, that national prejudice is a laudable partiality; but, however laudable it may be to indulge such a partiality, it ought not to render us blind to the merit of individuals of a rival nation.

General A———y, being one of those whose talents have been found too useful to the State to be suffered to remain in inaction, was obliged to attend at the *Conseil des Mines* soon after twelve o'clock, when the party separated. Just as I was taking leave, he did me the favour to put into my hand a copy of his *Histoire du Canal du Midi*, of which I shall say more when I have had leisure to peruse it.

I do not know that a man in good health, who takes regular exercise, is the worse for breakfasting on a beef-steak, in the long-exploded style of Queen Bess; but I am no advocate for all the accessories of a French *déjeûner à la fourchette*. The strong Mocha coffee which I swallowed, could not check the more powerful effect of the Madeira and *crême de rose*. I therefore determined on taking a long walk, which, when saddle-horses are not to be procured, I have always found the best remedy for the kind of restlessness created by such a breakfast.

I accordingly directed my steps across the *Pont & Place de la Concorde*, traversed the street of the same name; and, following the *Boulevard* for a certain distance, struck off to the left, that is, towards the north, in order to gain the summit of

MONTMARTRE.

In ancient times, there stood on this hill a temple dedicated to Mars, whence the name *Mons Martis*, of which has been made *Montmartre*. At the foot of it, was the *Campus Martius*, or *Champ de Mars*, where the French kings of the first race caused their throne to be erected every year on the first of May. They came hither in a car, decorated with green boughs and flowers, and drawn by four oxen. Such, indeed, was the town-equipage of king DAGOBERT,

"*Quatre bœufs attelés, d'un pas tranquil et lent,*
"*Promenaient dans Paris le monarque indolent.*"

Having seated themselves on the throne, they gave a public audience to the people, at the same time giving and receiving presents, which were called *estrennes*. Hence annual presents were afterwards termed *étrennes*, and this gave rise to the custom of making them.

On this hill too fell the head of Διονυσιος or *St. Denis*; and in latter times, this was the spot chosen by the Marshal DE BROGLIE, who commanded the thirty-five thousand troops by which the French capital was surrounded in May 1789, for checking the spirit of the turbulent Parisians, by battering their houses about their ears, and burying them under the ruins.

On the summit of *Montmartre*, is a circular terrace, in the centre of which stands a windmill, and not far from it, are several others. Round its brow are several *maisonettes*, or little country-boxes, and also some public gardens with bowers, where lovers often regale their mistresses. Hence you command a full view of the city of Paris. You behold roof rising above roof; and the churches towering above the houses have, at this distance, somewhat the appearance of lofty chimnies. You look down on the capital as far as the Seine, by which it is intersected: beyond that river, the surface of the land rises again in the form of an amphitheatre. On all sides, the prospect is bounded by eminences of various degrees of elevation, over which, as well as over the plains, and along the banks of the river, are scattered villas, windmills, country-seats, hamlets, villages, and coppices; but, from want of enclosures, the circumjacent country has not that rich and variegated aspect which delights the eye in our English rural scenery. This was always one of my favourite walks during my residence in Paris before the revolution; and I doubt not, when you visit the French capital, that you will have the curiosity to scale the heights of *Montmartre.*

As to the theatres, concerning which you interrogate me, I shall defer entering into any particular detail of them, till I have made myself fully acquainted with the attractions of each: this mode of proceeding will not occasion any material delay, as I generally visit one of them every evening, but always endeavour to go to that house where the *best* performers are to be seen, in their *best* characters, and in the *best* pieces. I mention this, in order that you may not think me inattentive to your request, by having hitherto omitted to point out to you the difference between the theatrical amusements here under the monarchy, and those of the republic.

The *théâtre des arts* or grand French opera, the *opera buffa* or Italian comic opera, the *théâtre Feydeau* or French comic opera, and the *théâtre Français*, chiefly engage my attention. Yesterday evening I went to the last-mentioned theatre purposely to see Mademoiselle Contat, who played in both pieces. The first was *Les Femmes Savantes*, a comedy, in which Molière, wishing to aim a blow at female pedantry, has, perhaps, checked, in some French women, a desire for improvement; the second was *La fausse Agnès*, a laughable afterpiece. Notwithstanding the enormous *embonpoint* which this celebrated comic actress has acquired since I saw her last on the Parisian stage upwards of ten years ago, she acquitted herself with her accustomed excellence. I happened to sit next to a very warm admirer of her superior talents, who told me that, bulky as she was become, he had been highly gratified in seeing her perform at *Rouen* not long since, in her favourite character of *Roxalane*, in *Les Trois Sultanes*. " She was much applauded, no doubt." observed I.—" Not at all," replied he, " for the " crowd was so great, that in no part of the " house was it possible for a man to use his " hands."

LETTER X.

Paris, November 2, 1801.

On reaching Paris, every person, whether Jew or Gentile, foreigner or not, coming from any department of the republic, except that of *La Seine*, in which the capital is situated, is now bound to make his appearance at the *Préfecture de Police*.

The new-comer, accompanied by two house-keepers, first repairs to the Police-office of the *arrondissement*, or district, in which he has taken up his residence, where he delivers his travelling passport; in lieu of which he receives a sort of certificate, and then he shews himself at the *Préfecture de Police*, or General Police-office, at present established in the *Cité*.

Here, his name and quality, together with a minute description of his person and his place of abode, are inserted in a register kept for that purpose, to which he puts his signature; and a printed paper, commonly called a *permis de séjour*, is given to him, containing a duplicate of all these matters, filled up in the blanks, which he also signs himself. It is intended that he should always carry this paper about him, in order that he may produce it when called on, or, in case of necessity, for verifying his person, on any particular occasion, such as passing by a guard-house on foot after eleven o'clock at night, or being unexpectedly involved in any affray. In a word, it answers to a stranger the same end as a *carte de sureté*, or ticket of safety, does to an inhabitant of Paris.

I accordingly went through this indispensable ceremony in due form on my arrival here; but, having neglected to read a *nota bene* in the margin of the *permis de séjour*, I had not been ten hours in my new apartments before I received a visit from an Inspector of Police of the *arrondissement*, who, very civilly reminding me of the omission, told me that I need not give myself the trouble of going to the Central Police-office, as he would report my removal. However, being determined to be strictly *en règle*, I went thither myself to cause my new residence to be inserted in the paper.

I should not have dwelt on the circumstance, were it not to shew you the precision observed in the administration of the police of this great city.

Under the old *régime*, every master of a ready-furnished hotel was obliged to keep a register, in which he inserted the name and quality of his lodgers for the inspection of the police-officers whenever they came: this regulation is not only strictly adhered to at present; but every person in Paris, who receives a stranger under his roof as an inmate, is bound, under penalty of a fine, to report him to the police, which is most vigilantly administered by Citizen Fouché.

Last night, not being in time to find good places at the *Théâtre des Arts*, or Grand French Opera, I went to the *Théâtre Louvois*, which is within a few paces of it, in hopes of being more successful. I shall not at present attempt to describe the house, as, from my arriving late, I was too ill accommodated to be able to view it to advantage.

However, I was well seated for seeing the performance. It consisted of three *petites pièces:* namely, *Une heure d'absence, La petite ville,* and *Le café d'une petite ville.* The first was entertaining; but the second much more so; and though the third cannot claim the merit of being well put together, I shall say a few words of it, as it is a production *in honour of peace,* and on that score alone, would, at this juncture, deserve notice.

After a few scenes somewhat languid, interspersed with common-place, and speeches of no great humour, a *dénouement,* by no means interesting, promised not to compensate the audience for their patience. But the author of the *Café d'une petite ville,* having eased himself of this burden, revealed his motive, and took them on their weak side, by making a strong appeal to French enthusiasm. This cord being adroitly struck, his warmth became communicative, and animating the actors, good-humour did the rest. The accessories were infinitely more interesting than the main subject. An allemande, gracefully danced by two damsels and a hero, in the character of a French hussar, returned home from the fatigues of war and battle, was much applauded; and a Gascoon poet, who declares that, for once in his life, he is resolved to speak truth, was loudly encored in the following couplets, adapted to the well-known air of " *Gai, le cœur à la danse.*"

" *Celui qui nous donne la paix,*
" *Comme il fit bien la guerre!*
" *Sur lui déjà force conplets....*
" *Mais il en reste à faire:*
" *Au diable nous nous donnions,*
" *Il revient, nous respirons....*
" *Il fait changer la danse;*
" *Par lui chez nous plus de discord;*
" *Il regle la cadence,*
" *Et nous voilà d'accord.*"

True it is, that BONAPARTE, as principal ballet-master, has changed the dance of the whole nation; he regulates their step to the measure of his own music, and *discord* is mute at the moment: but the question is, whether the French are bonâ-fide *d'accord*, (as the Gascoon affirms,) that is, perfectly reconciled to the new tune and figure? Let us, however, keep out of this maze; were we to enter it, we might remain bewildered there, perhaps, till old father Time came to extricate us.

The morning is inviting: suppose we take a turn in the *Tuileries*, not with a view of surveying this garden, but merely to breathe the fresh air, and examine the

PALAIS DU GOUVERNEMENT.

Since the Chief Consul has made it his town-residence, this is the new denomination given to the *Palais des Tuileries*, thus called, because a tile-kiln formerly stood on the site where it is erected. At that time, this part of Paris was not comprised within its walls, nothing was to be seen here, in the vicinity of the tile-kiln, but a few coppices and scattered habitations.

Catherine de Medicis, wishing to enlarge the capital on this side, visited the spot, and liking the situation, directed PHILIBERT DE L'ORME and JEAN BULLAN, two celebrated French architects, to present her with a plan, from which the construction of this palace was begun in May 1564. At first, it consisted only of the large square pavilion in the centre of the two piles of building, which have each a terrace towards the garden, and of the two pavilions by which they are terminated.

Henry IV enlarged the original building, and, in 1600, began the grand gallery which joins it to the *Louvre*, from the plan of Du Cerceau. Lewis XIII made some alterations in the palace; and in 1664, exactly a century from the date of its construction being begun, Lewis XIV directed Louis de Veau to finish it, by making the additions and embellishments which have brought it to its present state. These deviations from the first plan have destroyed the proportions required by the strict rules of art; but this defect would, probably, be overlooked by those who are not connoisseurs, as the architecture, though variously blended, presents, at first sight, an *ensemble* which is magnificent and striking.

The whole front of the palace of the *Tuileries* consists of five pavilions, connected by four piles of building, standing on the same line, and extending for the space of one thousand and eleven feet. The first order of the three middle piles is Ionic, with encircled columns. The two adjoining pavilions are also ornamented with Ionic pillars; but fluted, and embellished with foliage, from the third of their height to the summit. The second order of these two pavilions is Corinthian. The two piles of building, which come next, as well as the two pavilions of the wings, are of a Composite order with fluted pillars. From a tall iron spindle, placed on the pinnacle of each of the three principal pavilions, is now seen floating a horizontal tri-coloured streamer. Till the improvements made by Lewis XIV, the large centre pavilion had been decorated with the Ionic and Corinthian orders only; to these was added the Composite.

On the façade towards the *Place du Carrousel*, the pillars of all these orders are of brown and red marble. Here may be observed the marks of several cannon-balls, beneath each of which is inscribed, in black, 10 Août.

This tenth of August 1792, a day ever memorable in the history of France, has furnished many an able writer with the subject of an episode; but, I believe, few of them were, any more than myself, actors in that dreadful scene. While I was intently remarking the particular impression of a shot which struck the edge of one of the casements of the first floor of the palace, my *valet de place* came up to know at which door I would have the carriage remain in waiting.

On turning round, I fancied I beheld the man who " drew Priam's curtain in the dead of " night." That messenger, I am sure, could not have presented a visage more pale, more spiritless than my Helvetian. Recollecting that he had served in the Swiss guards, I was the less at a loss to account for his extreme agitation. " In what part of the *château* were you, Jean," said I, " when these balls were aimed at the " windows?"——" There was my post," replied he, recovering himself, and pointing to one of the centre casements.——" Is it true," continued I, " that, by way of feigning a reconciliation, you " threw down cartridges by handfuls to the " Marseillese below, and called out, *vive la na-* " *tion?*"——" It is but too true," answered Jean; " we then availed ourselves of the mo- " ment when they advanced under the persuasion " that they were to become our friends, and " opened on them a tremendous fire, by which " we covered the place with dead and dying. " But we became victims of our own treachery: " for our ammunition being, by this *ruse de* " *guerre*, the sooner expended, we presently had " no resource left but the bayonet, by which we " could not prevent the mob from closing on us." —" And how did you contrive to escape," said I?—" Having thrown away my Swiss uniform," replied he, " in the general confusion, I fortu- " nately possessed myself of the coat of a na- " tional volunteer, which he had taken off on " account of the hot weather. This garment, "bespattered with blood, I instantly put on, as well as his hat with a tri-coloured cockade."—"This disguise saved your life," interrupted I.—"Yes, indeed;" rejoined he. "Having got down to the vestibule, I could not find a passage into the garden; and, to prevent suspicion, I at once mixed with the mob on the place where we are now standing."—"How did you get off at last," said I?—"I was obliged," answered he, "to shout and swear with the *poissardes*, while the heads of many of my comrades were thrown out of the windows."—"The *poissardes*," added I, "set no bounds to their cruelty?"—"No," replied he, "I expected every moment to feel its effects; my disguise alone favoured my escape: on the dead bodies of my countrymen they practised every species of mutilation." Here Jean drew a picture of a nature too horrid to be committed to paper. My pen could not trace it.——In a word, nothing could exceed the ferocity of the infuriate populace; and the sacking of the palace of the Trojan king presents but a faint image of what passed here on the day which overset the throne of the Bourbons.

According to a calculation, founded as well on the reports of the police as on the returns of the military corps, it appears that the number of men killed in the attack of the palace of the

Tuileries on the 10th of August 1792, amounted in the whole to very near six thousand, of whom eight hundred and fifty-two were on the side of the besieged, and three thousand seven hundred and forty on the side of the besiegers.

The interior of this palace is not distinguished by any particular style of architecture, the kings who have resided here having made such frequent alterations, that the distribution throughout is very different from that which was at first intended. Here it was that Catherine de Medicis shut herself up with the Guises, the Gondis, and Birague, the chancellor, in order to plan the horrible massacre of that portion of the French nation whose religious tenets trenched on papal power, and whose spirit of independence alarmed regal jealousy.

Among the series of entertainments, given on the marriage of the king of Navarre with Marguerite de Valois, was introduced a ballet, in which the papists, commanded by Charles IX and his brothers, defended paradise against the huguenots, who, with Navarre at their head, were all repulsed and driven into hell. Although this pantomime, solely invented by Catherine, was evidently meant as a prelude to the dreadful proscription which awaited the protestants, they had no suspicion of it; and four days after was consummated the massacre, where that monster, to whom nature had given the form of a woman, feasted her eyes on the mangled corpses of thousands of bleeding victims!

No sooner was the Pope informed of the horrors of St. Bartholemew's day, by the receipt of Admiral de Coligny's head, which Catherine embalmed and sent to him, than he ordered a solemn procession, by way of returning thanks to heaven for the *happy event*. The account of this procession so exasperated a gentleman of Anjou, a protestant of the name of Bressaut de la Rouvraye, that he swore he would make eunuchs of all the monks who should fall into his hands; and he rendered himself famous by keeping his word, and wearing the trophies of his victory.

The *Louvre* and the palace of the *Tuileries* were alternately the residence of the kings of France, till Lewis XIV built that of Versailles, after which it was deserted till the minority o Lewis XV, who, when a little boy, was visited here by Peter the Great; but, in 1722, the court quitted Paris altogether for Versailles, where it continued fixed till the 5th of October 1789.

During this long interval, the palace was left under the direction of a governor, and inhabited only by himself, and persons of various ranks dependent on the bounty of the crown. When Lewis XVI and his family were brought hither at that period, the two wings alone were in proper order; the remainder consisted of spacious apartments, appropriated for the king's reception when he came occasionally to Paris, and ornamented with stately, old-fashioned furniture, which had not been deranged for years. The first night of their arrival, they slept in temporary beds, and on the king being solicited the next day to choose his apartments, he replied: "Let every one shift for himself; for my part, I am very well where I am." But this fit of ill-humour being over, the king and queen visited every part of the palace, assigning particular rooms to each person of their suite, and giving directions for sundry repairs and alterations.

Versailles was unfurnished, and the vast quantity of furniture collected in that palace, during three successive reigns, was transported to the *Tuileries* for their majesties' accommodation. The king chose for himself three rooms on the ground-floor, on the side of the gallery to the right as you enter the vestibule from the garden; on the entresol, he established his geographical study; and on the first floor, his bed-chamber: the apartments of the queen and royal family were adjoining to those of the king; and the attendants were distributed over the palace to the number of between six and seven hundred persons.

The greater part of the furniture, &c. in the

palace of the *Tuileries* was sold in the spring of 1793. The sale lasted six months, and, had it not been stopped, would have continued six months longer. Some of the king's dress-suits which had cost twelve hundred louis fetched no more than five. By the inventory taken immediately after the 10th of August 1792, and laid before the Legislative Assembly, it appears that the moveables of every description contained in this palace were valued at 12,540,158 livres (*circa* £522,560 sterling,) in which was included the amount of the thefts, committed on that day, estimated at 1,000,000 livres, and that of the dilapidations, at the like sum, making together about £84,000 sterling.

When Catherine de Medicis inhabited the palace of the *Tuileries*, it was connected to the *Louvre* by a garden, in the middle of which was a large pond, always well stocked with fish for the supply of the royal table. Lewis XIV transformed this garden into a spacious square or *place*, where in the year 1662, he gave to the queen dowager and his royal consort a magnificent fête, at which were assembled princes, lords, and knights, with their ladies, from every part of Europe. Hence the square was named

PLACE DU CARROUSEL.

Previously to the revolution, the palace of the

Tuileries, on this side, was defended by a wall, pierced by three gates opening into as many courts, separated by little buildings, which, in part, served for lodging a few troops and their horses. All these buildings are taken down; the *Place du Carrousel* is considerably enlarged by the demolition of various circumjacent edifices; and the wall is replaced by a handsome iron railing, fixed on a parapet about four feet high. In this railing are three gates, the centre one of which is surmounted by cocks, holding in their beak a civic crown over the letters R. F. the initials of the words *République Française*. On each side of it are small lodges, built of stone; and at the entrance are constantly posted two *vedettes*, belonging to the horse-grenadiers of the consular guard.

On the piers of the other two gates are placed the four famous horses of gilt bronze, brought from St. Mark's place at Venice, whither they had been carried after the capture of Byzantium. These productions are generally ascribed to the celebrated Lysippus, who flourished in the reign of Alexander the Great, about 325 years before the christian era; though this opinion is questioned by some distinguished antiquaries and artists. Whoever may be the sculptor, their destiny is of a nature to fix attention, as their removal has always been the consequence of a political revolution. After the conquest of Greece by the Romans, they were transported from Corinth to Rome, for the purpose of adorning the triumphal arch of Septimius Severus. Hence they were removed to Byzantium, when that city became the seat of the eastern empire. From Byzantium, they were conveyed to Venice, and from Venice they have at last reached Paris.

As on the plain of Pharsalia the fate of Rome was decided by Cæsar's triumph over Pompey, so on the *Place du Carrousel* was the fate of France by the triumph of the Convention over Robespierre and his satellites. Here, Henriot, one of his most devoted creatures, whom he had raised to the situation of commandant general of the Parisian guard, after having been carried prisoner before the Committee of Public Safety, then sitting in the palace of the *Tuileries*, was released by Coffinhal, the President of the Revolutionary Tribunal, who suddenly made his appearance at the head of a large body of horse and foot, supported by four pieces of cannon served by gunners the most devoted to Robespierre.

It was half past seven o'clock in the evening, when Coffinhal, decorated with his municipal scarf, presented himself before the Committee: all the members thought themselves lost, and their fright communicating to the very bosom of the Convention, there spread confusion and terror. But Coffinhal's presence of mind was not equal to his courage: he availed himself only in part of his advantage. After having, without the slightest resistance, disarmed the guards attached to the Convention, he loosened the fettered hands of Henriot and his aides-de-camp, and conducted them straight to the *Maison Commune.*

It is an incontestable fact that had either Coffinhal or Henriot imitated the conduct of Cromwell in regard to the Levellers, and marched at the head of their troops into the hall of the Convention, he might have carried all before him, and Robespierre's tyranny would have been henceforth established on a basis not to be shaken.

But, when Henriot soon after appeared on the *Place du Carrousel,* with his staff and a number of followers, he in vain endeavoured by haranguing the people to stir them up to act against the Convention; his voice was drowned in tumultuous clamours, and he was deserted by his hitherto-faithful gunners. The Convention had had time to recover from their panic, and to enlighten the Sections. Henriot was outlawed by that assembly, and, totally disconcerted by this news, he fled for refuge to the *Maison Commune,* where Robespierre and all his accomplices were soon surrounded, and fell into the hands of those whom but an instant before, they had proscribed as conspirators deserving of the most exemplary punishment.

Henriot, confused and terrified, sought his safety in flight, and was stealing along one of the galleries of the *Maison Commune,* when he met Coffinhal, who was also flying. At the sight of Henriot, who, on coming from the Committee, had pledged his life on the success of his measures, Coffinhal was unable to check his rage. " Coward!" said he to him, " to this then has " led your certain means of defence! Scoundrel! " you shall not escape the death you are en-" deavouring to avoid!" Saying these words, he seized Henriot by the middle, and threw him out of a window of the second story of the *Maison Commune.* Henriot falling on the roof of a building in a narrow street adjoining, was not killed; but he had scarcely recovered himself before he was recognized by some soldiers in quest of him: he then crawled into a sewer, close to the spot where he had fallen; when a soldier, thrusting his bayonet into the sewer, put out one of his eyes, and forced him to surrender.

Thus, the destiny of France, as is seen, hung by the thread of the moment. It will be recollected that Henriot had the arsenal at his disposal; he commanded the Parisian guard, and six thousand men encamped on the *Plaine des Sablons,* close to the capital: in a word, all the springs of the public force were in his hands. Had he seized the critical minute, and attacked the Convention at the instant of his release, the scene of the 10th of August would have been renewed, and the *Place du Carrousel* again stained with the blood of thousands.

LETTER XI.

Paris, November 5, 1801.

I RISE much later to-day than usual, in consequence of not having gone to bed till near seven o'clock this morning. Happening to call yesterday on a French lady of my acquaintance, I perceived some preparations which announced that she expected company. She did not leave me long in suspense, but invited me to her party for that evening.

This good lady, who is no longer in the flower of her age, was still in bed, though it was four o'clock when I paid my visit. On expressing my fears that she was indisposed, she assured me of the contrary, at the same time adding that she seldom rose till five in the afternoon, on account of her being under the necessity of keeping late hours. I was so struck by the expression, that I did not hesitate to ask her what was the *necessity* which compelled her to make a practice of turning day into night? She very courteously gave me a complete solution of this enigma, of which the following is the substance.

"During the reign of terror," said she, "several of us *ci-devant noblesse* lost our nearest relatives, and with them our property, which was either confiscated, or put under sequestration, so that we were absolutely threatened by famine. When the prisoners were massacred in September 1794, I left nothing unattempted to save the life of my uncle and grandfather, who were both in confinement in the *Abbaye*. All my efforts were unavailing. My interference served only to exasperate their murderers, and contributed, I fear, to accelerate their death, which it was my misfortune to witness. Their inhuman butchers, from whom I had patiently borne every species of insult, went so far as to present to me, on the end of a pike, a human heart, which had the appearance of having been broiled on the embers, assuring me that, as it was the heart of my uncle, I might eat it with safety."——Here an ejaculation, involuntarily escaping me, interrupted her for a moment.

"For my part," continued she, "I was so overwhelmed by a conflict of rage, despair, and grief, that I scarcely retained the use of

" my senses. The excess of my horror deprived
" me of utterance.—What little I was able to
" save from the wreck of my fortune, not afford-
" ing me sufficient means of subsistence, I was,
" however reluctantly, at length compelled to
" adopt a plan of life, by which I saw other
" women, in my forlorn situation, support a
" decent appearance. I therefore hired suitable
" apartments, and twice in each decade, I re-
" ceive company. On one of these two nights
" I give a ball and supper, and on the other,
" under the name of *société*, I have cards only.

" Having a numerous circle of female ac-
" quaintance," concluded she, " my balls are
" generally well attended: those who are not
" fond of dancing, play at the *bouillotte*;
" and the card-money defrays the expenses of
" the entertainment, leaving me a handsome
" profit. In short, these six parties, during the
" month, enable me to pay my rent, and produce
" me a tolerable pittance."

This melancholy recital affected me so much, that, on its being terminated, I was unable to speak; but I have reason to think that a favourable construction was put on my silence. A volume, of the size of a family-bible, would not be sufficient to display half the contrasts engendered by the revolution. Many a *Marquise* has been obliged to turn sempstress, in order to gain a livelihood; but my friend the *Comtesse* had much ready wit, though no talents of that description. Having soothed her mind by venting a few imprecations against the murderers of her departed relatives, she informed me that her company began to assemble between the hours of eleven and twelve, and begged that I would not fail to come to her

PRIVATE BALL.

About twelve o'clock, I accordingly went thither, as I had promised, when I found the rooms perfectly crowded. Among a number of very agreeable ladies, several were to be distinguished for the elegance of their figure, though there were no more than three remarkable for beauty. These terrestrial divinities would not only have embarrassed the Grand Signior for a preference, but even have distracted the choice of the Idalian shepherd himself. The dancing was already begun to an excellent band of music, led by Citizen JULIEN, a mulatto, esteemed the first player of country-dances in Paris. Of the dancers, some of the women really astonished me by the ease and gracefulness of their movements: steps, which are known to be the most difficult, seemed to cost them not the smallest exertion. Famous as they have ever been for

dancing, they seem now, in Cibber's words, " to
" outdo their usual outdoings."

In former times, an extraordinary degree of
curiosity was excited by any female who excelled
in this pleasing accomplishment. I remember to
have read that Don Juan of Austria, governor of
the Low Countries, set out post from Brussels,
and came to Paris *incog.* on purpose to see Marguerite de Valois dance at a dress-ball, this
princess being reckoned, at that time, the best
dancer in Europe. What then would be the admiration of such an *amateur*, could he now behold the perfection attained here by some of the
beauties of the present day?

The men, doubtless, determined to vie with
the women, seemed to pride themselves more on
agility than grace, and, by attempting whatever required extraordinary effort, reminded me of *figu-
rans* on the stage, so much have the Parisian
youth adopted a truly theatrical style of dancing.

The French country-dances (or cotilions, as
we term them in England) and waltzes, which
are as much in vogue here as in Germany, were
regularly interchanged. However, the Parisians, in
my opinion, cannot come up to the Germans in
this their native dance. I should have wished to
have had Lavater by my side, and heard his
opinion of the characters of the different female
waltzers. It is a very curious and interesting

spectacle to see one woman assume a languishing air, another a vacant smile, a third an aspect of stoical indifference; while a fourth seems lost in a voluptuous trance, a fifth captivates by an amiable modesty, a sixth affects the cold insensibility of a statue, and so on in ever-varying succession, though all turning to the animating changes of the same lively waltz. In short I observed that, in this species of dance, the eyes and feet of almost every woman appeared to be constantly at variance.

Without assuming the part of a moralist, I cannot help thinking that Werter was not altogether in the wrong when he swore, that, were it to cost him his life, no woman on whom he had set his affections, should ever waltz with any one but himself. I am not singular in this opinion; for I recollect to have met with the same ideas in a book written by M. JACOBI, I think, a German author.

Speaking of the waltz, "We either ought," says he, "not to boast so much of the propriety of our manners, or else not suffer that our wives and daughters, in a complete delirium, softly pressed in the arms of men, bosom to bosom, should thus be hurried away by the sound of intoxicating music. In this *whirligig* dance, every one seems to forget the rules of decorum; and though an innocent, young creature, exposed in this manner, were to remain pure and spotless, can she, without horror, reflect that she becomes the sport of the imagination of the licentious youths to whom she so abandons herself? It were to be wished," adds he, " that our damsels (I mean those who preserve any vestige of bashfulness), might, concealed in a private corner, hear sometimes the conversation of those very men to whom they yield themselves with so little reserve and caution."

To the best of my recollection, these are the sentiments of M. Jacobi, expressed twelve or fourteen years ago; yet I do not find that the waltz is discontinued, or even less practised, in Germany, than it was at the time when his work first appeared. This dance, like every other French fashion, has now found its way into England, and is introduced between the acts, by way of interlude I presume, at some of our grand private balls and assemblies. But, however I may be amused by the waltzing of the Parisian belles, I feel too much regard for my fair countrywomen to wish to see them adopt a dance, which, by throwing them off their guard, lays them completely open to the shafts of ridicule and malice.

Leaving this point to be settled by the worthy part of our British matrons, let us return to the

Parisian ball, from which I have been led into a little digression.

The dancing continued in this manner, that is, French country-dances and waltzes alternately, till four o'clock, when soup was brought round to all the company. This was dispatched *sans façon*, as fast as it could be procured. It was a prelude to the cold supper, which was presently served in another spacious apartment. No sooner were the folding-doors of an adjoining room thrown open, than I observed that, large as it was, it could not possibly afford accommodation to more than half of the number present. I therefore remained in the back-ground, naturally supposing that places would first be provided for all the women. Not so, my friend; several men seated themselves, and, in the twinkling of an eye, deranged the economy of the whole table; while the female bystanders were necessitated to seek seats at some temporary tables placed in the ball-room. Here too were they in luck if they obtained a few fragments from the grand board; for, such determined voracity was there exhibited, that so many vultures or cormorants could not have been more expeditious in clearing the dishes.

For instance, an enormous salmon, which would have done honour to the Tweed or the

Severn, graced the middle of the principal table. In less than five minutes after the company were seated, I turned round, and missing the fish, inquired whether it had proved tainted. No: but it is all devoured, was the reply of a young man, who, pointing to the bone, offered me a pear and a piece of bread, which he shrewdly observed was all that I might probably get to recruit my strength at this entertainment. I took the hint, and, with the addition of a glass of common wine, at once made my supper.

In half an hour, the tables being removed, the ball was resumed, and apparently with renewed spirit. The card-room had never been deserted. *Mind the main chance* is a wholesome maxim, which the good lady of the house seemed not to have forgotten. Assisted by a sort of *croupier*, she did the honours of the *bouillotte* with that admirable sang-froid which you and I have often witnessed in some of our hostesses of fashion; and, had she not communicated to me the secret, I should have been the last to suspect, while she appeared so indifferent, that she, like those ladies, had so great an interest in the card-party being continued till morning.

As an old acquaintance, she took an opportunity of saying to me, with joy in her eyes: " *Le jeu va bien ;*" but, at the same time, expressed her regret that the supper was such a scramble,

While we were in conversation, I inquired the name and character of the most striking women in the room, and found that, though a few of them might be reckoned substantial in fortune, as well as in reputation, the female part of the company was chiefly composed of ladies who, like herself, had suffered by the revolution; several were divorced from their husbands, but as incompatibility of temper was the general plea for such a disunion, that alone could not operate as a blemish.

To judge of the political predilection of these belles from their exterior, a stranger would, nine times out of ten, be led into a palpable error. He might naturally conclude them to be attached to a republican system, since they have, in general, adopted the Athenian form of attire as their model; though they have not, in the smallest degree, adopted the simple manners of that people. Their arms are bare almost to the very shoulder; their bosom is, in a great measure, uncovered; their ankles are encircled by narrow ribbands, in imitation of the fastenings of sandals; and their hair, turned up close behind, is confined on the crown of the head in a large knot, as we see it in the antique busts of Grecian beauties.

The rest of their dress is more calculated to display, than to veil the contours of their person.

It was thus explained to me by my friend, the *ci-devant Comtesse*, who at the same time assured me that young French women, clad in this airy manner, brave all the rigour of winter. "A simple piece of linen, slightly laced before," said she, "while it leaves the waist uncompressed, answers the purpose of a corset. If they put on a robe, which is not open in front, they dispense with petticoats altogether; their cambric *chemise* having the semblance of one, from its skirt being trimmed with lace. When attired for a ball, those who dance, as you may observe, commonly put on a tunic, and then a petticoat becomes a matter of necessity, rather than of choice. Pockets being deemed an incumbrance, they wear none: what money they carry, is contained in a little morocco leather purse; this is concealed in the centre of the bosom, whose form, in our well-shaped women, being that of the Medicean Venus, the receptacle occasionally serves for a little gold watch, or some other trinket, which is suspended to the neck by a collar of hair, decorated with various ornaments. When they dance, the fan is introduced within the zone or girdle; and the handkerchief is kept in the pocket of some sedulous swain, to whom the fair one has recourse when she has occasion for it. Some of the elderly ladies, like myself," added she, " carry these appendages in a sort of "work-bag, denominated a *ridicule*. Not long " since, this was the universal fashion first adopted " as a substitute for pockets; but, at present, it " is totally laid aside by the younger classes."

The men at this ball, were, for the most part, of the military class, thinly interspersed with returned emigrants. Some of the generals and colonels were in their hussar dress-uniform, which is not only exceedingly becoming to a well-formed man, but also extremely splendid and costly. All the seams of the jacket and pantaloons of the generals are covered with rich and tasteful embroidery, as well as their sabre-tash, and those of the colonels with gold or silver lace: a few even wore boots of red morocco leather.

Most of the Gallic youths, having served in the armies, either a few years ago under the requisition, or more recently under the conscription, have acquired a martial air, which is very discernible, in spite of their *habit bourgeois*. The brown coat cannot disguise the soldier. I have met with several young merchants of the first respectability in Paris, who had served, some two, others four years in the ranks, and constantly refused every sort of advancement. Not wishing to remain in the army, and relinquish the mercantile profession in which they had been educated, they cheerfully passed through their military servitude as privates, and, in that station, like true soldiers, gallantly fought their country's battles.

The hour of six being arrived, I was assailed, on all sides, by applications to set down this or that lady, as the morning was very rainy, and, independently of the long rank of hackney-coaches, which had been drawn up at the door, every vehicle that could be procured, had long been in requisition. The mistress of the house had informed two of her particular female friends that I had a carriage in waiting; and as I could accommodate only a certain number at a time, after having consented to take those ladies home first; I conceived myself at liberty, on my return, to select the rest of my convoy. To relieve beauty in distress was one of the first laws of ancient chivalry; and no knight ever accomplished that vow with greater ardour than I did on this occasion.

LETTER XII.

Paris, November 7, 1801.

My impatience is at length gratified: I have seen BONAPARTE. Yesterday, the 6th, as I mentioned in a former letter, was the day of the grand parade, which now takes place on the fifteenth only of every month of the Republican Calendar. The spot where this military spectacle is exhibited, is the court-yard of the palace of the *Tuileries*, which, as I have before observed, is enclosed by a low parapet wall, surmounted by a handsome iron railing.

From the kind attention of friends, I had the option of being admitted into the palace, or introduced into the hotel of Cⁿ. Maret, the Secretary of State, which adjoins to the palace, and standing at right angles with it, commands a full view of the court where the troops are assembled. In the former place, I was told, I should not, on account of the crowd, have an opportunity to see the parade, unless I took my station at a window two or three hours before it began; while from the latter, I should enjoy the sight without any annoyance or interruption.

Considering that an interval of a month, by producing a material change in the weather, might render the parade far less brilliant and attractive, and also that such an offer might not occur a second time, I made no hesitation in preferring Cⁿ. Maret's hotel.

Accompanied by my introducer, I repaired thither about half past eleven o'clock, and certainly I had every reason to congratulate myself on my election. I was ushered into a handsome room on the first-floor, where I found the windows partly occupied by some lovely women. Having paid my devoirs to the ladies, I entered into conversation with an officer of rank of my acquaintance, who had introduced me to them; and from him I gathered the following particulars respecting the

GRAND MONTHLY PARADE.

On the fifteenth of every month, the First Consul in person reviews all the troops of the consular guard, as well as those quartered in Paris, as a garrison, or those which may happen to be passing through this city.

The consular guard is composed of two battalions of foot-grenadiers, two battalions of light infantry, a regiment of horse-grenadiers, a regiment of mounted chasseurs or guides, and two companies of flying artillery. All this force may comprise between six and seven thousand men; but it is in contemplation to increase it by a squadron of Mamalûks, intermixed with Greeks and Syrians, mounted on Arabian horses.

This guard exclusively does duty at the palace of the *Tuileries*, and at *Malmaison*, BONAPARTE's country-seat: it also forms the military escort of the Consuls. At present it is commanded by General LASNES; but, according to rumour, another arrangement is on the point of being made.

The consular guard is soon to have no other chief than the First Consul, and under him are to command, alternately, four generals; namely, one of infantry, one of cavalry, one of artillery, and one of engineers; the selection is said to have fallen on the following officers, BESSIÈRES, DAVOUST, SOULT, and SONGIS.

The garrison (as it is termed) of Paris is not constantly of the same strength. At this moment it consists of three demi-brigades of the line, a demi-brigade of light infantry, a regiment of dragoons, two demi-brigades of veterans, the horse *gendarmerie*, and a new corps of choice *gendarmerie*, comprising both horse and foot, and commanded by the *Chef de brigade* SAVARY, aide-de-camp to the First Consul. This garrison may amount to about 15,000 effective men.

The consular guard and all these different corps, equipped in their best manner, repair to the parade, and, deducting the troops on duty, the number of men assembled there may, in general, be from twelve to fifteen thousand.

By a late regulation, no one, during the time of the parade, can remain within the railing of the court, either on foot or horseback, except the field and staff officers on duty; but persons enter the apartments of the *Tuileries*, by means of tickets, which are distributed to a certain number by the governor of the palace.

While my obliging friend was communicating to me the above information, the troops continued marching into the court below, till it was so crowded that, at first sight, it appeared impracticable for them to move, much less to manœuvre. The morning was extremely fine; the sun shone in full splendour, and the gold and silver lace and embroidery on the uniforms of the officers and on the trappings of their chargers, together with their naked sabres, glittered with uncommon lustre. The concourse of people without the iron railing was immense: in short, every spot or building, even to the walls and rafters of houses under demolition, whence a transient view of the parade could be obtained, was thronged with spectators.

By twelve o'clock, all the troops were drawn up in excellent order, and, as you may suppose, presented a grand *coup d'œil*. I never beheld a finer set of men than the grenadiers of the consular guard; but owing, perhaps, to my being accustomed to see our troops with short skirts, I thought that the extreme length of their coats detracted from their military air. The horses mostly of Norman breed, could not be compared to our English steeds, either for make or figure; but, sorry and rough as is their general appearance, they are, I am informed, capable of bearing much fatigue, and resisting such privations as would soon render our more sleek cavalry unfit for service. That they are active, and surefooted, I can vouch; for, in all their sudden wheelings and evolutions in this confined space, not one of them stumbled. They formed, indeed, a striking contrast to the beautiful white charger that was led about in waiting for the Chief Consul.

The band of the consular guard, which is both numerous and select, continued playing martial airs, till the colours having been brought down from the palace, under the escort of an officer and a small detachment, the drums beat *aux champs*, and the troops presented arms, when they were carried to their respective stations. Shortly after, the impatient steed, just mentioned, was conducted to the foot of the steps of the grand vestibule of the palace. I kept my eye stedfastly fixed on that spot; and such was the agility displayed by BONAPARTE in mounting his horse, that, to borrow the words of Shakspeare, he seemed to

"Rise from the ground like feather'd Mercury,
"And vaulted with such ease into his seat,
"As if an angel dropp'd down from the clouds
"To turn and wind a fiery Pegasus,
"And witch the world with noble horsemanship."

Off he went at a hand canter, preceded by his aides-de-camp, and attended, on his right, by

General Lasnes, and followed by other superior officers, particularly the general commanding the garrison of Paris, and him at the head of the district.

Bonaparte was habited in the consular dress, scarlet velvet embroidered with gold, and wore a plain cocked hat with the national cockade. As I purpose to obtain a nearer view of him, by placing myself in the apartments of the palace on the next parade day, I shall say nothing of his person till that opportunity offers, but confine myself to the military show in question.

Having rid rapidly along the several lines of infantry and cavalry, and saluted the colours as he passed, Bonaparte (attended by all his retinue, including a favourite Mamalûk whom he brought from Egypt), took a central position, when the different corps successively filed off before him with most extraordinary briskness; the corps composing the consular guard preceded those of the garrison and all the others: on inquiry, however, I find, that this order is not always observed.

It is no less extraordinary than true, that the news of the establishment of this grand parade produced on the mind of the late emperor of Russia the first impression in favour of the Chief Consul. No sooner did Paul I. hear of the cir-

cumstance, than he exclaimed: " BONAPARTE is,
" however, a great man."

Although the day was so favourable, the parade was soon over, as there was no distribution of arms of honour, such as muskets, pistols, swords, battle-axes, &c. which the First Consul presents with his own hand to those officers and soldiers who have distinguished themselves by deeds of valour or other meritorious service.

The whole ceremony did not occupy more than half an hour, when BONAPARTE alighted at the place where he had taken horse, and returned to his audience-room in the palace, for the purpose of holding his levee. I shall embrace a future opportunity to speak of the interior etiquette observed on this occasion in the apartments, and close this letter with an assurance that you shall have an early account of the approaching *fête*.

LETTER XIII.

Paris, November 8, 1801.

GREAT preparations for the *fête* of to-morrow have, for several days, employed considerable numbers of people: it therefore becomes necessary that I should no longer delay to give you an idea of the principal scene of action. For that purpose, we must direct our steps to the

JARDIN DES TUILERIES.

This garden, which is the most magnificent in Paris, was laid out by the celebrated LE NOTRE in the reign of Lewis XIV. It covers a space of three hundred and sixty toises* long by one hundred and sixty-eight broad. To the north and south, it is bordered, throughout its length, by two terraces, one on each side, which, with admirable art, conceal the irregularity of the ground, and join at the farther end in the form of a horse-shoe. To the east, it is limited by the palace of the *Tuileries*; and to the west, by the *Place de la Concorde*.

From the vestibule of the palace, the perspective produces a most striking effect: the eye first wanders for a moment over the extensive parterre, which is divided into compartments, planted with shrubs and flowers, and decorated with basins, *jets-d'eau*, vases, and statues in marble and bronze; it then penetrates through a venerable grove which forms a beautiful vista; and, following the same line, it afterwards discovers a fine road, bordered with trees, leading by a gentle ascent to *Pont de*

* The ratio between the English fathom and the French toise, as determined between the first astronomers of both countries, is as 72 to 76.734.

Neuilly, through the *Barrière de Chaillot*, where the prospect closes.

The portico of the palace has been recently decorated with several statues. On each side of the principal door is a lion in marble.

The following is the order in which the copies of antique statues, lately placed in this garden, are at present disposed.

On the terrace towards the river, are: 1. Venus *Anadyomene*. 2. An Apollo of Belvedere. 3. The group of Laocoon. 4. Diana, called by antiquaries, *Succincta*. 5. Hercules carrying Ajax.

In front of the palace: 1. A dying gladiator. 2. A fighting gladiator. 3. The flayer of Marsyas. 4. VENUS, styled *à la coquille,* crouched and issuing from the bath. N. B. All these figures are in bronze.

In the alley in front of the parterre, in coming from the terrace next the river: 1. Flora Farnese. 2. Castor and Pollux. 3. Bacchus instructing young Hercules. 4. Diana.

On the grass-plot, towards the *manège* or riding-house, Hippomenes and Atalanta. At the further end is an Apollo, in front of the horse-shoe walk, decorated with a sphynx at each extremity.

In the corresponding gras-plot towards the river, Apollo and Daphne; and at the further end, a Venus *Callypyga,* or (according to the French term) *aux belles fesses.*

In the compartment by the horse-chesnut trees, towards the riding-house, the Centaur. On the opposite side, the Wrestlers. Farther on, though on the same side, an Antinoüs.

In the niche, under the steps in the middle of the terrace towards the river, a Cleopatra.

In the alley of orange-trees, near the *Place de la Concorde*, Meleager; and on the terrace, next to the riding-house, Hercules Farnese.

In the niche to the right, in front of the octagonal basin, a Faun carrying a kid. In the one to the left, Mercury Farnese.

Independently of these copies after the antique, the garden is decorated with several other modern statues, by COYZEVOX, REGNAUDIN, COSTOU, LE GROS, LE PAUTRE, &c. which attest the degree of perfection that had been attained, in the course of the last century, by French sculptors. For a historical account of them, I refer you to a work, which I shall send you by the first opportunity, written by the learned MILLIN.

Here, in summer, the wide-spreading foliage of the lofty horse-chesnut trees afford a most agreeable shade; the air is cooled by the continual play of the *jets-d'eau*; while upwards of two hundred orange-trees, which are then set out, impregnate it with a delightful perfume. The garden is now kept in much better order than it was under the monarchy. The flower-beds are carefully cultivated; the walks are well gravelled, rolled, and occasionally watered; in a word, proper attention is paid to the convenience of the public.

But, notwithstanding these attractions, as long as it was necessary for every person entering this garden to exhibit to the sentinels the national cockade, several fair royalists chose to relinquish its charming walks, shaded by trees of a hundred years' growth, rather than comply with the republican mandate. Those anti-revolutionary *élégantes* resorted to other promenades; but, since the accession of the consular government, the wearing of this doubtful emblem of patriotism has been dispensed with, and the garden of the *Tuileries* is said to be now as much frequented in the fine season as at any period of the old *régime*.

The most constant visiters are the *quidnuncs*, who, according to the difference of the seasons, occupy alternately three walks; the *Terrasse des Feuillans* in winter; that which is immediately underneath in spring; and the centre or grand alley during the summer or autumn.

Before the revolution, this garden was not open to the populace, except on the festival of St. Lewis, and the eve preceding, when there was always a public concert, given under a temporary amphitheatre erected against the west façade of the palace: at present no person whatever is refused admittance.

There are six entrances, at each of which sentinels are regularly mounted from the grenadiers of the consular guard; and, independently of the grand guard-room over the vestibule of the palace, there is one at the end of the garden which opens on the *Place de la Concorde,* and another on the *Terrasse des Feuillans.*

But what is infinitely more interesting, on this terrace, is a new and elegant building, somewhat resembling a *casino,* which at once unites every accommodation that can be wished for in a coffee-house, a tavern, or a confectioner's. Here you may breakfast *à l'Anglaise* or *à la fourchette,* that is in the most substantial manner, in the French fashion, read the papers, dine, or sup sumptuously in any style you choose, or drink coffee and liqueurs, or merely eat ices. While thus engaged, you enjoy a full view of the company passing and repassing, and what adds beyond measure to the beauty of the scene, is the presence of the ladies, who not unfrequently come hither with their admirers to indulge in a *tête-à-tête,* or make larger parties to dine or sup at these fashionable rendezvous of good cheer.

According to the scandalous chronicle, Véry, the master of the house, is indebted to the charms of his wife for the occupation of this tasteful edifice, which had been erected by the government on a spot of ground that was national property, and, of course, at its disposal. Several candidates were desirous to be tenants of a building at once so elegant and so centrical. Véry himself had been unsuccessful, though he had offered a *pot de vin* (that is the Parisian term for *good-will*) of five hundred louis, and six thousand francs a year rent. His handsome wife even began to apprehend that her mission would be attended with no better fortune. She presented herself, however, to the then Minister of the Interior, who, unrelenting as he had hitherto been to all the competitors, did not happen to be a Scipio. On the contrary, he is said to have been so struck by the person of the fair supplicant, that he at once declared his readiness to accede to her request, on condition that she would favour him with her company to supper, and not forget to put her night-cap in her pocket. *Relata refero*.

Be this as it may, I assure you that Madame Véry, without being a perfect beauty, is what the French call a *beau corps de femme*, or, in plain English, a very desirable woman, and such as few ministers of Lⁿ. B————te's years would choose to dismiss unsatisfied. This is not the age of continence, and I am persuaded that any man who sees and converses with the amiable Madame Véry, if he do not envy the Minister the nocturnal sacrifice, will, on contemplating the elegance of her arrangements, at least allow that this spot of ground has not been disposed of to disadvantage.

Every step we take, in this quarter of Paris, calls to mind some remarkable circumstance of the history of the revolution. As the classic reader, in visiting *Troas,* would endeavour to trace the site of those interesting scenes described in the sublime numbers of the prince of poets; so the calm observer, in perambulating this garden, cannot but reflect on the great political events of which it has been the theatre. In front of the west façade of the palace, the unfortunate Lewis XVI, reviewed the Swiss, and some of the national guards, very early in the morning of the 10th of August 1792. On the right, close to the *Terrasse des Feuillans,* still stands the *manège* or riding-house, where the National Assembly at that time held their sittings, and whither the king, with his family, was conducted by ROEDERER, the deputy. That building, after having since served for various purposes, is at present shut up, and will, probably, be taken down, in consequence of projected improvements in this quarter.

In the centre of the west end of the garden, was the famous *Pont tournant,* by which, on the 11th of July 1789, the Prince de Lambesc entered it at the head of his regiment of cavalry, and, by maltreating some peaceable saunterers, gave the Parisians a specimen of what they were to expect from the disposition of the court. This inconsiderate *galopade*, as the French term it, was the first signal of the general insurrection.

The *Pont tournant* is destroyed, and the ditch filled up. Leaving the garden of the *Tuileries* by this issue, we enter the

PLACE DE LA CONCORDE.

This is the new name given to the *Place de Louis XV.* After the abolition of royalty in France, it was called the *Place de la Révolution.* When the reign of terror ceased, by the fall of Robespierre, it obtained its present appellation, which forms a strong contrast to the number of victims that have here been sacrificed to the demon of faction.

This square, which is seven hundred and eighty feet in length by six hundred and thirty in breadth, was planned after the treaty of Aix-la-Chapelle, and finished in 1763. It forms a parallelogram with its angles cut off, which are surrounded by ditches, guarded by balustrades, breast high. To repair from the *Tuileries* to the *Champs Elysées*, you cross it in a straight line from east to west, and from north to south, to proceed from the *Rue de la Concorde (ci-devant Rue Royale)* to the *Pont de la Concorde (ci-devant Pont de Louis XVI.)*

Near the intersection of these roads stood the

equestrian statue in bronze of Lewis XV, which caught the eye in a direct line with the centre of the grand alley of the garden of the *Tuileries*. It has since been replaced by a statue of Liberty. This colossal figure was removed a few days ago, and, by all accounts, will not be re-erected.

The north part of this square, the only one that is occupied by buildings, presents, on each side of the *Rue de la Concorde*, two edifices, each two hundred and forty-eight feet in front, decorated with insulated columns of the Corinthian order, to the number of twelve, and terminated by two pavilions, with six columns, crowned by a pediment. On the ground-floor of these edifices, one of which, that next the *Tuileries*, was formerly the *Garde-Meuble de la Couronne*, are arcades that form a gallery, in like manner as the colonnade above, the cornice of which is surmounted by a balustrade. I have been thus particular in describing this façade, in order to enable you to judge of the charming effect which it must produce, when illuminated with thousands of lamps on the occasion of the grand *fête* in honour of peace, which takes place to-morrow.

It was in the right hand corner of this square, as you come out of the garden of the *Tuileries* by the centre issue, that the terrible guillotine was erected. From the window of a friend's room, where I am now writing, I behold the very spot which has so often been drenched with the mixed blood of princes, poets, legislators, philosophers, and plebeians. On that spot too fell the head of one of the most powerful monarchs in Europe.

I have heard much regret expressed respecting this execution; I have witnessed much lamentation excited by it both in England and France; but I question whether any of those loyal subjects, who deserted their king when they saw him in danger, will ever manifest the sincere affection, the poignant sensibility of Dominique Sarrède.

To follow Henry IV to the battle of Ivry in 1583, Sarrède had his wounded leg cut off, in order that he might be enabled to sit on horseback. This was not all. His attachment to his royal master was so great, that, in passing through the *Rue de la Ferronnerie* two days after the assassination of that prince, and surveying the fatal place where it had been committed, he was so overcome by grief, that he fell almost dead on the spot, and actually expired the next morning. I question, I say, whether any one of those emigrants, who made so officious a display of their zeal, when they knew it to be unavailing, will ever moisten with a single tear the small space of earth stained with the blood of their unfortunate monarch.

Since I have been in Paris, I have met with a

person of great respectability, totally unconnected with politics, who was present at several of those executions: at first he attended them from curiosity, which soon degenerated into habit, and at last became an occupation. He successively beheld the death of Charlotte Corday, Madame Roland, Louis XVI, Marie Antoinette, Madame Elizabeth, Philippe Egalité, Madame du Barry, Danton, Robespierre, Couthon, St. Just, Henriot, Fouquier-Tinville, *cum multis aliis*, too numerous to mention.

Among other particulars, this person informed me that Lewis XVI struggled much, by which the fatal instrument cut through the back of his head, and severed his jaw: the queen was more resigned; on the scaffold, she even apologized to Samson, the executioner in chief, for treading accidentally on his toe. Madame Roland met her fate with the calm heroism of a Roman matron. Charlotte Corday died with a serene and dignified countenance; one of the executioners having seized her head when it fell, and given it several slaps, this base act of cowardice raised a general murmur among the people.

As to Robespierre, no sooner had he ascended the scaffold, amid the vociferous acclamations of the joyful multitude, than the executioner tore off the dirty bandage in which his wounded head was enveloped, and which partly concealed his pale and ferocious visage. This made the wretch roar like a wild beast. His under jaw then falling from the upper, and streams of blood gushing from the wound, gave him the most ghastly appearance that can be imagined. When the national razor, as the guillotine was called by his partisans, severed Robespierre's head from his body; and the executioner, taking it by the hair, held it up to the view of the spectators, the plaudits lasted for twenty minutes. Couthon, St. Just, and Henriot, his heralds of murder, who were placed in the same cart with himself, next paid the debt of their crimes. They were much disfigured, and the last had lost an eye. Twenty-two persons were guillotined at the same time with Robespierre, all of them his satellites. The next day, seventy members of the *commune,* and the day following twelve others, shared the fate of their atrocious leader, who, not many hours before, was styled the virtuous and incorruptible patriot.

You may, probably, imagine that, whatever dispatch might be employed, the execution of seventy persons, would demand a rather considerable portion of time, an hour and a half, or two hours, for instance. But, how wide of the mark! Samson, the executioner of Paris, worked the guillotine with such astonishing quickness, that, including the preparatives of the punishment, he has been known to cut off no less than forty-five heads, the one after the other, in the short space of fifteen minutes; consequently, at this expeditious rate of three heads in one minute, it required no more than twenty-three minutes and twenty seconds to decapitate seventy persons.

Guillotin, the physician, who invented or rather improved this machine, which is called after his name with a *feminine* termination, is said to have been a man of humanity; and, on that principle alone, he recommended the use of it, from the idea of saving from painful sensations criminals condemned to die. Seeing the abuse made of it, from the facility which it afforded of dispatching several persons in a few minutes, he took the circumstance so much to heart that grief speedily shortened his existence.

According to Robespierre, however, the axe of the guillotine did not do sufficient execution. One of his satellites announced to him the invention of an instrument which struck off nine heads at once: the discovery pleased him, and he caused several trials of this new machine to be made at *Bicêtre*. It did not answer; but human nature gained nothing by its failure. Instead of half a dozen victims a day, Robespierre wished to have daily fifty or sixty, or more; and he was but too well obeyed. Not only had he his own private lists of proscription; but all his creatures, from the president of the revolutionary tribunal down to the under-jailers, had similar lists; and the *almanac royal,* or French court calendar, was converted into one by himself.

The inhabitants of the streets through which the unfortunate sufferers were carried, wearied at length by the daily sight of so melancholy a spectacle, ventured to utter complaints. Robespierre, no less suspicious than cruel, was alarmed, and, dreading an insurrection, removed the scene of slaughter. The scaffold was erected on the *Place de la Bastille:* but the inhabitants of this quarter also murmured, and the guillotine was transferred to the *Barrière St. Antoine.*

Had not this modern Nero been cut off in the midst of his cruelties, it is impossible to say where he would have stopped. Being one day asked the question, he coolly answered: " The " generation which has witnessed the old *régime,* " will always regret it. Every individual who was " more than fifteen in 1789, must be put to " death: this is the only way to consolidate the " revolution."

It was the same in the departments as in Paris. Every where blood ran in streams. In all the principal towns the guillotine was rendered permanent, in order, as Robespierre expressed himself, to *regenerate the nation.* If this sanguinary monster did not intend to " wade through slaugh-

"ter to a throne," it is certain at least that he
"shut the gates of mercy on mankind."

But what cannot fail to excite your astonishment and that of every thinking person, is, that, in the midst of these executions, in the midst of these convulsions of the state, in the midst of these struggles for power, in the midst of these outcries against the despots of the day, in the midst of famine even, not artificial, but real; in short, in the midst of an accumulation of horrors almost unexampled, the fiddle and tambourin never ceased. Galas, concerts, and balls were given daily in incredible numbers; and no less than from fifteen to twenty theatres, besides several other places of public entertainment, were constantly open, and almost as constantly filled.

P. S. I am this moment informed of the arrival of Lord Cornwallis.

LETTER XIV.

Paris, November 10, 1801.

On the evening of the 8th, there was a representation *gratis* at all the theatres, it being the eve of the great day, of the occurrences of which I shall now, agreeably to my promise, endeavour to give you a narrative. I mean the

NATIONAL FÊTE,
In honour of Peace.
Celebrated on the 18*th of Brumaire, year* X, *the anniversary of* Bonaparte's *accession to the consulate.*

Notwithstanding the prayers which the Parisians had addressed to the sun for the preceding twenty-four hours,

" ———*Nocte pluit totâ, redeunt spectacula mane,*"

it rained all night, and was still raining yesterday morning, when the day was ushered in by discharges of artillery from the saluting battery at the *Hôtel des Invalides.* This did not disturb me; I slept soundly till, about eight o'clock, a tintamarre of trumpets, kettle-drums, &c. almost directly under my window, roused me from my peaceful slumber. For fear of losing the sight, I immediately presented myself at the casement, just as I rose, in my shirt and nightcap. The officers of the police, headed by the Prefect, and escorted by a party of dragoons, came to the *Place des Victoires,* as the third station, to give publicity, by word of mouth, to the Proclamation of the Consuls, of which I inclose you a printed copy. The civil officers were habited in their dresses of parade, and decorated with tricoloured sashes; the heads of their steeds, which, by the bye, were not of a fiery, mettlesome race, being adorned in like manner.

This ceremony being over, I returned not to bed, but sat down to a substantial breakfast, which I considered necessary for preparing my strength for the great fatigues of so busy a day. Presently the streets were crowded with people moving towards the river-side, though small, but heavy rain continued falling all the forenoon. I therefore remained at home, knowing that there was nothing yet to be seen for which it was worth while to expose myself to a good wetting.

At two o'clock the sun appeared, as if to satisfy the eager desire of the Parisians; the mist ceased, and the weather assumed a promising aspect. In a moment the crowd in the streets was augmented by a number of persons who had till now kept within doors, in readiness to go out, like the Jews keeping Easter, *cincti renibus & comedentes festinantur.* I also sallied forth, but alone, having previously refused every invitation from my friends and acquaintance to place myself at any window, or join any party, conceiving that the best mode to follow the bent of my humour was to go unaccompanied, and, not confining myself to any particular spot or person, stroll about wherever the most interesting objects presented themselves.

With this view, I directed my steps towards

the *Tuileries*, which, in spite of the immense crowd, I reached without the smallest inconvenience. The appearance of carriages of every kind had been strictly prohibited, with the exception of those belonging to the British ambassador; a compliment well intended, no doubt, and very gratifying when the streets were so extremely dirty.

For some time I amused myself with surveying the different countenances of the groups within immediate reach of my observation, and which to me was by no means the least diverting part of the scene; but on few of them could I discover any other impression than that of curiosity: I then took my station in the garden of the *Tuileries*, on the terrace next the river. Hence was a view of the *Temple of Commerce* rising above the water, on that part of the Seine comprised between the *Pont National* and the *Pont Neuf*. The quays on each side were full of people; and the windows, as well as the roofs of all the neighbouring houses, were crowded beyond conception. In the newspapers, the sum of 500 francs, or £20 sterling, was asked for the hire of a single window of a house in that quarter.

Previously to my arrival, a flotilla of boats, decked with streamers and flags of different colours, had ascended the river from *Chaillot* to this temple, and were executing divers evolutions around it, for the entertainment of the Parisians, who quite drowned the music by their more noisy acclamations.

About half after three, the First Consul appeared at one of the windows of the apartments of the Third Consul, LEBRUN, which, being situated in the *Pavillon de Flore*, as it is called, at the south end of the palace of the *Tuileries*, command a complete view of the river. He and LEBRUN were both dressed in their consular uniform.

In a few minutes, a balloon, previously prepared at this floating *Temple of Commerce*, and adorned with the flags of different nations, ascended thence with majestic slowness, and presently took an almost horizontal direction to the south-west. In the car attached to it were Garnerin, the celebrated aëronaut, his wife, and two other persons, who kept waving their tricoloured flags, but were soon under the necessity of putting them away for a moment, and getting rid of some of their ballast, in order to clear the steeples and other lofty objects which appeared to lie in their route. The balloon, thus lightened, rose above the grosser part of the atmosphere, but with such little velocity as to afford the most gratifying spectacle to an immense number of spectators.

While following it with my eyes, I began to draw comparisons in my mind, and reflect on the rapid improvement made in these machines, since

I had seen Blanchard and his friend, Dr. Jefferies, leave Dover Cliff in January 1785. They landed safely within a short distance of Calais, as every one knows: yet few persons then conceived it possible, or at least probable, that balloons could ever be applied to any useful purpose, still less to the art of war. We find, however, that at the battle of Fleurus, where the Austrians were defeated, Jourdan, the French General, was not a little indebted for his victory to the intelligence given him of the enemy's dispositions by his aëronautic reconnoitring-party.

The sagacious Franklin seems to have had a presentiment of the future utility of this invention. On the first experiments being made of it, some one asked him: " Of what use are balloons?" —" Of what use is a new-born child!" was the philosopher's answer.

Garnerin and his fellow-travellers being now at such a distance as not to interest an observer unprovided with a telescope, I thought it most prudent to gratify that ever-returning desire, which, according to Dr. Johnson, excites once a day a serious idea in the mind even of the most thoughtless. I accordingly retired to my own apartments, where I had taken care that dinner should be provided for myself and a friend, who, assenting to the propriety of allowing every man the indulgence of his own caprice, had, like me, been taking a stroll alone among the innumerable multitude of Paris.

After dinner, my friend and I sat chatting over our dessert, in order that we might not arrive too soon at the scene of action. At six, however, we rose from table, and separated. I immediately proceeded to the *Tuileries*, which I entered by the centre gate of the *Place du Carrousel*. The whole façade of the palace, from the base of the lowest pillars up to the very turrets of the pavilions, comprising the entablatures, &c. was decorated with thousands of *lampions*, whence issued a steady, glaring light. By way of parenthesis, I must inform you that these *lampions* are nothing more than little circular earthen pans, somewhat resembling those which are used in England as receptacles for small flower-pots. They are not filled with oil, but with a substance prepared from the offals of oxen and in which a thick wick is previously placed. Although the body of light proceeding from *lampions* of this description braves the weather, yet the smoke which they produce, is no inconsiderable drawback on the effect of their splendour.

Nothing could exceed the brilliancy of the *coup d'œil* from the vestibule of the palace of the *Tuileries*. The grand alley, as well as the end of the parterre on each side and the edges of the basins, was illuminated in a style equally tasteful and splendid. The frame-work on which the lamps were disposed by millions, represented lofty arcades of elegant proportion, with their several pillars, cornices, and other suitable ornaments. The eye, astonished, though not dazzled, penetrated through the garden, and, directed by this avenue of light, embraced a view of the temporary obelisk erected on the ridge of the gradual ascent, where stands the *Barrière de Chaillot*; the road on each side of the *Champs Elysées* presenting an illuminated perspective, whose vanishing point was the obelisk before-mentioned.

After loitering a short time to contemplate the west façade of the palace, which, excelling that of the east in the richness of its architecture, also excelled it in the splendour of its illuminations, I advanced along the centre or grand alley to the *Place de la Concorde*. Here, rose three *Temples* of correct design and beautiful symmetry, the most spacious of which, placed in the centre, was dedicated to *Peace*, that on the right hand to the *Arts*, and that on the left to *Industry*.

In front of these temples, was erected an extensive platform, about five feet above the level of the ground, on which was exhibited a pantomime, representing, as I was informed, the horrors of war succeeded by the blessings of peace. Though I arrived in time to have seen at least a part of it, I saw nothing, except the back of the spectators immediately before me, and others, mounted on chairs and benches, some of whom seemed to consider themselves fortunate if they recovered their legs, when they came now and then to the ground, by losing their equilibrium. These little accidents diverted me for the moment; but a misadventure of a truly-comic nature afforded me more entertainment than any pantomime I ever beheld, and amply consoled me for being thus confined to the back-ground.

A lusty young Frenchman, who, from his head-dress *à la Titus*, I shall distinguish by that name, escorting a lady whom, on account of her beautiful hair, I shall style *Berenice*, stood on one of the hindmost benches. The belle, habited in a tunic *à la Grecque*, with a species of sandals which displayed the elegant form of her leg, was unfortunately not of a stature sufficiently commanding to see over the heads of the other spectators. It was to no purpose that the gentleman called out " *à bas les chapeaux!*" When the hats were off, the lady still saw no better. What will not gallantry suggest to a man of fashionable education? Our considerate youth perceived, at no great distance, some persons standing on a plank supported by a couple of casks. Confiding the fair *Berenice* to my care, he vanished: but, almost in an instant, he reappeared, followed by two men, bearing an empty hogshead, which, it seems, he procured from the tavern at the west entrance of the *Tuileries*. To place the cask near the feet of the lady, pay for it, and fix her on it, was the business of a moment. Here then she was, like a statue on its pedestal, enjoying the double gratification of seeing and being seen. But, for enjoyment to be complete, we must share it with those we love. On examining the space where she stood, the lady saw there was room for two, and accordingly invited the gentleman to place himself beside her. In vain he resisted her entreaties; in vain he feared to incommode her. She commanded; he could do no less than obey. Stepping up on the bench, he thence nimbly sprang to the cask; but, O! fatal catastrophe! while, by the light of the neighbouring clusters of lamps, every one around was admiring the mutual attention of this sympathizing pair, in went the head of the hogshead.

Our till-then-envied couple fell suddenly up to the middle of the leg in the wine-lees left in the cask, by which they were bespattered up to their very eyes. Nor was this all: being too eager to extricate themselves, they overset the cask, and came to the ground, rolling in it and its offensive contents. It would be no easy matter to picture the ludicrous situation of Citizen *Titus* and Madame *Berenice*. This being the only mischief resulting from their fall, a universal burst of laughter seized the surrounding spectators, in which I took so considerable a share, that I could not immediately afford my assistance.

LETTER XV.

Paris, November 11, 1801.

WHAT fortunate people are the Parisians! Yesterday evening so thick a fog came on, all at once, that it was almost impossible to discern the lamps in the streets, even when they were directly over-head. Had the fog occurred twenty-four hours earlier, the effect of the illuminations would have been entirely lost; and the blind would have had the advantage over the clear-sighted. This assertion experience has proved: for, some years ago, when there was, for several successive days, a duration of such fogs in Paris, it was found necessary, by persons who had business to transact out of doors, to hire the blind men belonging to the hospital of the *Quinze-Vingts*, to lead them about the streets. These guides, who were well acquainted with the topography of the capital, were paid by the hour, and sometimes, in the course of the day, each of them cleared five louis.

Last night, persons in carriages, were compelled to alight, and grope their way home as they could: in this manner, after first carefully ascertaining where I was, and keeping quite close to the wall, I reached my lodgings in safety, in spite of numberless interrogations put to me by people who had, or pretended to have, lost themselves.

When I was interrupted in my account of the *fête*, we were, if I mistake not, on the *Place de la Concorde*.

Notwithstanding the many loads of small gravel scattered here, with a view of keeping the place clean, the quantity of mud collected in the space of a few hours was really astonishing. *N'importe* was the word. No fine lady, by whatever motive she was attracted hither, regretted at the moment being up to her ankles in dirt, or having the skirt of her dress bemired. All was busy curiosity, governed by peaceable order.

For my part, I never experienced the smallest uncomfortable squeeze, except, indeed, at the conclusion of the pantomime, when the impatient crowd rushed forward, and, regardless of the fixed bayonets of the guards in possession of the platform, carried it by storm. Impelled by the torrent, I fortunately happened to be nearly in front of the steps, and, in a few seconds, I found myself safely landed on the platform.

The guard now receiving a seasonable reinforcement, order was presently restored without bloodshed; and, though several persons were under the necessity of making a retrograde movement, on my declaring that I was an Englishman, I was suffered to retain my elevated position, till the musicians composing the orchestras, appropriated to each of the three temples, had taken their stations. Admittance then became general, and the temples were presently so crowded that the dancers had much difficulty to find room to perform the figures.

Good-humour and decorum, however, prevailed to such a degree that, during the number of hours I mixed in the crowd, I witnessed not the smallest disturbance.

Between nine and ten o'clock, I went to the *Pont de la Concorde* to view the fireworks played off from the *Temple of Commerce* on the river; but these were, as I understand, of a description far inferior to those exhibited at the last National Fête of the 14th of July, the anniversary of the taking of the Bastille.

This inferiority is attributed to the precaution dictated, by the higher authorities, to the authors of the fireworks to limit their ingenuity; as, on the former occasion, some accidents occurred of a rather serious nature. The spectators, in general, appeared to me to be disappointed by the mediocrity of the present exhibition.

I was compensated for the disappointment by the effect of the illumination of the quays, which, being faced with stone, form a lofty rampart on each embankment of the river. These were decorated with several tiers of lamps from the top of the parapet to the water's edge; the parapets and cornices of the bridges, together with the circumference of the arches, were likewise illuminated, as well as the gallery of the *Louvre*, and the stately buildings adjoining the quays.

The palace of the Legislative Body, which faces the south end of the *Pont de la Concorde*, formed a striking object, being adorned, in a magnificent style, with variegated lamps and transparencies. No less splendid, and in some respects more so, from the extent that it presented, was the façade of the *ci-devant Garde-Meuble*, and the corresponding buildings, which form the north side of the *Place de la Concorde*, whither I now returned.

The effect of the latter was beautiful, as you may judge from the description which I have already given you of this façade, in one of my preceding letters. Let it suffice then to say, that, from the base of the lower pillars to the upper cornice, it was covered with lamps so arranged as to exhibit, in the most brilliant manner, the style and richness of its architecture.

The crowd, having now been attracted in various directions, became more penetrable; and, in regaining the platform on the *Place de la Concorde*, I had a full view of the turrets, battlements, &c. erected behind the three temples, in which the skilful machinist had so combined his plan, by introducing into it a sight of the famous horses brought from *Marly*, and now occupying the entrance of the *Champs Elysées*, that these beautiful marble representations of that noble animal seemed placed here on purpose to embellish his scenery.

Finding myself chilled by standing so many hours exposed to the dampness of a November night, I returned to the warmer atmosphere of the temples, in order to take a farewell view of the dancers. The scene was truly picturesque, the male part of the groups being chiefly composed of journeymen of various trades, and the females consisting of a ludicrous medley of all classes; but it required no extraordinary penetration to perceive, that, with the exception of a few particular attachments, the military bore the bell, and, all things considered, this was no more than justice. Independently of being the best dancers, after gaining the laurels of victory in the hard-fought field, who can deny that they deserved the prize of beauty?

The dancing was kept up with the never-flagging vivacity peculiar to this nation, and, as I conclude, so continued till a very late hour in the morning. At half past eleven I withdrew, with a friend whom I chanced to meet, to Véry's, the famous *restaurateur's* in the *Tuileries*, where we supped. On comparing notes, I found that I had been more fortunate than he, in beholding to advantage all the sights of the day: though it was meant to be a day of jubilee, yet it was far from being productive of that mirth or gaiety which I expected. The excessive dearness of a few articles of the first necessity may, probably, be one cause of this gloom among the people. Bread, the staff of life, (as it may be justly termed in France, where a much greater proportion is, in general, consumed than in any other country,) is now at the enormous price of eighteen *sous* (nine-pence sterling) for the loaf of four pounds. Besides, the Parisians have gone through so much during the revolution, that I apprehend they are, to a certain degree, become callous to the spontaneous sensations of joy and pleasure. Be the cause what it may, I am positively assured that the people expressed not so much hilarity at this fête as at the last, I mean that of the 14th of July.

In my way home, I remarked that few houses were illuminated, except those of the rich in the streets which are great thorough-fares. People here, in general, I suppose, consider themselves dispensed from lighting up their private residence from the consideration that they collectively contribute to the public illumination, the expenses of which are defrayed by the government out of the national coffers.

Several songs have been composed and published in commemoration of this joyful event. Among those that have fallen under my notice, I have selected the following, of which our friend M――s, with his usual facility and taste, will, I dare say, furnish you an imitation.

Chant d'Allégresse,
Pour la paix.

Air : *de la Marche Triomphante.*

" Reviens pour consoler la terre,
　" Aimable Paix, descends des cieux,
" Depuis assez long-tems la guerre
　" Afflige un peuple généreux,
" Ah ! quell' aurore pure & calme
　" S'offre à nos regards satisfaits !
" Nous obtenons la double palme
　" De la victoire & de la paix.　　　bis.

" *Disparaissez tristes images,*
  " *D'un tems malheureux qui n'est plus,*
" *Nous réparerons nos dommages*
  " *Pàr la sagesse & les vertus.*
" *Que la paix enfin nous rallie !*
  " *Plus d'ingrats ni de mécontens,*
" *O triomphe de la patrie !*
  " *Plus de Français indifférens.*   bis.

" *Revenez phalanges guerrières,*
  " *Héros vengeurs de mon pays,*
" *Au sein d'une épouse, d'un père,*
  " *De vos parens, de vos amis,*
" *Revenez dans votre patrie*
  " *Après tant d'effrayans hazards,*
" *Trouver ce qui charme la vie,*
  " *L'amitié, l'amour, et les arts.*   bis.

" *Oh ! vous qui, sous des catacombes,*
  " *Etes couchés au champ d'honneur,*
" *Nos yeux sont fixés sur vos tombes,*
  " *En chantant l'hymne du vainqueur,*
" *Nous transmettrons votre mémoire*
  " *Jusqu' aux siécles à venir,*
" *Avec le burin de l'histoire,*
  " *Et les larmes du souvenir."*   bis.

Song of Joy,

In honor of peace.

Imitated from the French.

To the same tune: *de la Marche Triomphante.*

Come, lovely Peace, from heav'n descending,
 Thy presence earth at length shall grace;
Those terrible afflictions ending,
 That long have griev'd a gen'rous race:
We see Aurora rise refulgent;
 Serene she comes to bless our sight;
While Fortune to our hopes indulgent,
 Bids victory and peace unite.

Be gone, ye dark imaginations,
 Remembrances of horrors past:
Virtue's and Wisdom's reparations
 Shall soon be made, and ever last:
Now peace to happiness invites us;
 The bliss of peace is understood:
With love fraternal peace delights us,
 Our private ease, and country's good.

Re-enter, sons of war, your houses;
 Heroic deeds for peace resign:
Embrace your parents and your spouses,
 And all to whom your hearts incline:
Behold your countrymen invite you,
 With open arms, with open hearts;
Here find whatever can delight you;
 Here friendship, love, and lib'ral arts.

Departed heroes, crown'd with glory,
  While you are laid in Honour's bed,
Sad o'er your tombs we'll sing the story,
  How Gallia's warriors fought and bled:
And, proud to shew to future ages
  The claims to patriot valour due,
We'll vaunt, in our historic pages,
  The debt immense we owe to you.

LETTER XVI.

Paris, November 13, 1801.

ENRICHED, as this capital now is, with the spoils of Greece and Italy, it may literally be termed the repository of the greatest curiosities existing. In the CENTRAL MUSEUM are collected all the prodigies of the fine arts, and, day after day, you may enjoy the sight of these wonders.

I know not whether you are satisfied with the abridged account I gave you of the GALLERY OF ANTIQUES; but, on the presumption that you did not expect from me a description of every work of sculpture contained in it, I called your attention to the most pre-eminent only; and I shall now pursue the same plan respecting the master-pieces of painting exhibited in the great

GALLERY OF THE LOUVRE.

This gallery, which is thirteen hundred and

sixty-five feet in length by thirty in breadth, runs north and south all along the quays of the river Seine, and joins the *Louvre* to the palace of the *Tuileries*. It was begun by Charles IX, carried as far as the first wicket by Henry IV, to the second by Lewis XIII, and terminated by Lewis XIV. One half, beginning from a narrow strip of ground, called the *Jardin de l'Infante*, is decorated externally with large pilasters of the Composite order, which run from top to bottom, and with pediments alternately triangular and elliptical, the tympanums of which, both on the side of the *Louvre*, and towards the river, are charged with emblems of the Arts and Sciences. The other part is ornamented with coupled pilasters, charged with vermiculated rustics, and other embellishments of highly-finished workmanship.

In the inside of this gallery are disposed the *chefs d'œuvre* of all the great masters of the Italian, Flemish, and French schools. The pictures, particularly the historical ones, are hung according to the chronological order of the painters' birth, in different compartments, the number of which, at the present period, amounts to fifty-seven; and the productions of each school and of each master are as much as possible assembled; a method which affords the advantage of easily comparing one school to another, one master to another, and a master to himself. If the chronology of past ages be considered as a book from which instruction is to be imbibed, the propriety of such a classification requires no eulogium. From the pictures being arranged chronologically, the GALLERY OF THE LOUVRE becomes a sort of dictionary, in which may be traced every degree of improvement or decline that the art of painting has successively experienced.

The entrance to the great GALLERY OF PAINTINGS is precisely the same as that to the GALLERY OF ANTIQUES. After ascending a noble stone stair-case, and turning to the left, you reach the

SALOON OF THE LOUVRE.

This apartment, which serves as a sort of antichamber to the great Gallery, is, at the present moment, appropriated to the annual monthly exhibition of the productions of living painters, sculptors, architects, engravers, and draughtsmen. Of these modern works, I shall, perhaps, speak on a future occasion. But, in the course of a few days, they will give place to several master-pieces of the Italian School, some of which were under indispensable repair, when the others were arranged in the great Gallery.

It would be no easy task to express the various sentiments which take possession of the mind of the lover of the arts, when, for the first time, he enters this splendid repository. By frequent visits, however, the imagination becomes somewhat less distracted, and the judgment, by degrees, begins to collect itself. Although I am not, like you, conversant in the Fine Arts, would you tax me with arrogance, were I to presume to pass an opinion on some of the pictures comprised in this matchless collection?

Painting being a representation of nature, every spectator, according to the justness of his ideas, may form an opinion how far the representation is happily pourtrayed, and in beholding it, experience a proportionate degree of pleasure: but how different the sensations of him who, combining all the requisites of a connoisseur, contemplates the composition of a masterly genius! In tracing the merits of such a production, his admiration gradually becomes inflamed, as his eye strays from beauty to beauty.

In painting or sculpture, beauty, as you well know, is either natural, or generally admitted: the latter depends on the perfection of the performance, on certain rules established, and principles settled. This is what is termed *ideal* beauty, which is frequently not within the reach of the vulgar; and the merit of which may be lost on him who has not learned to know and appreciate it. Thus, one of the finest pictures, ever conceived and executed by man, might not, perhaps, make an impression on many spectators. Natural beauty, on the contrary, is a true imitation of nature: its effect is striking and general, so that it stands not in need of being pointed out, but is felt and admired by all.

Notwithstanding this truth, be assured that I should never, of my own accord, have ventured to pronounce on the various degrees of merit of so many *chefs d'œuvre*, which all at once solicit attention. This would require a depth of knowledge, a superiority of judgment, a nicety of discrimination, a fund of taste, a maturity of experience, to none of which have I any pretension. The greatest masters, who have excelled in a particular branch, have sometimes given to the world indifferent productions; while artists of moderate abilities have sometimes produced master-pieces far above their general standard. In a picture, which may, on the whole, merit the appellation of a *chef d'œuvre*, are sometimes to be found beauties which render it superior, negligences which border on the indifferent, and defects which constitute the bad. Genius has its flights and deviations; talent, its successes, attempts, and faults; and mediocrity even, its flashes and chances.

Whatever some persons may affect, a true knowledge of the art of painting is by no means an easy acquirement; it is not a natural gift, but demands much reading and study. Many there are, no doubt, who may be able to descant speciously enough, perhaps, on the perfections and defects of a picture; but, on that account alone, they are not to be regarded as real judges of its intrinsic merit.

Know then, that, in selecting the most remarkable productions among the vast number exhibited in the CENTRAL MUSEUM, I have had the good fortune to be directed by the same firstrate connoisseur who was so obliging as to fix my choice in the GALLERY OF ANTIQUES. I mean M. VISCONTI.

Not confining myself either to alphabetical or chronological order, I shall proceed to point out to you such pictures of each school as claim particular notice.

ITALIAN SCHOOL.

N. B. *Those pictures to which no number is prefixed, are not yet publicly exhibited.*

RAFFAELLO.

N° 55. (Saloon.) *The Virgin and Child, &c.* commonly known by the name of the *Madonna di Foligno.*

This is one of the master-pieces of RAPHAEL for vigour of colouring, and for the beauty of the heads and of the child. It is in his second manner; although his third is more perfect, seldom are the pictures of this last period entirely executed by himself. This picture was originally painted on pannel, and was in such a lamentable state of decay, that doubts arose whether it could safely be conveyed from Italy. It has been recently transferred to canvass, and now appears as fresh and as vivid, as if, instead of a lapse of three centuries, three years only had passed since it was painted. Never was an operation of the like nature performed in so masterly a manner. The process was attended by a Committee of the National Institute, appointed at the particular request of the Administration of the Museum. The *Madonna di Foligno* is to be engraved from a drawing taken by that able draughtsman Du Tertre.

N° (   ) *The Holy Family.*

This valuable picture of RAPHAEL's third manner is one of the most perfect that ever came from his pencil. It belonged to the old collection of the crown, and is engraved by EDELINCK. Although superior to the *Madonna di Foligno* as to style and composition, it is inferior in the representation of the child, and in vigour of colouring.

N° (   ) *The Transfiguration of Christ on Mount Tabor.*

This is the last production of RAPHAEL, and his most admirable *chef d'œuvre* as to composition and grace of the contours in all its figures. It is not yet exhibited, but will be shortly. This picture is in perfect preservation, and requires only to be cleaned from a coat of dust and smoke which has been accumulating on it for three centuries, during which it graced the great altar of St. Peter's church at Rome.

Among the portraits by RAPHAEL, the most surprising are:

N° 58. (Saloon.) *Baltazzare Castiglione*, a celebrated writer in Italian and Latin.

N° (   ) *Leo X.*

Every thing that RAPHAEL's pencil has produced is in the first order. That master has something greatly superior in his manner: he really appears as a god among painters. Addison seems to have been impressed with the truth of this sentiment, when he thus expresses himself:

" Fain would I RAPHAEL's godlike art rehearse,
" And shew th' immortal labours in my verse,
" When from the mingled strength of shade and light,
" A new creation rises to my sight:

" Such heav'nly figures from his pencil flow,
" So warm with life his blended colours glow,
" From theme to theme with secret pleasure lost,
" Amidst the soft variety I'm lost."

Leonardo da Vinci.

There are several pictures by this master in the present exhibition; but you may look here in vain for the portrait of *La Gioconda*, which he employed four years in painting, and in which he has imitated nature so closely, that, as a well-known author has observed, " the eyes have all " the lustre of life, the hairs of the eye brows and " lids seem real, and even the pores of the skin " are perceptible."

This celebrated picture is now removed to the palace of the *Tuileries*; but the following one, which remains, is an admirable performance.

N° (   ) *Portrait of Charles VIII.*

Fra Bartolomeo.

N° 28. (Saloon.) *St. Mark the Evangelist.*
N° 29. (Saloon.) *The Saviour of the world.*

These two pictures, which were in the *Pitti* palace at Florence, give the idea of the most noble simplicity, and of no common taste in the distribution of the lights and shades,

Giulio Romano.

N° 35. (Saloon.) *The Circumcision.*

This picture belonged to the old collection of the crown. The figures in it are about a foot and a half in height. It is a real *chef d'œuvre*, and has all the grace of the antique bas-reliefs.

Tiziano.

N° 69. (Saloon.) *The Martyrdom of St. Peter.*

This large picture, which presents a grand composition in colossal figures, with a country of extraordinary beauty in the back-ground, is considered as the *chef d'œuvre* of Titian. It was painted on pannel; but, having undergone the same operation as the *Madonna di Foligno*, is now placed on canvass, and is in such a state as to claim the admiration of succeeding ages.

N° 74. (Saloon.) *The Portraits of Titian and his mistress.*

70. (Saloon.) *Portrait of the Marquis del Guasto with some ladies.*

Both these pictures belonged to the old collection of the crown, and are to be admired for grace and beauty.

N° 940. (Gallery.) *Christ crowned with thorns.*
941. (Gallery.) *Christ carried to the grave.*

There is a wonderful vigour of colouring in these two capital pictures.

The preceding are the most admirable of the productions which are at present exhibited of this inimitable master, the first of painters for truth of colouring.

Correggio.

N° 753. (Gallery.) *The Virgin, the infant Jesus, Mary Magdalen, and St. Jerome.*

This picture, commonly distinguished by the appellation of the *St. Jerome* of Correggio, is undoubtedly his *chef d'œuvre.* In the year 1749, the king of Portugal is said to have offered for it a sum equal in value to £18,000 sterling.

N° 756. (Gallery.) *The Marriage of St. Catherine.*
757. (Gallery.) *Christ taken down from the cross.*

This last-mentioned picture has just been engraved in an excellent manner by an Italian artist, M. Rosa-Spina.

The grace of his pencil and his *chiaro oscuro* place Correggio in the first class of painters, where he ranks the third after Raphael and Titian. He is inferior to them in design and composition; however the scarceness of his pictures frequently gives them a superior value. Poor CORREGGIO! It grieves one to recollect that he lost his life, in consequence of the fatigue of staggering home under a load of *copper* coin, which avaricious monks had given him for pictures now become so valuable that they are not to be purchased for their weight, even in *gold*.

No collection is so rich in pictures of CORREGGIO as that of the CENTRAL MUSEUM.

PAOLO VERONESE.

N° 44. (Saloon.) *The Wedding at Cana.*
45. (Saloon.) *The Repast at the house of Levi.*
51. (Saloon.) *The Pilgrims of Emmaüs.*

These are astonishing compositions for their vast extent, the number and beauty of the figures and portraits, and the variety and truth of the colouring. Nothing in painting can be richer.

ANDREA DEL SARTO.

N° 4. (Saloon.) *Christ taken down from the cross.*

ANDREA SQUAZZELLI (his pupil.)

N°   (   ) *Christ laid in the tomb.*

This capital picture is not in the catalogue.

Giorgione del Castel-Franco.

N° 32. (Saloon.) *A Concert containing three portraits.*

This master-piece is worthy of Titian.

Guercino.

N° 33 (Saloon.) *St. Petronilla.*

This large picture was executed for St. Peter's church in the Vatican, where it was replaced by a copy in Mosaic, on being removed to the pontificate palace of Monte Cavallo, at Rome.

In the great Gallery are exhibited no less than twenty-three pictures by Guercino: but to speak the truth, though, in looking at some of his productions, he appears an extremely agreeable painter, as soon as you see a number of them, you can no longer bear him. This is what happens to *mannerists.* The dark shades at first astonish you, afterwards they disgust you.

Andrea Sacchi.

N° 65. (Saloon.) *St. Remuald.*

This picture was always one of the most esteemed of those in the churches at Rome. It was the altar-piece of the church of St. Remuald in that city.

ALBANO.

N° 676. (Gallery.) *Fire.*
 677. *Air.*
 678. *Water.*
 679. *Earth.*

In the Gallery are twenty-nine pictures of this master, and all of them graceful; but the preceding four, representing the elements, which were taken from the royal cabinet of Turin, are the most remarkable.

BAROCCIO.

N° 686. (Gallery.) *The Virgin, St Anthony, and St. Lucia.*
 688. *St. Michaelina.*

These are the best pictures of BAROCCIO already exhibited. His colouring is enchanting. It is entirely transparent, and seems as if impregnated with light: however, his forms, and every thing else, bespeak the *mannerist.*

ANNIBALE CARACCI.

N° 721. (Gallery.) *Christ dead on the knees of the Virgin.*
 723. *The Resurrection of Christ.*
 728. *The Nativity of Christ.*
 730. *Christ laid in the tomb,*

Of the CARRACCI, ANNIBALE is the most perfect. He is also remarkable for the different manners which he has displayed in his works. They appear to be by two or three different painters. Of more than twenty in the Gallery, the above are the best of his productions.

MICHAEL ANGELO DA CARAVAGGIO.

N° 744. (Gallery.) *Christ laid in the tomb.*

This wonderful picture, which was brought from Rome, is, for vigour of execution and truth of colouring, superior to all the others by the same master. Every one of his works bears the stamp of a great genius.

DOMENICHINO.

N° 763. (Gallery.) *The Communion of St. Jerome.*

This picture, the master-piece of DOMENICHINO, comes from the great altar of the church of *San Geronimo della Carità*, at Rome. It will appear incredible that for a work of such importance, which cost him so much time, study, and labour, he received no more than the sum of about £10 sterling.

N° 769. (Gallery.) *St. Cecilia.*

This capital performance is now removed to

the drawing-room of the First Consul, in the palace of the *Tuileries*.

After RAPHAEL, DOMENICHINO is one of the most perfect masters; and his *St. Jerome*, together with RAPHAEL's Transfiguration, are reckoned among the most famous *chefs d'œuvre* of the art of painting.

GUIDO.

N° 797. (Gallery.) *The Crucifixion of St. Peter.*
800. *Fortune.*

These are the finest of the twenty pictures by that master, now exhibited in the CENTRAL MUSEUM. They both came from Rome; the former, from the Vatican; the latter, from the Capitol.

GUIDO is a noble and graceful painter; but, in general, he betrays a certain negligence in the execution of several parts.

LUINI.

N° 860. (Gallery.) *The Holy Family.*

In this picture, LUINI has fallen little short of his master, LEONARDO DA VINCI.

ANDREA SOLARIO.

N° 896. (Gallery.) *The Daughter of Herodias receiving the head of St. John.*

SOLARIO is another worthy pupil of LEONARDO.

This very capital picture belonged to the collection of the crown, and was purchased by Lewis XIV.

Pierino del Vaga.

N° 928. (Gallery.) *The Muses challenged by the Pïerides.*

An excellent picture from Versailles.

Baltassare Peruzzi.

N° 929. (Gallery.) *The Virgin discovering the infant Jesus asleep.*

A remarkably fine production.

Sebastiano del Piombo.

N°   (   ) *Portrait of the young sculptor, Baccio Bomdinelli.*

This picture is worthy of the pencil of Raphael. It is not yet exhibited.

Pietro da Cortona.

N° 52. (Saloon.) *The Birth of the Virgin.*
53. *Remus and Romulus.*

These are the finest pictures in the collection by this master.

We have now noticed the best productions of

the Italian School: in our next visit to the CENTRAL MUSEUM, I shall point out the most distinguished pictures of the French and Flemish Schools.

P. S. Lord Cornwallis is sumptuously entertained here, all the ministers giving him a grand dinner, each in rotation. After having viewed the curiosities of Paris, he will, in about a fortnight, proceed to the congress at Amiens. On his Lordship's arrival, I thought it my duty to leave my name at his hotel, and was most agreeably surprised to meet with a very old acquaintance in his military Secretary, Lieut. Col. L————s. For any of the ambassador's further proceedings, I refer you to the English newspapers, which seem to anticipate all his movements.

LETTER XVII.

Paris, November 15, 1801.

THE more frequently I visit the CENTRAL MUSEUM OF THE ARTS, the more am I inclined to think that such a vast number of pictures, suspended together, lessen each other's effect. This is the first idea which now presents itself to me, whenever I enter the

GALLERY OF THE LOUVRE.

Were this collection rendered apparently less numerous by being subdivided into different apartments, the eye would certainly be less dazzled than it is, at present, by an assemblage of so many various objects, which, though arranged as judiciously as possible, somehow convey to the mind an image of confusion. The consequence is that attention flags, and no single picture is seen to advantage, because so many are seen together.

In proportion as the lover of the arts becomes more familiarized with the choicest productions of the pencil, he perceives that there are few pictures, if any, really faultless. In some, he finds beauties, which are general, or forming, as it were, a whole, and producing a general effect; in others, he meets with particular or detached beauties, whose effect is partial: assembled, they constitute the beautiful: insulated, they have a merit which the amateur appreciates, and the artist ought to study. General or congregated beauties always arise from genius and talent: particular or detached beauties belong to study, to labour, that is, to the *nulla die sine lineâ*, and sometimes solely to chance, as is exemplified in the old story of Protogenes, the celebrated Rhodian painter,

To discover some of these beauties, requires no extraordinary discernment; a person of common observation might decide whether the froth at the mouth of an animal, panting for breath, was naturally represented: but a spectator, possessing a cultivated and refined taste, minutely surveys every part of a picture, examines the grandeur of the composition, the elevation of the ideas, the nobleness of the expression, the truth and correctness of the design, the grace scattered over the different objects, the imitation of nature in the colouring, and the masterly strokes of the pencil.

Our last visit to the CENTRAL MUSEUM terminated with the Italian School; let us now continue our examination, beginning with the

FRENCH SCHOOL.

LE BRUN.

N° 17. (Gallery) *The Defeat of Porus.*
    18. *The Family of Darius at the feet of Alexander.*
    19. *The Entrance of Alexander into Babylon.*
        The Passage of the Granicus.
    14. *Jesus asleep, or Silence.*
    16. *The Crucifix surrounded by angels.*

The compositions of LE BRUN are grand and rich; his costume well-chosen, and tolerably scientific; the tone of his pictures well-suited to the subject. But, in this master, we must not look for purity and correctness of drawing, in an eminent degree. He much resembles PIETRO DA CORTONA. LE BRUN, however, has a taste more in the style of RAPHAEL and the antique, though it is a distant imitation. The colouring of PIETRO DA CORTONA is far more agreeable and more captivating.

Among the small pictures by LE BRUN, N^{os}, 14 and 16 deserve to be distinguished; but his *chefs d'œuvre* are the achievements of Alexander. When the plates from these historical paintings, engraved by AUDRAN, reached Rome, it is related that the Italians, astonished, exclaimed: " *Povero Raffaello! non sei più il primo.*" But, when they afterwards saw the originals, they restored to RAPHAEL his former pre-eminence.

CLAUDE LORRAIN.

N° 43. (Gallery.) *View of a sea-port at sun-set.*
   45. *A Sea-piece on a fine morning.*
   46. *A Landscape enlivened by the setting sun.*

The superior merit of CLAUDE in landscape-painting is too well known to need any eulogium. The three preceding are the finest of his pictures in this collection. However, at Rome, and in England, there are some more perfect than those in the

Central Museum. One of his *chefs d'œuvre*, formerly at Rome, is now at Naples, in the Gallery of Prince Colonna.

Jouvenet.

N° 54. (Gallery.) *Christ taken down from the cross.*

The above is the most remarkable picture here by this master.

Mignard.

N° 57. (Gallery.) *The Virgin,* called *La Vièrge à la grappe,* because she is taking from a basket of fruit a bunch of grapes to present to her son.

Nicolas Poussin.

N° 70. (Gallery.) *The Fall of the manna in the desert.*
75. *Rebecca and Eleazar.*
77. *The Judgment of Solomon.*
78. *The blind Men of Jericho.*
82. *Winter or the Deluge.*

In this collection, the above are the finest historical paintings of Poussin; and of his landscapes, the following deserve to be admired.

N° 76. (Gallery.) *Diogenes throwing away his porringer.*
83. *The Death of Eurydice.*

Poussin is the greatest painter of the French school. His compositions bear much resemblance to those of RAPHAEL, and to the antique; though they have not the same *naïveté* and truth. His back-grounds are incomparable; his landscapes, in point of composition, superior even to those of CLAUDE. His large altar-pieces are the least beautiful of his productions. His feeble colouring cannot support proportions of the natural size: in these pictures, the charms of the background are also wanting.

LE SUEUR.

N° 98. (Gallery.) *St Paul preaching at Ephesus.*

This is the *chef d'œuvre* of LE SUEUR, who is to be admired for the simplicity of his pencil, as well as for the beauty of his compositions.

VALENTINO.

N° 111. (Gallery.) *The Martyrdom of St. Processa and St. Martinian.*
112. *Cæsar's Tribute.*

These are the finest productions of this master, who was a worthy rival of CARAVAGGIO.

Vernet.

N° 121. (Gallery.) *A Sea-port at sun-set.*

This painter's style is generally correct and agreeable. In the above picture he rivals Claude.

We now come to the school which, of all others, is best known in England. This exempts me from making any observations on the comparative merits of the masters who compose it. I shall therefore confine myself to a bare mention of the best of their performances, at present exhibited in the Central Museum.

FLEMISH SCHOOL.

Rubens.

N° 485. (Gallery.) *St. Francis, dying, receives the sacrament.*

503. *Christ taken down from the cross,* a celebrated picture from the cathedral of Antwerp.

507. *Nicholas Rockox, a burgomaster of the city of Antwerp, and a friend of* Rubens.

509. *The Crucifixion of St. Peter.*

513. *St. Roch interceding for the people attacked by the plague.*

526. *The Village-Festival.*

In this repository, the above are the most remarkable productions of Rubens.

VANDYCK.

N° 255. (Gallery.) *The Mother of pity.*
  264. *The portraits of Charles I, elector palatine, and his brother, prince Robert.*
  265. *A full-length portrait of a man holding his daughter by the hand.*
  266. *A full-length portrait of a lady with her son.*

These are superior to the other pictures by VANDYCK in this collection.

CHAMPAGNE.

N° 216. (Gallery.) *The Nuns.*

The history of this piece is interesting. The eldest daughter of CHAMPAGNE was a nun in the convent of *Port-Royal* at Paris. Being reduced to extremity by a fever of fourteen months' duration, and given over by her physicians, she falls to prayers with another nun, and recovers her health.

CRAYER.

N° 227. (Gallery.) *The Triumph of St. Catherine.*

GERHARD DOUW.

N° 234. (Gallery.) *The dropsical Woman.*

Hans Holbein.

N° 319. (Gallery.) *A young woman, dressed in a yellow veil, and with her hands crossed on her knees.*

Jordaens.

N° 351. (Gallery.) *Twelfth-Day.*
352. *The Family-Concert.*

Adrian Van Ostade.

N° 428. (Gallery.) *The family of Ostade, painted by himself.*
430. *A smoking Club.*
431. *The Schoolmaster, with the ferula in his hand, surrounded by his scholars.*

Paul Potter.

N° 446. (Gallery.) *An extensive pasture, with cattle.*

This most remarkable picture represents, on the fore-ground, near an oak, a bull, a ewe with its lamb, and a herdsman, all as large as life.

Rembrandt.

N° 457. (Gallery.) *The head of a woman with ear-rings, and dressed in a fur-cloak.*
458. *The good Samaritan.*

N° 465. *The Cabinet-maker's family.*

466. *Tobias and his family kneeling before the angel Raphael, who disappears from his sight, after having made himself known.*

469. *The Presentation of Jesus in the temple.*

The pictures, exhibited in the *Saloon* of the *Louvre*, have infinitely the advantage of those in the *Great Gallery*; the former apartment being lighted from the top; while in the latter, the light is admitted through large windows, placed on both sides, those on the one side facing the compartments between those on the other; so that, in this respect, the master-pieces in the *Gallery* are viewed under very unfavourable circumstances.

The *Gallery* of the *Louvre* is still capable of containing more pictures, one eighth part of it (that next to the *Tuileries)*, being under repair for the purpose*. It has long been a question with the French republican government, whether the palace of the *Tuileries* should not be connected to the *Louvre*, by a gallery parallel to that which borders the Seine. Six years ago, I understand,

---

* In the great *Gallery* of the *Louvre* are suspended about nine hundred and fifty pictures; which, with ninety in the *Saloon*, extend the number of the present exhibition to one thousand and forty.

the subject was agitated, and dropped again, on consideration of the state of the country in general, and particularly the finances. It is now revived; and I was told the other day, that a plan of construction had absolutely been adopted. This, no doubt, is more easy than to find the sums of money necessary for carrying on so expensive an undertaking.

If the fact were true, it is of a nature to produce a great sensation in modern art, since it is affirmed that the object of this work is to give a vast display to every article appropriated to general instruction; for, according to report, it is intended that these united buildings, should, in addition to the National Library, contain the collections of statues, pictures, &c. &c. still remaining at the disposal of the government. I would not undertake to vouch for the precise nature of the object proposed; but it cannot be denied that, in this project, there is a boldness well calculated to flatter the ambition of the Chief Consul.

However, I think it more probable that nothing, in this respect, will be positively determined in the present state of affairs. The expedition to St. Domingo will cost an immense sum, not to speak of the restoration of the French navy, which must occasion great and immediate calls for money. Whence I conclude that the erection of the new Gallery, like that of the National

Column, will be much talked of, but remain among other projects in embryo, and the discussion be adjourned *sine die.*

Leaving the *Great Gallery*, we return to the *Saloon* of the *Louvre*, which, being an intermediate apartment, serves as a point of communication between it and the

GALLERY OF APOLLO.

The old gallery of this name, first called *La petite galérie du Louvre*, was constructed under the reign of Henry IV, and, from its origin, ornamented with paintings. This gallery having been consumed by fire in 1661, owing to the negligence of a workman employed in preparing a theatre for a grand ballet, in which the king was to dance with all his court, Lewis XIV immediately ordered it to be rebuilt and magnificently decorated.

Le Brun, who then directed works of this description in France, furnished the designs of all the paintings, sculpture, and ornaments, which are partly executed. He divided the vault of the roof into eleven principal compartments; in that which is in the centre, he intended to represent *Apollo* in his car, with all the attributes peculiar to the Sun, which was the king's device. The *Seasons* were to have occupied the four nearest compartments; in the others, were to have been *Even-*

ing and *Morning, Night* and *Day-break,* the *Waking of the Waters,* and that of the *Earth at Sun-rise.*

Unfortunately for his fame, this vast project of LE BRUN was never completed. Lewis XIV, captivated by Versailles, soon turned all his thoughts towards the embellishment of that palace. The works of the GALLERY OF APOLLO were entirely abandoned, and, of all this grand composition, LE BRUN was enabled to execute no more than the following subjects:

1. *Evening,* represented by Morpheus, lying on a bed of poppies, and buried in a profound sleep.

2. *Night* succeeding to day, and lighted by the silvery disk of the Moon, which, under the figure of Diana, appears in a car drawn by hinds.

3. *The Waking of the Waters.* Neptune and Amphitrite on a car drawn by sea-horses, and accompanied by Tritons, Nereïds, and other divinities of the waters, seem to be paying homage to the rising sun, whose first rays dispel the Winds and Tempests, figured by a group to the left; while, to the right, Polyphemus, seated on a rock, is calling with his loud instrument to his Galatea.

The other compartments, which LE BRUN could not paint, on account of the cessation of the works, remained a long time vacant, and would have been so at this day, had not the *ci-devant* Academy of Painting, to whom the king, in 1764, granted the use of the GALLERY OF APOLLO, resolved that, in future, the historical painters who might be admitted members, should be bound to paint for their reception one of the subjects which were still wanting for the completion of the ceiling. In this manner, five of the compartments, which remained to be filled, were successively decorated, namely:

1. *Summer*, by DURAMEAU.
2. *Autumn*, by TARAVAL.
3. *Spring*, by CALLET.
4. *Winter*, by LAGRENÉE the younger.
5. *Morning*, or day-break, by RENOU.

The GALLERY OF APOLLO now making part of the CENTRAL MUSEUM, it would be worthy of the government to cause its ceiling to be completed, by having the three vacant compartments painted by skilful French artists.

Under the compartments, and immediately above the cornice, are twelve medallions, which were to represent the *twelve months of the year*, characterized by the different occupations peculiar to them: eight only are executed, and these are the months of summer, autumn, and winter.

The rich borders in gilt stucco, which serve as frames to all these paintings, the caryatides which support them, as well as the groups of Muses,

Rivers, and Children, that are distributed over the great cornice, are worthy of remark. Not only were the most celebrated sculptors then in France, GASPAR and BALTHAZAR MARSY, REGNAUDIN, and GIRARDON, chosen to execute them; but their emulation was also excited by a premium of three hundred louis, which was promised to him who should excel. GIRARDON obtained it by the execution of the following pieces of sculpture :

1. The figure representing a river which is under the *Waking of the Waters*; at the south extremity of the gallery.

2. The two trophies of arms which are near that river.

3. The caryatides that support one of the octagonal compartments towards the quay, at the foot of which are seen two children; the one armed with a sickle, the other leaning on a lion.

4. The group of caryatides that supports the great compartment where *Summer* is represented, and below which is a child holding a balance.

5. The two grouped figures of Tragedy and Comedy, which rest on the great cornice.

In the GALLERY OF APOLLO will be exhibited in succession, about twelve thousand original drawings of the Italian, Flemish, and French schools, the greater part of which formerly belonged to the crown. This valuable collection had been successively enriched by the choice of those of JABAK, LANOUE, MONTARSIS, LE BRUN, CROZAT, MARIETTE, &c. yet never rendered public. Private and partial admission to it had, indeed, been granted; but artists and amateurs, in general, were precluded from so rich a source of study. By inconceivable neglect, it seemed almost to have escaped the attention of the old government, having been for a hundred years shut up in a confined place, instead of being exhibited to public view.

The variety of the forms and dimensions of these drawings having opposed the more preferable mode of arranging them by schools, and in chronological order, the most capital drawings of each master have been selected (for, in so extensive a collection, it could not be supposed that they were all equally interesting); and these even are sufficiently numerous to furnish several successive exhibitions.

The present exhibition consists of upwards of two hundred drawings by the most distinguished masters of the Italian school, about one hundred by those of the Flemish, and as many, or rather more, by those of the French. They are placed in glazed frames, so contrived as to admit of the subjects being changed at pleasure. Among the drawings by RAPHAEL, is the great cartoon of the Athenian School, a valuable fragment which served for the execution of the grand *fresco* painting in the Vatican, the largest and finest of all his productions. It was brought from the Ambrosian library at Milan, and is one of the most instructive works extant for a study.

Besides the drawings, is a frame containing a series of portraits of illustrious personages who made a figure in the reign of Lewis XIV. They are miniatures in enamel, painted chiefly by the celebrated PETITOT of Geneva.

Here are also to be seen some busts and antique vases. The most remarkable of the latter is one of Parian marble, about twenty-one inches in height by twelve in diameter. It is of an oval form; the handles, cut out of the solid stone, are ornamented with four swans' heads, and the neck with branches of ivy. On the swell is a bas-relief, sculptured in the old Greek style, and in the centre is an altar on which these words may be decyphered.

ΣΟΣΙΒΙΟΣ ΑΘΗΝΑΙΟΣ ΕΠΟΙΕΙ.
Sosibios of Athens fecit.

This beautiful vase* is placed on a table of violet African breccia, remarkable for its size,

---

* Whatever may be the beauty of this vase, two others are to be seen in Paris, which surpass it, according to the opinion of one of the most celebrated antiquaries of the age, M. VISCONTI. They are now in the possession of M. AUBRI, being twelve feet in length, three feet ten inches in breadth, and upwards of three inches in thickness.

It might, at first, be supposed that the indiscriminate admission of persons of all ranks to a Museum, which presents so many attractive objects, would create confusion, and occasion breaches of decorum. But this is by no means the case. *Savoyards, poissardes,* and the whole motley assemblage of the lower classes of both sexes in Paris, behave themselves with as much propriety as the more refined visiters; though their remarks,

---

doctor of Physic, residing at N°. 272, *Rue St. Thomas du Louvre,* but they formerly graced the cabinet of the *Villa-Albani* at Rome. In this apartment, Cardinal Alessandro had assembled some of the most valuable ornaments of antiquity. Here were to be seen the Apollo *Sauroctonos* in bronze, the Diana in alabaster, and the *unique* bas-relief of the apotheosis of Hercules. By the side of such rare objects of art, these vases attracted no less attention. To describe them as they deserve, would lead me too far; they need only to be seen to be admired. Although their form is antique, the execution of them is modern, and ascribed to the celebrated sculptor, SILVIO DA VELETRI, who lived in the beginning of the seventeenth century. Indeed, M. VISCONTI affirms that antiquity affords not their equal; assigning as a reason that porphyry was introduced into Rome at a period when the fine arts were tending to their decline. Notwithstanding the hardness of the substance, they are executed with such taste and perfection, that the porphyry is reduced to the thinness of china.

perhaps, may be expressed in language less polished. In conspicuous places of the various apartments, boards are affixed, on which is inscribed the following significant appeal to the uncultivated mind, " *Citoyens, ne touchez à rien;* " *mais respectez la Propriété Nationale.*" Proper persons are stationed here and there to caution such as, through thoughtlessness or ignorance, might not attend to the admonition.

On the days appropriated to the accommodation of students, great numbers are to be seen in different parts of the Museum, some mounted on little stages, others standing or sitting, all sedulously employed in copying the favourite object of their studies. Indeed, the epithet CENTRAL has been applied to this establishment, in order to designate a MUSEUM, which is to contain the choicest productions of art, and, of course, become the *centre* of study. Here, nothing has been neglected that could render such an institution useful, either in a political light, or in regard to public instruction. Its magnificence and splendour speak to every eye, and are calculated to attract the attention of foreigners from the four quarters of the globe; while, as a source of improvement, it presents to students the finest models that the arts and sciences could assemble. In a philosophical point of view, such a Museum may be compared to a torch, whose light will not only dispel the remnant of that bad taste which, for a century, has predominated in the arts dependent on design, but also serve to guide the future progress of the rising generation.

LETTER XVIII.

Paris, November 17, 1801.

THE *Louvre*, the *Tuileries*, together with the *National Fête* in honour of Peace, and a crowd of interesting objects, have so engrossed our attention, that we seem to have overlooked the *ci-devant Palais Royal*. Let us then examine that noted edifice, which now bears the name of

PALAIS DU TRIBUNAT.

In 1629, Cardinal Richelieu began the construction of this palace. When finished, in 1636, he called it the *Palais Cardinal*, a denomination which was much criticized, as being unworthy of the founder of the French Academy.

Like the politic Wolseley, who gave Hampton-Court to Henry VIII, the crafty Richelieu, in 1639, thought proper to make a present of this palace to Lewis XIII. After the death of that king, Anne of Austria, queen of France and regent of the kingdom, quitted the *Louvre* to inhabit the *Palais Cardinal*, with her sons Lewis XIV and the Duke of Anjou.

The first inscription was then removed, and this palace was called *le Palais Royal*, a name which it preserved till the revolution, when, after the new title assumed by its then owner, it was denominated *la Maison Égalité*, till, under the consular government, since the Tribunate have here established their sittings, it has obtained its present appellation of *Palais du Tribunat*.

In the sequel, Lewis XIV granted to Monsieur, his only brother, married to Henrietta Stuart, daughter of Charles I, the enjoyment of the *Palais Royal*, and afterwards vested the property of it in his grandson, the Duke of Chartres.

That prince, become Duke of Orleans, and regent of France, during the minority of Lewis XV, resided in this palace, and (to use Voltaire's expression) hence gave the signal of voluptuousness to the whole kingdom. Here too, he ruled it with principles the most daring; holding men, in general, in great contempt, and conceiving them to be all as insidious, as servile, and as covetous as those by whom he was surrounded. With the superiority of his character, he made a sport of governing this mass of individuals, as if the task was unworthy of his genius. The fact is illustrated by the following anecdote.

At the commencement of his regency, the

debts of the State were immense, and the finances exhausted: such great evils required extraordinary remedies; he wished to persuade the people that paper-money was better than specie. Thousands became the dupes of their avarice, and too soon awoke from their dream only to curse the authors of a project which ended in their total ruin. It is almost needless to mention that I here allude to the Mississippi bubble.

In circumstances so critical, the Parliament of Paris thought it their duty to make remonstrances. They accordingly sent deputies to the regent, who was persuaded that they wished to stir up the Parisians against him. After having listened to their harangue with much phelgm, he gave them his answer in four words: " Go and be d———n'd." The deputy, who had addressed him, nothing disconcerted, instantly replied : " Sir, it is the cus-
" tom of the Parliament to enter in their registers
" the answers which they receive from the throne:
" shall they insert this ?"

The principles of the regent's administration, which succeeded those of Lewis XIV, form in history, a very striking shade. The French nation, which, plastic as wax, yields to every impression, was new-modelled in a single instant. As a rotten speck, by spreading, contaminates the finest fruit, so was the *Palais Royal* the corrupt spot, whence the contagion of debauchery was propagated, even to the remotest parts of the kingdom.

This period, infinitely curious and interesting, paved the way to the present manners. If the basis of morality be at this day overthrown in France, the regency of Philip of Orleans, by completing what the dissolute court of Lewis XIV had begun, has occasioned that rapid change, whose influence was felt long before the revolution, and will, in all probability, last for ages. At least, I think that such a conclusion is exemplified by what has occurred in England since the profligate reign of Charles II, the effects of whose example have never been done away.

Different circumstances have produced considerable alterations in this palace, so that, at the present day, its numerous buildings preserve of the first architect, LE MERCIER, no more than a small part of the second court.

The principal entrance of the *Palais du Tribunat* is from the *Rue St. Honoré*. The façade, on this side, which was constructed in 1763, consists of two pavilions, ornamented by Doric and Ionic pillars, and connected by a lofty stone-wall, perforated with arches, to three grand gates, by which you enter the first court. Here, two elegant wings present themselves, decorated with pilasters, also of the Doric and Ionic orders, which are likewise employed for the pillars of the avant-corps in the centre. This avant-corps is pierced with three arches, which serve as a passage into the second court, and correspond with the three gates before-mentioned.

Having reached the vestibule, between the two courts, where large Doric pillars rise, though partly concealed by a number of little shops and stalls, you see, on the right, the handsome elliptical stair-case, which leads to the apartments. It branches off into two divisions at the third step, and is lighted by a lofty dome. The balustrade of polished iron is beautiful, and is said to have cost thirty-two workmen two years' labour. Before the revolution, strangers repaired hither to admire the cabinet of gems and engraved stones, the cabinet of natural history, the collection of models of arts, trades, and manufactures, and the famous collection of pictures, belonging to the *last* duke of Orleans, and chiefly assembled, at a vast expense, by his grandfather, the regent.

This second court is larger than the first; but it still remains in an incomplete state. The right-hand wing only is finished, and is merely a continuation of that which we have seen in the other court. On the left hand, is the site of the new hall intended for the sittings of the Tribunate. Workmen are now employed in its construction; heaps of stones and mortar are lying about, and the building seems to proceed with tolerable expedition. Here, in the back-ground, is a crowd of little stalls for the sale of various articles, such as prints, plays, fruit, and pastry. In front stand such carriages as remain in waiting for those who may have been set down at this end of the palace. Proceeding onward, you pass through two parallel wooden galleries, lined on each side with shops, and enter the formerly-enchanting regions of the

JARDIN DU PALAIS DU TRIBUNAT.

The old garden of the *Palais Royal*, long famous for its shady walks, and for being the most fashionable public promenade in Paris, had, from its centrical situation, gradually attracted to its vicinity a considerable number of speculators, who there opened ready-furnished hotels, coffee-houses, and shops of various descriptions. The success of these different establishments awakened the cupidity of its wealthy proprietor, then Duke of Chartres, who, conceiving that the ground might be made to yield a capital augmentation to his income, fixed on a plan for enclosing it by a magnificent range of buildings.

Notwithstanding the clamours of the Parisian public, who, from long habit, considered that they had a sort of prescriptive right to this favourite promenade, the axe was laid to the celebrated *arbre de Cracovie* and other venerable trees, and their stately heads were soon levelled to the ground. Every one murmured as if these trees had been his own private property, and cut down against his will and pleasure. This will not appear extraordinary, when it is considered that, under their wide-spreading branches, which afforded a shelter impervious to the sun and rain, politicians by day, adjusted the balance of power, and arbiters of taste discussed the fashions of the moment; while, by night, they presented a canopy, beneath which were often arranged the clandestine bargains of opera-girls and other votaries of Venus.

After venting their spleen in vague conjectures, witty epigrams, and lampoons, the Parisians were silent. They presently found that they were, in general, not likely to be losers by this devastation. In 1782, the execution of the new plan was begun: in less than three years, the present inclosure was nearly completed, and the modern garden thrown open to the public, uniting to the advantages of the ancient one, a thousand others more refined and concentrated.

The form of this garden is a parallelogram, whose length is seven hundred and two feet by three hundred in breadth, taken at its greatest dimensions. It is bordered, on three of its sides, by new, uniform buildings, of light and elegant architecture. Rising to an elevation of forty-two feet, these buildings present two regular stories, exclusively of the *mansarde,* or attic story, decorated by festoons, bas-reliefs, and large Composite fluted pillars, bearing an entablature in whose frieze windows are pierced. Throughout its extent, the whole edifice is crowned by a balustrade, on the pedestals of which vases are placed at equal distances.

In the middle of the garden stood a most singular building, partly subterraneous, called a *Cirque.* This circus, which was first opened in 1789, with concerts, balls, &c. was also appropriated to more useful objects, and, in 1792, a *Lyceum of Arts* was here established; but in 1797, it was consumed by fire, and its site is now occupied by a grass-plot. On the two long sides of the garden are planted three rows of horse-chesnut trees, not yet of sufficient growth to afford any shade; and what is new, is a few shrubs and flowers in inclosed compartments. The walks are of gravel, and kept in good order.

On the ground-floor, a covered gallery runs entirely round the garden. The shops, &c. on this floor, as well as the apartments of the *entresol* above them, receive light by one hundred and eighty porticoes, which are open towards the garden, and used to have each a glass lantern, with reflectors, suspended in the middle of their arch. In lieu of these, some of a less brilliant description are now distributed on a more economical plan under the piazzas; but, at the close of day, the rivalship of the shopkeepers, in displaying their various commodities, creates a blaze of light which would strike a stranger as the effect of an illumination.

The fourth side of the garden towards the *Rue St. Honoré* is still occupied by a double gallery, constructed, as I have already mentioned, of wood, which has subsisted nearly in its present state ever since I first visited Paris in 1784. It was to have been replaced by a colonnade for the inclosure of the two courts. This colonnade was to have consisted of six rows of Doric pillars, supporting a spacious picture-gallery, (intended for the whole of the Orleans collection), which was to have constituted the fourth façade to the garden, and have formed a covered walk, communicating with the galleries of the other three sides.

These galleries, whose whole circumference measures upwards of a third of a mile, afford to the public, even in bad weather, a walk equally agreeable and convenient, embellished, on the one side, by the aspect of the garden, and, on the other, by the studied display of every thing that taste and fashion can invent to captivate the attention of passengers.

No place in Paris, however, exhibits such a

contrast to its former attractions as this once-fashionable rendezvous. The change of its name from *Palais Royal* to *Maison Égalité* conveys not to the imagination a dissimilitude more glaring than is observable between the present frequenters of this favourite promenade, and those who were in the habit of flocking hither before the revolution.

At that period, the scene was enlivened by the most brilliant and most captivating company in the capital, both in point of exterior and manners. At this day, the medal is exactly reversed. In lieu of well-dressed or well-behaved persons of both sexes, this garden, including its purlieus, presents, morning and evening, nothing but hordes of stock-jobbers, money-brokers, gamblers, and adventurers of every description. The females who frequent it, correspond nearly to the character of the men; they are, for the greater part, of the most debauched and abandoned class: for a Laïs of *bon ton* seldom ventures to shew herself among this medley of miscreants. In the crowd, may be occasionally remarked a few strangers attracted by curiosity, and other individuals of respectable appearance called hither on business, as well as some inoffensive newsmongers, resorting to the coffee-houses to read the papers. But, in general, the great majority of the company, now seen here, is of a cast so extremely low, that no decent woman, whether married or single, thinks of appearing in a place where she would run a risk of being put out of countenance in passing alone, even in the day-time. In the evening, the company is of a still worse complexion; and the concourse becomes so great under the piazzas, particularly when the inclemency of the weather drives people out of the garden, that it is sometimes difficult to cross through the motley assemblage. At the conclusion of the performances in the neighbouring theatres, there is a vast accession of the inferior order of nymphs of the Cyprian corps; and then, amorous conversation and dalliance reach the summit of licentious freedom.

The greater part of the political commotions which have, at different times, convulsed Paris, took their rise in the *ci-devant Palais Royal,* or it has, in some shape, been their theatre. In this palace too originated the dreadful reverse of fortune which the queen experienced; and, indeed, when the cart in which her majesty was carried to the scaffold, passed before the gates of this edifice, she was unable to repress a sign of indignation.

All writers who have spoken of the inveterate hatred, which existed between the queen and M. d'Orléans, have ascribed it to despised love, whose pangs, as Shakspeare tells us, are not patiently endured. Some insist that the duke, enamoured of the charms of the queen, hazarded a declaration, which her majesty not only received with disdain, but threatened to inform the king of in case of a renewal of his addresses. Others affirm that the queen, at one time, shewed that the duke was not indifferent to her, and that, on a hint being given to him to that effect, he replied: " Every one may be ambitious to please " the queen, except myself. Our interests are " too opposite for Love ever to unite them." On this foundation is built the origin of the animosity which, in the end, brought both these great personages to the scaffold.

Whatever may have been the motive which gave rise to it, certain it is that they never omitted any opportunity of persecuting each other. The queen had no difficulty in pourtraying the duke as a man addicted to the most profligate excesses, and in alienating from him the mind of the king: he, on his side, found it as easy, by means of surreptitious publications, to represent her as a woman given to illicit enjoyments; so that, long before the revolution, the character both of the queen and the duke were well known to the public; and their example tended not a little to increase the general dissoluteness of morals. The debaucheries of the one served as a model to all the young rakes of fashion; while the levity of the other was imitated by what were termed the *amiable* women of the capital.

After his exile in 1788, the hatred of M. d'Orléans towards the queen roused that ambition which he inherited from his ancestors. In watching her private conduct, in order to expose her criminal weaknesses, he discovered a certain political project, which gave birth to the idea of his forming a plan of a widely-different nature. Hitherto he had given himself little trouble about State affairs; but, in conjunction with his confidential friends, he now began to calculate the means of profiting by the distress of his country.

The first shocks of the revolution had so electrified the greater part of the Parisians, that, in regard to the Duke of Orleans, they imperceptibly passed from profound contempt to blind infatuation. His palace became the rendezvous of all the malcontents of the court, and this garden the place of assembly of all the demagogues. His exile appeared a public calamity, and his recall was celebrated as a triumph. Had he possessed a vigour of intellect, and a daring equal to the situation of leader of a party, there is little doubt that he might have succeeded in his plan, and been declared regent. His immense income, amounting to upwards of three hundred thousand pounds sterling, was employed to gain partisans, and secure the attachment of the people.

After the taking of the Bastille, it is admitted that his party was sufficiently powerful to effect a revolution in his favour; but his pusillanimity prevailed over his ambition. The active vigilance of the queen thwarting his projects, he resolved to get rid of her: and in that intention was the irruption of the populace directed to Versailles. This fact seems proved: for, on some one complaining before him in 1792, that the revolution proceeded too slowly. " It would have been " terminated long ago," replied he, " had the " queen been sacrificed on the 5th of October " 1789."

Two months before the fall of the throne, M. d'Orléans still reckoned to be able to attain his wishes; but he soon found himself egregiously mistaken. The factions, after mutually accusing each other of having him for their chief, ended by deserting him; and, after the death of the king, he became a stranger to repose, and, for the second time, an object of contempt. The necessity of keeping up the exaltation of the people, had exhausted his fortune, great as it was; and want of money daily detached different agents from his party. His plate, his pictures, his furniture, his books, his trinkets, his gems, all went to purchase the favour, and at length the protection, of the Maratists. Not having it in his power to satisfy their cupidity, he opened loans on all sides, and granted illusory mortgages. Having nothing more left to dispose of, he was reduced, as a last resource, to sell his body-linen. In this very bargain was he engaged, when he was apprehended and sent to Marseilles.

Although acquitted by the criminal tribunal, before which he was tried in the south of France, he was still detained there in prison. At first, he had shed tears, and given himself up to despair, but now hope once more revived his spirits, and he availed himself of the indulgence granted him, by giving way to his old habits of debauchery. On being brought to Paris after six months' confinement, he flattered himself that he should experience the same lenity in the capital. The jailer of the *Conciergerie,* not knowing whether M. d'Orléans would leave that prison to ascend the throne or the scaffold, treated him with particular respect; and he himself was impressed with the idea that he would soon resume an ascendency in public affairs. But, on his second trial, he was unanimously declared guilty of conspiring against the unity and indivisibility of the Republic, and condemned to die, though no proof whatever of his guilt was produced to the jury. One interrogatory put to him is deserving of notice. It was this: " Did you not one day say "to a deputy: *What will you ask of me when I am king?* And did not the deputy reply: *I will ask you for a pistol to blow out your brains?*"

Every one who was present at the condemnation of M. d'Orléans, and saw him led to the guillotine, affirms that if he never shewed courage before, he did at least on that day. On hearing the sentence, he called out: " Let it be executed directly." From the revolutionary tribunal he was conducted straight to the scaffold, where, notwithstanding the reproaches and imprecations which accompanied him all the way, he met his fate with unshaken firmness.

LETTER XIX.

Paris, November 18, 1801.

But if the *ci-devant Palais Royal* has been the mine of political explosions, so it still continues to be the epitome of all the trades in Paris. Under the arcades, on the ground-floor, here are, as formerly, shops of jewellers, haberdashers, artificial florists, milliners, perfumers, print-sellers, engravers, tailors, shoemakers, hatters, furriers, glovers, confectioners, provision-merchants, woollen-drapers, mercers, cutlers, toymen, money-changers, and booksellers, together with several coffee-houses, and lottery-offices, all in miscellaneous succession.

Among this enumeration, the jewellers' shops are the most attractive in point of splendour. The name of the proprietor is displayed in large letters of artificial diamonds, in a conspicuous compartment facing the door. This is a sort of signature, whose brilliancy eclipses all other names, and really dazzles the eyes of the spectators. But at the same time it draws the attention both of the learned and the illiterate: I will venture to affirm that the name of one of these jewellers is more frequently spelt and pronounced than that of any great man recorded in history, either ancient or modern.

With respect to the price of the commodities exposed for sale in the *Palais du Tribunat*, it is much the same as in *Bond Street*, you pay one third at least for the idea of fashion annexed to the name of the place where you make the purchase, though the quality of the article may be nowise superior to what you might procure elsewhere. As in Bond Street too, the rents in this building are high, on which account the shopkeepers are, in some measure, obliged to charge higher than those in other parts of the town. Not but I must do them the justice to acknowledge that they make no scruple to avail themselves of every prejudice formerly entertained in favour of this grand emporium, in regard to taste, novelty, &c. by a still further increase of their prices. No small advantage to the shopkeepers established here is the chance custom, arising from such a variety of trades being collected together so conveniently, all within the same inclosure. A person resorting hither to procure one thing, is sure to be reminded of some other want, which, had not the article presented itself to his eye, would probably have escaped his recollection; and, indeed, such is the thirst of gain, that several tradesmen keep a small shop under these piazzas, independently of a large warehouse in another quarter of Paris.

Pamphlets and other ephemeral productions usually make their first appearance in the *Palais du Tribunat*; and strangers may rely on being plagued by a set of fellows who here hawk about prohibited publications, of the most immoral tendency, embellished with correspondent engravings; such as *Justine, ou les malheurs de la vertu, Les quarante manières, &c.* They seldom, I am told, carry the publication about them, for fear of being unexpectedly apprehended, but keep it at some secret repository hard by, whence they fetch it in an instant. It is curious to see with what adroitness these vagrants elude the vigilance of the police. I had scarcely set my foot in this building before a Jew-looking fellow, coming close to me, whispered in my ear: "*Monsieur* "*veut-il la vie polissonne de Madame*―――?" Madame who do you think? You will stare when I tell you to fill up the blank with the name of her who is now become the first female personage in France? I turned round with astonishment; but the ambulating book-vender had vanished, in consequence, as I conclude, of being observed by some *mouchard*. Thus, what little virtue may remain in the mind of youth is contaminated by precept, as well as example; and the rising generation is in a fair way of being even more corrupted than that which has preceded it.

" *Ætas parentum, pejor avis, tulit*
" *Nos nequiores, mox daturos*
" *Progeniem vitiosiorem.*"

Besides the shops, are some auction-rooms, where you may find any article of wearing apparel or household furniture, from a lady's wig *à la Caracalla* to a bed *à la Grecque:* here are as many puffers as in a mock auction in London; and should you be tempted to bid, by the apparent cheapness of the object put up for sale, it is fifty to one that you soon repent of your bargain. Not so with the *magazins de confiance à prix fixe,* where are displayed a variety of articles, marked at a fixed price, from which there is no abatement.

These establishments are extremely convenient, not only to ingenious mechanics, who have invented or improved a particular production of art, of which they wish to dispose, but also to purchasers. You walk in, and if any article strikes your fancy, you examine it at your ease; you consider the materials, the workmanship, and lastly the price, without being hurried by a loquacious shopkeeper into a purchase which you may shortly regret. A commission of from five to one half per cent, in graduated proportions, according to the value of the article, is charged to the seller, for warehouse-room and all other expenses.

Such is the arrangement of the ground-floor; the apartments on the first floor are at present occupied by *restaurateurs,* exhibitions of various kinds, billiard-tables, and *académies de jeu,* or public gaming-tables, where all the passions are let loose, and all the torments of hell assembled.

The second story is let out in lodgings, furnished or unfurnished, to persons of different descriptions, particularly to the priestesses of Venus. The rooms above, termed *mansardes,* in the French architectural dialect, are mostly inhabited by old batchelors, who prefer economy to show; or by artists, who subsist by the employment of their talents. These chambers are spacious, and though the ceilings are low, they receive a more uninterrupted circulation of fresh air, than the less exalted regions.

Over the *mansardes*, in the very roof, are nests of little rooms, or cock-lofts, resembling, I am told, the cells of a beehive. Journeymen shopkeepers, domestics, and distressed females are said to be the principal occupiers of these aërial abodes.

I had nearly forgot to mention a species of apartment little known in England: I mean the *entresol*, which is what we should denominate a low story, (though here not so considered), immediately above the ground-floor, and directly under the first-floor. In this building, some of the *entresols* are inhabited by the shopkeepers below; some, by women of no equivocal calling, who throw out their lures to the idle youths sauntering under the arcades; and others again are now become *maisons de prêt*, where pawnbrokers exercise their usurious dealings.

In the *Palais du Tribunat*, as you may remark, not an inch of space is lost; every hole and corner being turned to account: here and there, the cellars even are converted into scenes of gaiety and diversion, where the master of the house entertains his customers with a succession of vocal and instrumental music, while they are taking such refreshments as he furnishes.

This speculation, which has, by all accounts, proved extremely profitable, was introduced in the early part of the revolution. Since that period, other speculations, engendered by the luxury of the times, have been set on foot within the precincts of this palace. Of two of these, now in full vigour and exercise, I must say a few words, as they are of a nature somewhat curious.

The one is a *cabinet de décrotteur*, where the art of blacking shoes is carried to a pitch of perfection hitherto unknown in this country.

Not many years ago, it was common, in Paris, to see counsellors, abbés, and military officers, as well as *petits-maîtres* of every denomination, full dressed, that is, with their hat under their arm, their sword by their side, and their hair in a bag, standing in the open street, with one leg cocked up on a stool, while a rough Savoyard or Auvergnat hastily cleaned their shoes with a coarse mixture of lamp-black and rancid oil. At the present day, the *décrotteurs* or shoe-blacks still exercise their profession on the *Pont Neuf* and in other quarters; but, as a refinement of the art, there is also opened, at each of the principal entrances of the *Palais du Tribunat*, a *cabinet de décrotteur*, or small apartment, where you are invited to take a chair, and presented with the daily papers.

The artist, with due care and expedition, first removes the dirt from your shoes or boots with a sponge occasionally moistened in water, and by means of several pencils, of different sizes, not unlike those of a limner, he then covers them with a jetty varnish, rivaling even japan in lustre. This operation he performs with a gravity and consequence that can scarcely fail to excite laughter. Yet, according to the trite proverb, it is not the customer who ought to indulge in mirth, but the *artist*. Although his price is much dearer than that demanded by the other professors of this art, his cabinet is seldom empty from morning to night; and, by a simple calculation, his pencil is found to produce more than that of some good painters of the modern French school.

At the first view of the matter, it should appear that the other speculation might have been hit on by any man with a nose to his face; but, on more mature consideration, one is induced to think that its author was a person of some learning, and well read in ancient history. He, no doubt, took the hint from VESPASIAN. As that emperor blushed not to make the urine of the citizens of Rome a source of revenue, so the learned projector in question rightly judged that, in a place of such resort as the *Palais du Tribunat*, he might, without shame or reproach, levy a small tax on the Parisians, by providing for their convenience in a way somewhat analogous. His penetration is not unhandsomely rewarded; for he derives an income of 12,000 francs, or £500 sterling, from his *cabinets d'aisance*.

Since political causes first occasioned the shutting up of the old *Théâtre Français* in the *Faubourg St. Germain*, now reduced to a shell by fire, Melpomene and Thalia have taken up their abode in the south-west angle of the *Palais du Tribunat*, and in its north-west corner is another theatre, on a smaller scale, where Momus holds his court; so that be you seriously, sentimentally, or humorously disposed, you may, without quitting the shelter of the piazzas, satisfy your inclination. Tragedy, Comedy, and Farce all lie before you within the purlieus of this extraordinary edifice.

To sum up all the conveniences of the *Palais du Tribunat*, suffice it to say, that almost every want, natural or artificial, almost every appetite, gross or refined, might be gratified without passing its limits; for, while the extravagant voluptuary is indulging in all the splendour of Asiatic luxury, the parsimonious sensualist need not depart unsatisfied.

Placed in the middle of Paris, the *Palais du Tribunat* has been aptly compared to a sink of vice, whose contagious effects would threaten society with the greatest evils, were not the scandalous scenes of the capital here concentrated into one focus. It has also been mentioned, by the same writer, Mercier, as particularly worthy of remark, that, since this building is become a grand theatre, where cupidity, gluttony, and licentiousness shew themselves under every form and excess, several other quarters of Paris are, in a manner, purified by the accumulation of vices which flourish in its centre.

Whether or not this assertion be strictly correct, I will not pretend to determine: but, certain it is that the *Palais du Tribunat* is a vortex of dissipation where many a youth is ingulfed. The natural manner in which this may happen I shall endeavour briefly to explain, by way of conclusion to this letter.

A young Frenchman, a perfect stranger in Paris, arrives there from the country, and, wishing to equip himself in the fashion, hastens to the *Palais du Tribunat*, where he finds wearing apparel of every description on the *ground-floor*: prompted by a keen appetite, he dines at a *restaurateur's* on the *first-floor*: after dinner, urged by mere curiosity, perhaps, if not decoyed by some sharper on the look-out for novices, he visits a public gaming-table on the same story. Fortune not smiling on him, he retires; but, at that very moment, he meets, on the landing-place, a captivating damsel, who, like Virgil's Galatea, flies to be pursued; and the inexperienced youth, after ascending another flight of stairs, is, on the *second-floor*, ushered into a brothel. Cloyed or disgusted there, he is again induced to try the humour of the fickle goddess, and repairs once more to the gaming-table, till, having lost all his money, he is under the necessity of descending to the *entresol* to pawn his watch, before he can even procure a lodging in a *garret* above.

What other city in Europe can boast of such an assemblage of accommodation? Here, under the same roof, a man is, in the space of a few minutes, as perfectly equipped from top to toe, as if he had all the first tradesmen in London at his command; and shortly after, without setting his foot into the street, he is as completely stripped, as if he had fallen into the hands of a gang of robbers.

To cleanse this Augæan stable, would, no doubt, be a Herculean labour. For that purpose, Merlin (of Douay), when Minister of the police, proposed to the Directory to convert the whole of the buildings of the *ci-devant Palais Royal* into barracks. This was certainly striking at the root of the evil; but, probably, so bold a project was rejected, lest its execution, in those critical times, should excite the profligate Parisians to insurrection.

LETTER XX.

Paris, November 20, 1801.

ONE of the private entertainments here in great vogue, and which is understood to mark a certain pre-eminence in the *savoir-vivre* of the present day, is a nocturnal repast distinguished by the insignificant denomination of a

THÉ.

A stranger might, in all probability, be led to suppose that he was invited to a tea-drinking party, when he receives a note couched in the following terms:

"*Madame R——prie Monsieur B—— de lui*
"*faire l'honneur de venir au thé qu'elle doit don-*
"*ner le 5 de ce mois.*"

Considering in that light a similar invitation which I received, I was just on the point of sending an apology, when I was informed that a *thé* was nothing more or less than a sort of rout, followed by substantial refreshments, and generally commencing after the evening's performance was ended at the principal theatres.

On coming out of the opera-house then the other night, I repaired to the lady's residence in question, and arriving there about twelve o'clock, found that I had stumbled on the proper hour. As usual, there were cards, but for those only disposed to play; for, as this lady happened not to be under the necessity of recurring to the *bouillotte* as a financial resource, she gave herself little or no concern about the card-tables. Being herself a very agreeable, sprightly woman, she had invited a number of persons of both sexes of her own character, so that the conversation was kept up with infinite vivacity till past one o'clock, when tea and coffee were introduced. These were immediately followed by jellies, sandwiches, pâtés, and a variety of savoury viands, in the style of a cold supper, together with different sorts of wines and liqueurs. In the opinion of some of the Parisian sybarites, however, no *thé* can be complete without the addition of an article, which is here conceived to be a perfect imitation of fashionable English cheer. This is hot punch.

It was impossible for me to refuse the cheerful and engaging *dame du logis* to taste her *ponche*, and, in compliment to me as an Englishman, she presented me with a glass containing at least a treble allowance. Not being overfond of punch, I would willingly have relinquished the honour of drinking her health in so large a portion, apprehending that this beverage might, in quality, resemble that of the same name which I had tasted here a few evenings ago in one of the principal coffeehouses. The latter, in fact, was a composition of new rum, which reminded me of the trash of that kind distilled in New England, acidulated with rotten lemons, sweetened with capillaire, and increased by a *quantum sufficit* of warm water. My hostess's punch, on the contrary, was made of the best ingredients, agreeably to the true standard; in a word, it was proper lady's punch, that is, hot, sweet, sour, and strong. It was distributed in tea-pots, of beautiful porcelaine, which, independently of keeping it longer warm, were extremely convenient for pouring it out without spilling. Thus concluded the entertainment.

About half past two o'clock the party broke up, and I returned home, sincerely regretting the change in the mode of life of the Parisians.

Before the revolution, the fashionable hour of dinner in Paris was three o'clock, or at latest four: public places then began early; the curtain at the grand French opera drew up at a quarter past five. At the present day, the workman dines at two; the tradesman, at three; the clerk in a public office, at four; the rich upstart, the money-broker, the stock-jobber, the contractor, at five;

the banker, the legislator, the counsellor of state, at six; and the ministers, in general, at seven, nay not unfrequently at eight.

Formerly, when the performance at the opera, and the other principal theatres, was ended at nine o'clock, or a quarter past, people of fashion supped at ten or half after; and a man who went much into public, and kept good company, might retire peaceably to rest by midnight. In three-fourths of the houses in Paris, there is now no such meal as supper, except on the occasion of a ball, when it is generally a mere scramble. This, I presume, is one reason why substantial breakfasts are so much in fashion.

" *Déjeûners froids et chauds,*" is an inscription which now generally figures on the exterior of a Parisian coffeehouse, beside that of " *Thé à l'An-glaise, Café à la crême, Limonade, &c.*" Solids are here the taste of the times. Two ladies, who very gallantly invited themselves to breakfast at my apartments the other morning, were ready to turn the house out of the window, when they found that I presented to them nothing more than tea, coffee, and chocolate. I was instantly obliged to provide cold fowl, ham, oysters, white wine, &c. I marvel not at the strength and vigour of these French belles. In appetite, they would cope with an English ploughman, who had just turned up an acre of wholesome land on an empty stomach.

Now, though a *thé* may be considered as a substitute for a supper, it cannot, in point of agreeableness, be compared to a *petit souper*. If a man must sup, and I am no advocate for regular suppers, these were the suppers to my fancy. A select number of persons, well assorted, assembled at ten o'clock, after the opera was concluded, and spent a couple of hours in a rational manner. Sometimes a *petit souper* consisted of a simple *tête-à-tête*, sometimes of *partie quarrée*, or the number was varied at pleasure. But still, in a *petit souper*, not only much gaiety commonly prevailed, but also a certain *épanchement de cœur*, which animated the conversation to such a degree as to render a party of this description the *acme* of social intercourse, " the feast of reason and the " flow of soul."

Under the old *régime*, not a man was there in office, from the *ministre d'état* to the *commis*, who did not think of making himself amends for the fatigues of the morning by a *petit souper:* these *petits soupers*, however, were, in latter times, carried to an excessive pitch of luxurious extravagance. But for refinements attempted in luxury, though, I confess, of a somewhat dissolute nature, our countryman eclipsed all the French *bons vivans* in originality of conception.

Being in possession of an ample fortune, and willing to enjoy it according to his fancy, he purchased in Paris a magnificent house, but constructed on a small scale, where every thing that the most refined luxury could suggest was assembled. The following is the account given by one of his friends, who had been an eye-witness to his manner of living.

" Mr. B—— had made it a rule to gratify his five senses to the highest degree of enjoyment of which they were susceptible. An exquisite table, perfumed apartments, the charms of music and painting; in a word, every thing most enchanting that nature, assisted by art, could produce, successively flattered his sight, his taste, his smell, his hearing, and his feeling.

" In a superb saloon, whither he conducted me," says this gentleman, " were six young beauties, dressed in an extraordinary manner, whose persons, at first sight, did not appear unknown to me: it struck me that I had seen their faces more than once, and I was accordingly going to address them, when Mr. B——, smiling at my mistake, explained to me the cause of it."
" I have, in my amours," said he, " a particular fancy. The choicest beauty of Circassia would have no merit in my eyes, did she not resemble

the portrait of some woman, celebrated in past ages: and while lovers set great value on a miniature which faithfully exhibits the features of their mistress, I esteem mine only in proportion to their resemblance to ancient portraits.

" Conformably to this idea," continued Mr. B——, " I have caused the intendant of my pleasures to travel all over Europe, with select portraits, or engravings, copied from the originals. He has succeeded in his researches, as you see, since you have conceived that you recognized these ladies on whom you have never before set your eyes; but whose likenesses you may, undoubtedly, have met with. Their dress must have contributed to your mistake: they all wear the attire of the personage they represent; for I wish their whole person to be picturesque. By these means, I have travelled back several centuries, and am in possession of beauties whom time had placed at a great distance."

" Supper was served up. Mr. B—— seated himself between Mary, queen of Scots, and Anne Bullein. I placed myself opposite to him," concludes the gentleman, " having beside me Ninon de l'Enclos, and Gabrielle d'Estrées. We also had the company of the fair Rosamond and Nell Gwynn; but at the head of the table was a vacant elbow-chair, surmounted by a canopy, and destined for Cleopatra, who was coming from Egypt, and of whose arrival Mr. B—— was in hourly expectation."

LETTER XXI.

Paris, November 21, 1801.

OFTEN as we have heard of the extraordinary number of places of public entertainment in Paris, few, if any, persons in England have an idea of its being so considerable as it is, even at the present moment. But, in 1799, at the very time when we were told over and over again in Parliament, that France was unable to raise the necessary supplies for carrying on the war, and would, as a matter of course, be compelled not only to relinquish her further projects of aggrandisement, but to return to her ancient territorial limits; at that critical period, there existed in Paris, and its environs, no less than seventy

PUBLIC PLACES
OF VARIOUS DESCRIPTIONS.

Under the old *régime*, nothing like this number was ever known. Such an almost incredible variety of amusements is really a phenomenon, in the midst of a war, unexampled in its consumption of blood and treasure. It proves that, whatever may have been the public distress, there was at least a great *show* of private opulence. Indeed, I have been informed that, at the period alluded to, a spirit of indifference, prodigality, and dissipation, seemed to pervade every class of society. Whether placed at the bottom or the top of Fortune's wheel, a thirst of gain and want of economy were alike conspicuous among all ranks of people. Those who strained every nerve to obtain riches, squandered them with equal profusion.

No human beings on earth can be more fond of diversion than the Parisians. Like the Romans of old, they are content if they have but *panem et circenses*, which a Frenchman would render by *spectacles et de quoi manger*. However divided its inhabitants may be on political subjects, on the score of amusement at least the Republic is one and indivisible. In times of the greatest scarcity, many a person went dinnerless to the theatre, eating whatever scrap he could procure, and consoling himself by the idea of being amused for the evening, and at the same time saving at home the expense of fire and candle.

The following list of public places, which I have transcribed for your satisfaction, was communicated to me by a person of veracity; and, as far as it goes, its correctness has been confirmed by my own observation. Although it falls short of the number existing here two years ago, it will enable you to judge of the ardour still prevalent among the Parisians, for " running at the ring of pleasure." Few of these places are shut up, except for the winter; and new ones succeed almost daily to those which are finally closed. However, for the sake of perspicuity, I shall annex the letter S to such as are intended chiefly for summer amusement.

1. *Théâtre des Arts, Rue de la Loi.*
2. ———— *Français, Rue de la Loi.*
3. ———— *Feydeau, Rue Feydeau.*
4. ———— *Louvois, Rue de Louvois.*
5. ———— *Favart,* now *Opéra Buffa.*
6. ———— *de la Porte St. Martin.*
7. ———— *de la Société Olympique* (late *Opéra Buffa.*)
8. ———— *du Vaudeville, Rue de Chartres.*
9. ———— *Montansier, Palais du Tribunat.*
10. ———— *de l'Ambigu Comique, Boulevard du Temple.*
11. ———— *de la Gaiété, Boulevard du Temple.*
12. ———— *des Jeunes Artistes, Boulevard St. Martin,*
13. ———— *des Jeunes Elèves, Rue de Thionville.*
14. ———— *des Délassemens Comiques, Boulevard du Temple.*
15. ———— *sans Prétension, Boulevard du Temple.*

16. *Théâtre du Marais, Rue Culture Ste. Catherine.*
17. ——— *de la Cité, vis-à-vis le Palais de Justice.*
18. ——— *des Victoires, Rue du Bacq.*
19. ——— *de Molière, Rue St. Martin.*
20. ——— *de l'Estrapade.*
21. ——— *de Mareux, Rue St. Antoine.*
22. ——— *des Aveugles, Rue St. Denis.*
23. ——— *de la Rue St. Jean de Beauvais.*
24. *Bal masqué de l'Opéra, Rue de la Loi.*
25. ——————— *de l'Opéra Buffa, Rue de la Victoire.*
26. *Bal du Sallon des Étrangers, Rue Grange Batelière.*
27. ——— *de l'Hôtel de Salm, Rue de Lille, Faubourg St. Germain.*
28. ——— *de la Rue Michaudière.*
29. *Soirées amusantes de l'Hôtel Longueville, Place du Carrousel.*
30. *Veillées de la Cité, vis-à-vis le Palais de Justice.*
31. *Phantasmagorie de Robertson, Cour des Capucines.*
32. *Concert de Feydeau.*
33. *Ranelagh au bois de Boulogne.*
34. *Tivoli, Rue de Clichy,* S.
35. *Frascati, Rue de la Loi,* S.
36. *Idalie,* S.

37. *Hameau de Chantilly, aux Champs Élysées.*
38. *Paphos, Boulevard du Temple.*
39. *Vauxhall d'hiver.*
40. ———— *d'été*, S.
41. ———— *à Mousseaux*, S.
42. ———— *à St. Cloud*, S.
43. ———— *au Petit Trianon*, S.
44. *Jardin de l'hôtel Biron, Rue de Varenne*, S.
45. ——— *Thélusson, Chaussée d'Antin*, S.
46. ——— *Marbœuf, Grille de Chaillot*, S.
47. ——— *de l'hôtel d'Orsay*, S.
48. *Fêtes champêtres de Bagatelle*, S.
49. *La Muette, à l'entrée du Bois de Boulogne*, S.
50. *Colisée, au Parc des Sablons*, S.
51. *Amphithéâtre d'équitation de Franconi, aux Capucines.*
52. *Panorama, même lieu.*
53. *Exhibition de Curtius, Boulevard du Temple.*
54. *Expériences Physiques, au Palais du Tribunat.*
55. *La Chaumière, aux Nouveaux Boulevards.*
56. *Cabinet de démonstration de Physiologie et de Pathologie, au Palais du Tribunat; No. 38, au premier.*

Although, previously to the revolution, the taste for dramatic amusements had imperceptibly spread, Paris could then boast of no more than three principal theatres, exclusively of *l'Opéra Buffa*, introduced in 1788. These were *l'Opéra*, *les Français*, and *les Italiens*, which, with six inferior ones, called *petits spectacles*, brought the whole of the theatres to ten in number. The subaltern houses were incessantly checked in their career by the privileges granted to the *Comédie Française*, which company alone enjoyed the right to play first-rate productions: it also possessed that of censorship, and sometimes exercised it in the most despotic manner. Authors, ever in dispute with the comedians, who dictated the law to them, solicited, but in vain, the opening of a second French theatre. The revolution took place, and the unlimited number of theatres was presently decreed. A great many new ones were opened; but the attraction of novelty dispersing the amateurs, the number of spectators did not always equal the expectation of the managers; and the profits, divided among so many competitors, ceased to be sufficiently productive for the support of every establishment of this description. The consequence was, that several of them were soon reduced to a state of bankruptcy.

Three theatres of the first and second rank have been destroyed by fire within these two years, yet upwards of twenty are at present open, almost every night, exclusively of several associations of self-denominated *artistes-amateurs*.

Amidst this false glare of dramatic wealth, theatres of the first rank have imperceptibly declined, and at last fallen. It comes not within my province or intention to seek the causes of this in the defects of their management.; but the fact is notorious. The *Théâtres Favart* and *Feydeau*, at each of which French comic operas were chiefly represented, have at length been obliged to unite the strength of their talents, and the disgrace which they have experienced, has not affected any of those inferior playhouses where subaltern performers establish their success on an assemblage of scenes more coarse, and language more unpolished.

At the present moment, the government appear to have taken this decline of the principal theatres into serious consideration. It is, I understand, alike to be apprehended, that they may concern themselves too little or too much in their welfare. Hitherto the persons charged with the difficult task of upholding the falling theatres of the first rank, have had the good sense to confine their measures to conciliation; but, of late, it has been rumoured that the stage is to be subjected to its former restrictions. The benefit resulting to the art itself and to the public, from a rivalship of theatres, is once more called in question: and some people even go so far as to assert that, with the exception of a few abuses, the direction of the *Gentils-hommes de la chambre* was extremely good: thence it should seem that the only difficulty is to find these lords of the bed-chamber, if there be any still in being, in order to restore to them their dramatic sceptre*.

Doubtless, the liberty introduced by the revolution has been, in many respects, abused, and in too many, perhaps, relative to places of public amusement. But must it, on that account, be entirely lost to the stage, and falling into a contrary excess, must recourse be had to arbitrary measures, which might also be abused by those to whose execution they were intrusted? The unlimited number of theatres may be a proper subject for the interference of the government: but as to the liberty of the theatres, included in the number that may be fixed on to represent pieces of every description, such only excepted as may be hurtful to morals, seems to be a salutary and incontestable principle. This it is that, by disengaging the French comic opera from the narrow sphere to which it was confined, has, in a great measure, effected a musical revolution, at which all persons of taste must rejoice, by introducing on that stage the harmonic riches of Italy. This too it is

---

* During the old *régime*, the theatres were under the control of the *Gentils-hommes de la chambre*; but at the establishment of the directorial government, they were placed in the power of the Minister of the Interior, in whose department they have since continued. Of late, however, it is asserted, that they are each to be under the direction of a Prefect of the Palace.

that has produced, on theatres of the second and third rank, pieces which are neither deficient in regularity, connexion, representation, nor decoration. The effect of such a principle was long wanted here before the revolution, when the independent spirit of dramatic authors was fettered by the procrastinations of a set of privileged comedians, who discouraged them by ungracious refusals, or disgusted them by unjust preferences. Hence, the old adage in France that, when an author had composed a good piece, he had performed but half his task; this was true, as the more difficult half, namely, the getting it read and represented, still remained to be accomplished.

As for the multiplicity of playhouses, it certainly belongs to the government to limit their number, not by privileges which might be granted through favour, or obtained, perhaps, for money. The taste of the public for theatrical diversions being known, the population should first be considered, as it is that which furnishes both money and spectators. It would be easy to ascertain the proportion between the population of the capital and the number of theatres which it ought to comprise. Public places should be free as to the species of amusement, but limited in their number, so as not to exceed the proportion which the population can bear. The houses would then be constantly well attended, and the proprietors, actors, authors, and all those concerned in their success, secure against the consequences of failure, and the true interest of the art be likewise promoted. In a word, neither absolute independence, nor exclusive privilege should prevail; but a middle course be adopted, in order to fix the fate of those great scenic establishments, which, by forming so essential a part of public diversion, have a proportionate influence on the morals of the nation.

I have been led, by degrees, into these observations, not only from a review of the decline of some of the principal playhouses here, but also from a conviction that their general principle is applicable to every other capital in Europe. What, for example, can be more absurd than, in the dog-days, when room and air are particularly requisite, that the lovers of dramatic amusement in the British métropolis are to be crammed into a little theatre in the Haymarket, and stewed year after year, as in a sweating-room at a bagnio, because half a century ago an exclusive privilege was inconsiderately granted?

The playhouses here, in general, have been well attended this winter, particularly the principal ones; but, in Paris, every rank has not exactly its theatre as at a ball. From the *spectacles* on the *Boulevards* to those of the first and second rank, there is a mixture of company. Formerly, the lower classes confined themselves solely to the former; at present, they visit the latter. An increase of wages has enabled the workman to gratify his inclination for the indulgence of a species of luxury; and, by a sort of instinct, he now and then takes a peep at those scenes of which he before entertained, from hearsay, but an imperfect idea.

If you wish to see a new or favourite piece, you must not neglect to secure a seat in proper time; for, on such occasions, the house is full long before the rising of the curtain. As to taking places in the manner we do in England, there is no such arrangement to be made, except, indeed, you choose to take a whole box, which is expensive. In that case you pay for it at the time you engage it, and it is kept locked the whole evening, or till you and your party make your appearance*.

At all the *spectacles* in Paris, you are literally kept on the outside of the house till you have received a ticket, in exchange for your money, through an aperture in the exterior wall. Within a few paces of the door of the principal theatres

---

* Independently of the boxes reserved for the officers of the staff of the city of Paris, and those at the head of the police, who have individually free admission to all the *spectacles* on producing their ivory ticket, there is also a box at each theatre appropriated to the Minister of Public Instruction.

are two receiver's offices, which are no sooner open, than candidates for admission begin to form long ranks, extending from the portico into the very street, and advance to them two abreast in regular succession. A steady sentinel, posted at the aperture, repeats your wishes to the receiver, and in a mild, conciliating manner, facilitates their accomplishment. Other sentinels are stationed for the preservation of order, under the immediate eye of the officer, who sees that every one takes his turn to obtain tickets: however, it is not uncommon, for forestallers to procure a certain number of them, especially at the representation of a new or favourite piece, and offer them privately at a usurious price, which many persons are glad to pay rather than fall into the rear of the ranks.

The method I always take to avoid this unpleasant necessity, I will recommend to you as a very simple one, which may, perhaps, prevent you from many a theatrical disappointment. Having previously informed myself what *spectacle* is best worth seeing, while I am at dinner I send my *valet de place*, or if I cannot conveniently spare him, I desire him to dispatch a *commissionnaire* for the number of tickets wanted, so that when I arrive at the theatre, I have only to walk in, and place myself to the best advantage.

It is very wisely imagined not to establish the

receiver's offices in the inside of the house, as in our theatres. By this plan, however great may be the crowd, the entrance is always unobstructed, and those violent struggles and pressures, which among us have cost the lives of many, are effectually prevented. You will observe that no half-price is taken at any theatre in Paris; but in different parts of the house, there are offices, called *bureaux de supplément*, where, if you want to pass from one part of it to another, you exchange your counter-mark on paying the difference.

Nothing can be better regulated than the present police, both interior and exterior, of the theatres in Paris. The eye is not shocked, as was formerly the case, by the presence of black-whiskered grenadiers, occupying different parts of the house, and, by the inflexible sternness of their countenance, awing the spectators into a suppression of their feelings. No fusileer, with a fixed bayonet and piece loaded with ball, now dictates to the auditors of the pit that such a seat must hold so many persons, though several among them might, probably, be as broad-bottomed as Dutchmen. If you find yourself incommoded by heat or pressure, you are at liberty to declare it without fear of giving offence. The criticism of a man of taste is no longer silenced by the arbitrary control of a military despot, who, for an exclamation or gesture, not exactly coinciding with his own prepossessions, pointed him out to his myrmidons, and transferred him at once to prison. You may now laugh with Moleire, or weep with Racine, without having your mirth or sensibility thus unseasonably checked in its expansion.

The existence of this despotism has been denied; but facts are stubborn things, and I will relate to you an instance in which I saw it most wantonly exercised. Some years ago I was present at the *Théâtre Français*, when, in one of Corneille's pieces, Mademoiselle Raucourt, the tragic actress, was particularly negligent in the delivery of a passage, which, to do justice to the author, required the nicest discrimination. An amateur in the *parterre* reproved her, in a very gentle manner, for a wrong emphasis. Being at this time a favourite of the queen, she was, it seems, superior to admonition, and persisted in her misplaced shrieks, till it became evident that she set the audience at defiance: other persons then joined the former in expressing their disapprobation. Instantly the *major* singled out the leading critic: two grenadiers forced their way to the place where he was seated, and conveyed him to prison for having had the audacity to reprove an actress in favour at court. From such improper exercise of authority, the following verse had become a proverb:

"*Il est bien des sifflets, mais nous avons la garde.*"

Many there are, I know, who approved of this manner of bridling the fickle Parisians, on the ground that they were so used to the curb that they could no longer dispense with it. A guard on the outside of a theatre is unquestionably necessary, and proper for the preservation of order; but that the public should not be at liberty to approve or condemn such a passage, or such an actor, is at once to stifle the expression of that general opinion which alone can produce good performers. The interior police of the theatre being at present almost entirely in the hands of the public themselves, it is, on that account, more justly observed and duly respected.

Considering the natural impetuosity of their character, one is surprised at the patient tranquillity with which the French range themselves in their places. Seldom do they interrupt the performance by loud conversation, but exchange their thoughts in a whisper. When one sees them applaud with rapture a tender scene, which breathes sentiments of humanity or compassion, speaks home to every feeling heart, and inspires the most agreeable sensations, one is tempted to question whether the Parisians of the present day belong to the identical race that could, at one time, display the ferocity of tigers, and, at another, the tameness of lambs, while their nearest relations and best friends were daily bleeding on the scaffold?

By the existing regulations, many of which are worthy of being adopted in London, no theatre can be opened in Paris without the permission of the police, who depute proper persons to ascertain that the house is solidly built, the passages and outlets unincumbered and commodious, and that it is provided with reservoirs of water, and an adequate number of fire-engines.

Every public place that may be open, is to be shut up immediately, if, for one single day, the proprietors neglect to keep the reservoirs full of water, the engines in proper order, and the firemen ready.

No persons can be admitted behind the scenes, except those employed in the service of the theatre. Nor is the number of tickets distributed to exceed that of the persons the house can conveniently hold.

No coachman, under any pretext whatever, can quit the reins of his horses, while the persons he has driven, are getting out of or into their carriage. Indeed, the necessity of his doing so is obviated by porters stationed at the door of the theatres, and appointed by the police. They are distinguished by a brass plate, on which their permission and the name of the theatre are engraved.

At all the theatres in Paris, there is an exterior guard, which is at the disposal of the *civil* officer, stationed there for the preservation of order. This guard cannot enter the inside of the theatre but in case of the safety of the public being exposed, and at the express requisition of the said officer, who can never introduce the armed force into the house, till after he has, in a loud voice, apprized the audience of his intention.

Every citizen is bound to obey, *provisionally*, the officer of police. In consequence, every person invited by the officer of police, or summoned by him, to quit the house, is immediately to repair to the police-office of the theatre, in order to give such explanations as may be required of him. The said officer may either transfer him to the competent tribunal, or set him at liberty, according to circumstances.

Proper places are appointed for carriages to wait at. When the play is ended, no carriage in waiting can move till the first crowd coming out of the house has disappeared. The commanding officer of the guard on duty decides the moment when carriages may be called.

No carriage can move quicker than a foot-pace, and but on a single rank, till it has got clear of the streets in the vicinity of the theatre. Nor can it arrive thither but by the streets appointed for that purpose.

Two hours before the rising of the curtain, sentinels are placed in sufficient number to facilitate the execution of these orders, and to prevent any obstruction in the different avenues of the theatre.

Indeed, obstruction is now seldom seen: I have more than once had the curiosity to count, and cause to be counted, all the *private* carriages in waiting at the grand French opera, on a night when the boxes were filled with the most fashionable company. Neither I nor my *valet de place* could ever reckon more than from forty to fifty; whereas, formerly, it was not uncommon to see here between two and three hundred; and the noise of so many equipages rattling through the streets, from each of the principal theatres, sufficiently indicated that the performance was ended.

By the number of advertisements in the *petites affiches* or daily advertiser of Paris, offering a reward for articles lost, no doubt can exist of there being a vast number of pickpockets in this gay capital; and a stranger must naturally draw such an inference from observing where the pockets are placed in men's clothes: in the coat, it is in the inside of the facing, parallel to the breast: in the waistcoat, it is also in the inside, but lower down, so that when a Frenchman wants to take out his money, he must go through the ceremony of unbuttoning first his surtout, if he wears one in winter, then his coat, and lastly his waistcoat. In this respect, the ladies have the advantage; for, as I have already mentioned, they wear no pockets.

LETTER XXII.

Paris, November 23, 1801.

YESTERDAY being the day appointed for the opening of the session of the Legislative Body, I was invited by a member to accompany him thither, in order to witness their proceedings. No one can be admitted without a ticket; and by the last constitution it is decreed, that not more than two hundred strangers are to be present at the sittings. The gallery allotted for the accommodation of the public, is small, even in proportion to that number, and, in general, extremely crowded. My friend, aware of this circumstance, did me the favour to introduce me into the body of the hall, where I was seated very conveniently, both for seeing and hearing, near the *tribune*, to the left of the President.

This hall was built for the Council of Five Hundred, on the site of the grand apartments of the *Palais Bourbon*. Since the accession of the consular government, it has been appropriated to the sittings of the Legislative Body, on which account the palace has aken their name, and over the principal entrance is inscribed, in embossed characters of gilt bronze:

PALAIS DU CORPS LÉGISLATIF.

The palace stands on the south bank of the Seine, facing the *Pont de la Concorde*. It was begun, in 1722, for Louise-Françoise de Bourbon, a legitimated daughter of Lewis XIV. GIRARDINI, an Italian architect, planned the original building, the construction of which was afterwards superintended by LASSURANCE and GABRIEL. The Prince de Condé having acquired it by purchase, he caused it to be considerably augmented and embellished, at different times, under the direction of BARRAU, CARPENTIER, and BÉLISARD.

Had the *Pont de la Concorde* subsisted previously to the erection of the *Palais Bourbon*, the principal entrance would, probably, have been placed towards the river; but it faces the north, and is preceded by a paltry square, now called *Place du Corps Législatif.*

In the centre of a peristyle, of the Corinthian

order, is the grand gateway, crowned by a sort of triumphal arch, which is connected, by a double colonnade, to two handsome pavilions. The lateral buildings of the outer court, which is two hundred and eighty feet in length, are decorated with the same order, and a second court of two hundred and forty feet, includes part of the original palace, which is constructed in the Italian style.

The principal entrances to the right and left lead to two halls; the one dedicated to *Peace*; the other, to *Victory*. On the one side, is a communication to the apartments of the old palace; on the other, are two spacious rooms. The room to the left, inscribed to *Liberty*, is intended for petitioners, &c.: that to the right, inscribed to *Equality*, is appropriated to conferences. Between the halls of Liberty and Equality, is the hall of the sittings of the Legislative Body.

The form of this hall is semicircular; the benches, rising gradually one above the other, as in a Roman amphitheatre, are provided with backs, and well adapted both for ease and convenience. They are intersected by passages, which afford to the members the facility of reaching or quitting their places, without disturbance or confusion. Every seat is distinguished by a number, so that a deputy can never be at a loss to find his place. In the centre, is an elevated rostrum, with a seat for the President, directly under which is the *tribune*, also elevated, for the orator addressing the assembly. The tribune is decorated by a bas-relief, in white marble, representing France writing her constitution, and Fame proclaiming it. The table for the four secretaries is placed facing the tribune, beneath which the *huissiers* take their station. The desk and seat of the President, formed of solid mahogany, are ornamented with *or moulu*. The folding doors, which open into the hall, to the right and left of the President's chair, are also of solid mahogany, embellished in the same manner. Their frames are of white marble, richly sculptured. Independently of these doors, there are others, serving as a communication to the upper-seats, by means of two elegant stone stair-cases.

In six niches, three on each side of the tribune, are so many statues of Greek and Roman legislators. On the right, are Lycurgus, Solon, and Demosthenes: on the left, Brutus, Cato, and Cicero. The inside of the hall is in stucco, and the upper part is decorated by a colonnade of the Ionic order. The light proceeds from a cupola, glazed in the centre, and the remainder of which is divided into small compartments, each ornamented by an emblematical figure. The floor is paved with marble, also in compartments, embellished with allegorical attributes.

Having made you acquainted with the hall of the sittings, I think it may not be uninteresting to give you an account of the forms observed in opening the session.

When I arrived, with my friend, at the Palace of the Legislative Body, most of the members were already assembled in the apartments of their library. At noon, they thence repaired to the hall, preceded by the *huissiers*, messengers of state, and secretaries.

The opening of the session was announced by the report of artillery.

The oldest member, in point of years, took the President's chair, provisionally.

The four youngest members of the assembly were called to the table to discharge the office of secretaries, also provisionally.

The provisional President then declared, that the members of the Legislative Body were assembled by virtue of Article XXXIII of the constitution, for the session of the year X; that, being provisionally organized, the sitting was opened; and that their names were going to be called over, for the purpose of ascertaining the number of members present, and for forming definitive arrangements, by the nomination of a president and four secretaries.

The names were then called over alphabetically, and, after they were all gone through, they were recalled.

This ceremony being terminated, four committees, each composed of four members, whose names were drawn by lot by the President, proceeded, in presence of the assembly, to scrutinize the ballot.

It thence resulted, that the number of members present was two hundred and twenty-eight;

That Citizen Dupuis was elected President by a majority of votes;

That Citizens Dubosc, Bord, Estaque, and Clavier were individually elected, by a similar majority, to officiate as secretaries.

In consequence, Citizen Dupuis was proclaimed President, and took the chair. He then moved the following resolution, which was agreed to:

" The Legislative Body declares, that it is
" definitely constituted, and decrees that the
" present declaration shall be carried to the Con-
" servative Senate, to the Tribunate, and to the
" Consuls of the Republic, by a messenger of
" State."

The President next addressed the assembly in these words:

".Citizens Legislators,

" After twelve years of a painful and glo-
" rious struggle against all Europe, in order to
" insure the triumph of the liberty of man and
" that of nations, the moment is at length
" arrived when Peace is on the point of crown-
" ing the efforts of the French people, and se-
" curing the Republic on a foundation never
" to be shaken. For this peace, which will
" unite by the bonds of friendship two great na-
" tions, already connected by esteem, we are
" indebted to the valour and wisdom of the he-
" roic pacificator, to the wise administration of
" the government, to the bravery of our invin-
" cible armies, to the good understanding sub-
" sisting between all the constituted authorities,
" and, above all, to that spirit of moderation
" which has known how to fix limits to vic-
" tory itself. The name of peace, so dear to
" the friend of human nature, ought to im-
" pose silence on all malignant passions, cor-
" dially unite all the children of the same
" country, and be the signal of happiness to
" the present generation, as well as to our
" posterity.

" How gratifying is it to us, Citizens Le-
" gislators, after having passed through the

"storms of a long revolution, to have at length
"brought safely into port the sacred bark of
"the Republic, and to begin this session by
"the proclamation of peace to the world, as
"those who preceded us opened theirs by the
"proclamation of the Rights of Man and that
"of the Republic! To crown this great work,
"nothing more remains for us but to make
"those laws so long expected, which are to
"complete social organization, and regulate the
"interests of citizens. This code, already pre-
"pared by men of consummate prudence, will, I
"hope, be soon submitted to your examination
"and sanction; and the present session will
"be the most glorious epoch of our Republic:
"for there is nothing more glorious to man
"than to insure the happiness of his fellow-
"creatures, and scatter beforehand the first seeds
"of the liberty of the world."

"*L'impression! L'impression!*" was the cry that instantly proceeded from bench to bench on the close of this speech, which was deliver-ed in a manner that did honour to the President's feelings. But, though you have it, as it were, at second-hand, and cannot be struck by Citizen Dupuis' manner, I hope you will deem the matter sufficiently interesting to justify its insertion in this letter.

Three orators, deputed by the government,

were next announced, and introduced in form. They were habited in their dress of Counsellors of State, that is, a scarlet coat, richly embroidered in shaded silks of the same colour, over which they wore a tricoloured silk sash.

One of them, having ascended the tribune, and obtained leave to speak, read an extract from the registers of the Council of State, dated the 24th of Brumaire, purporting that the First Consul had nominated the Counsellors of State, REGNIER, BÉRENGER, and DUMAS to repair to the present sitting. Citizen REGNIER then addressed the assembly in the name of the government. He read his speech from a paper which he held in his hand. It began by announcing the signature of the preliminaries of peace with England, and informed the Legislative Body that measures had been taken by the government for regulating the various branches of the interior administration, and of its intention to submit to them the civil code. It was replete with language of a conciliating nature, and concluded with a wish that the most unalterable harmony might subsist between the first authorities of the State, and strengthen in the mind of the people the confidence which they already testified.

From the tenour of this speech, I think it may be inferred that the government is apprehensive of a difference of opinion respecting the civil code; not so much in this place, for, by the constitution, the lips of the deputies are sealed, but in the Tribunate, where a warm discussion may be expected.

The President made a short and apt reply to the orators of the government, who then retired with the same ceremony with which they had entered. Both these speeches were ordered to be printed.

The Conservative Senate addressed to the Legislative Body, by a message read by the President, the different acts emanated from its authority since the last session. Ordered to be inserted in the Journals. A few letters were also read by the President from different members, excusing themselves for non-attendance on account of indisposition. Several authors having addressed a copy of their works to the Legislative Body, these presents were accepted, and ordered to be placed in their library.

The administrative commission of the Legislative Body announced that the ambassador of the Cisalpine Republic had sent a present of three hundred medals, struck on occasion of the peace and of the *forum Bonaparte*, which medals were distributed to the members.

The assembly then broke up, the next sitting being appointed for the following day at noon.

Lord Cornwallis and suite sat in the box allotted to Foreign Ministers, facing the President, as did the Marquis de Lucchesini, the Prussian ambassador, and some others. A small box is likewise appropriated to reporters, who take down the proceedings. The members were all habited in their appointed dress, which consists of a dark blue coat embroidered with gold, blue pantaloons and white waistcoat, also embroidered, a tricoloured silk sash, worn above the coat, and ornamented with a rich gold fringe. They wore a plain cocked hat, with the national cockade, and short boots. This meeting of legislators, all in the same dress, undoubtedly presents a more imposing spectacle than such a variegated assemblage as is sometimes to be seen in our House of Commons.

By the present constitution, you will see that no new law can be promulgated, unless decreed by the Legislative Body.

The votes in this assembly being taken by ballot, and the laws being enacted without any discussion, on the part of its members, on the plans debated before it by the orators of the Tribunate and of the government, it necessarily follows that the sittings present far less interest to strangers, than would result from an animated delivery of the opinion of a few leading orators.

Before I take leave of this palace, I must introduce you into the suite of rooms formerly distinguished by the appellation of *petits appartemens du Palais Bourbon*, and which, before the revolution, constituted one of the curiosities of Paris.

In the distribution of these, BÉLISARD had assembled all the charms of modern elegance. The vestibule, coloured in French gray, contains, in the intervals between the doors, figures of Bacchantes, and, in the ceiling, wreaths of roses and other ornaments painted in imitation of relief. The eating-room, which comes next, is decorated so as to represent a verdant bower, the paintings are under mirrors, and tin-plate, cut out in the Chinese manner, seems to shew light through the foliage. In two niches, made in the arbour-work, in the form of porticoes, which Cupids are crowning with garlands, are placed two statues from the antique, the one representing Venus *pudica*, and the other, Venus *callypyga*, or *aux belles fesses:* mirrors, placed in the niches, reflect beauties which the eye could not discover.

The drawing-room, another enchanting place, is of a circular form, surrounded with Ionic pillars. In the intercolumniations, are arches lined with mirrors, and ornamented with the most tasteful hangings. Under each arch is a sopha. The ceiling represents caryatides supporting a circular gallery, between which are different subjects, such as the Toilet of Venus, the Departure of Adonis, &c. Every thing here is gallant and rich; but mark the secret wonder. You pull a string; the ceiling rises like a cloud, and exhibits to view an extensive sky, with which it becomes confounded. The music of an invisible orchestra, placed above the ceiling, used to be heard through the opening, and produced a charming effect, when entertainments were given in these apartments.

This is not all. You pull another string; and, by means of concealed machinery, the aperture of the three casements suddenly becomes occupied by pannels of mirrors, so that you may here instantly turn day into night. The bed-chamber, the *boudoir*, the study, &c., are all decorated in a style equally elegant and tasteful.

LETTER XXIII.

Paris, November 25, 1801.

OF all the public edifices in this capital, I know of none whose interior astonishes so much, at first sight, and so justly claims admiration, especially from those who have a knowledge of architecture or mechanics, as the

HALLE AU BLÉ.

This building is destined for the reception of corn and flour: it was begun in 1762, on the site of the ancient *Hôtel de Soissons*, which was purchased by the city of Paris. In the space of three years, the hall and the circumjacent houses were finished, under the direction of the architect, CAMUS DE MEZIÈRE.

The circular form of this hall, the solidity of its construction, its insulated position, together with the noble simplicity of its decoration, perfectly accord with the intention and character of the object proposed. Twenty-five arches, all of equal size, serve each as an entrance. On the ground-floor are pillars of the Tuscan order, supporting vast granaries, the communication to which is by two stair-cases of well-executed design.

The court is covered by a cupola of one hundred and twenty feet in diameter, forming a perfect semicircle, whose centre, taken on a level with the cornice, is forty-four feet from the ground. The dome of the Pantheon at Rome, which is the largest known, exceeds that of the *Halle au Blé* by thirteen feet only. This cupola is entirely composed of deal boards, a foot in breadth, an inch in thickness, and about four feet in length. It is divided into twenty-five lateral openings, which give as many rays of light diverging from the centre-opening, whose diameter is twenty-four feet. These openings are all glazed, and the wood-work of the dome is covered with sheets of tinned copper.

PHILIBERT DE L'ORME, architect to Henry II, was the original author of this new method of covering domes, though he never carried it into execution. As a homage for the discovery, MOLINOS and LEGRAND, the architects of the cupola, have there placed a medallion with his portrait. It is said that this experiment was deemed so hazardous, that the builder could find no person bold enough to strike away the shores, and was under the necessity of performing that task in person. To him it was not a fearful one; but the workmen, unacquainted with the principles of this manner of roofing buildings, were astonished at the stability of the dome, when the shores were removed.

No place in Paris could well be more convenient for giving a banquet than the *Halle au Blé*; twelve or fourteen hundred persons might here be accommodated at table; and little expense would be required for decoration, as nothing can be more elegant than the cupola itself.

Several periodical publications give a statement;

more or less exact, of the quantity of flour lodged in this spacious repository, which is filled and emptied regularly every four or five days. But these statements present not the real consumption of Paris, since several bakers draw their supply directly from the farmers of the environs; and, besides, a great quantity of loaves are brought into the capital from some villages, famous for making bread, whose inhabitants come and retail them to the Parisians.

The annual consumption of bread-corn in this capital has, on an average, been computed at twenty-four millions of bushels. But it is not the consumption only that it is useful to know: the most material point to be ascertained, is the method of providing effectually for it; so that, from a succession of unfavourable harvests, or any other cause, the regular supplies may not experience even a momentary interruption. When it is considered that Paris contains eight or nine hundred thousand of the human race, it is evident that this branch of administration requires all the vigilance of the government.

Bread is now reckoned enormously dear, nineteen *sous* for the loaf of four pounds; but, during the winter of 1794, the Parisians felt all the horrors of a real famine. Among other articles of the first necessity, bread was then so scarce, that long ranks of people were formed at the doors of the bakers' shops, each waiting in turn to receive a scanty portion of two ounces.

The consumption of flour here is considerably increased by the immense number of dogs, cats, monkies, parrots, and other birds, kept by persons of every class, and fed chiefly on bread and biscuit.

No poor devil that has not in his miserable lodging a dog to keep him company: not being able to find a friend among his own species, he seeks one in the brute creation. A pauper of this description, who shared his daily bread with his faithful companion, being urged to part with an animal that cost him so much to maintain: " Part with him!" rejoined he; " who then shall " I get to love me?"

Near the *Halle au Blé*, stands a large fluted pillar of the Doric order, which formerly belonged to the *Hôtel de Soissons*, and served as an observatory to Catherine de Medicis. In the inside, is a winding stair-case, leading to the top, whither that diabolical woman used frequently to ascend, accompanied by astrologers, and there perform several mysterious ceremonies, in order to discover futurity in the stars. She wore on her stomach a skin of parchment, strewn with figures, letters, and characters of different colours; which skin she was persuaded had the virtue of insuring her from any attempt against her person.

Much about that period, 1572, there were

reckoned, in Paris alone, no less than thirty thousand astrologers. At the present day, the ambulating magicians frequent the *Old Boulevards*, and there tell fortunes for three or four *sous*; while those persons that value science according to the price set on it, disdaining these two-penny conjurers, repair to fortune-tellers of a superior class, who take from three to six francs, and more, when the opportunity offers. The TROPHONIUS of Paris is Citizen Martin, who lives at N° 1773 *Rue d'Anjou*: the PHEMONOË is Madame Villeneuve, *Rue de l'Antechrist*.

Formerly, none but courtesans here drew the cards; now, almost every female, without exception, has recourse to them. Many a fine lady even conceives herself to be sufficiently mistress of the art to tell her own fortune; and some think they are so skilled in reading futurity in the cards, that they dare not venture to draw them for themselves, for fear of discovering some untoward event.

This rage of astrology and fortune-telling is a disease which peculiarly affects weak intellects, ruled by ignorance, or afflicted by adversity. In the future, such persons seek a mitigation of the present; and the illusive enjoyments of the mind make them almost forget the real sufferings of the body. According to Pope,

" Hope springs eternal in the human breast,
" Man never *is*, but always *to be* blest."

At the foot of the above pillar, the only one of the sort in Paris, is erected a handsome fountain, which furnishes water from the Seine. At two-thirds of its height is a dial of a singular kind, which marks the precise hour at every period of the day, and in all seasons. It is the invention of Father Pingré, who was a regular canon of St. Geneviève, and member of the *ci-devant* Academy of Sciences.

While we are in this quarter, let us avail ourselves of the moment; and, proceeding from the *Halle au Blé* along the *Rue Oblin*, examine the

CHURCH OF SAINT EUSTACHE.

This church, which is one of the most spacious in Paris, is situated at the north extremity of the *Rue des Prouvaires*, facing the *Rue du Jour*. It was begun in 1532, but not finished till the year 1642.

Notwithstanding the richness of its architecture, it presents not an appearance uniformly handsome, on account of the ill-combined mixture of the Greek and Gothic styles : besides, the pillars are so numerous in it, that it is necessary to be placed in the nave to view it to the best advantage.

The new portal of *St. Eustache*, which was constructed in 1754, is formed of two orders, the Doric and the Ionic, the one above the other. At each extremity of this portal, rise two insulated towers, receding from all the projection of the inferior order, and decorated by Corinthian columns with pilasters, on an attic serving as a socle. These two towers were to have been crowned by a balustrade; one alone has been finished.

Several celebrated personages have been interred in this church. Among them, I shall particularize one only; but that one will long live in the memory of every convivial British seaman. Who has not heard the lay which records the defeat of Tourville? Yes—

> He who " on the main triumphant rode
> " To meet the gallant Russel in combat o'er the deep;
> Who " led his noble troops of heroes bold
> " To sink the English admiral and his fleet."

Though considered by his countrymen, as one of the most eminent seamen that France ever produced, and enjoying at the time of his death the dignity of Marshal, together with that of Vice-admiral of the kingdom, Tourville never had an epitaph. He died on the 28th of May 1701, aged 59.

Some of the monuments which existed here

have been transferred to the Museum in the *Rue des Petits Augustins*, where may be seen the sarcophagus of Colbert, Minister to Lewis XIV, and the medallion of Cureau de la Chambre, physician to that king, and also his physiognomist, whom he is said to have constantly consulted in the selection of his ministers. Among the papers of that physician there still exists, in an unpublished correspondence with Lewis XIV, this curious memorandum: " Should I die before his " majesty, he would run a great risk of making, " in future, many a bad choice."

It is impossible to enter one of these sanctuaries without reflecting on the rapid progress of irreligion among a people who, six months before, were, on their knees, adoring the effigies which, at that period, they were eager to mutilate and destroy. Iron crows and sledge-hammers were almost in a state of requisition. In the beginning, it was a contest who should first aim a blow at the nose of the Virgin Mary, or break the leg of her son. In one day, contracts were entered into with masons for defacing images which, for centuries, had been partly concealed under the dusty webs of generations of spiders.

As for the statues within reach of swords and pikes, it was a continual scene of amusement to the licentious to knock off the ear of one angel, and scratch the face of another. Not an epitaph was left to retrace the patriotic deeds of an upright statesman, or the more brilliant exploits of a heroic warrior; not a memento, to record conjugal affection, filial piety, or grateful friendship. The iconoclasts proceeded not with the impetuous fury of fanatics, but with the extravagant foolery of atheistical buffoons.

All the gold and silver ornaments disappeared: a great part of them were dissolved in the crucibles of the mint, after having been presented as a homage to the Convention, some of whose members danced the *carmagnole* with those who presented them at their bar, loaded on the back of mules and asses, bedecked with all the emblems of catholic worship; while several of the rubies, emeralds, &c. which had formerly decorated the glory, beaming round the head of a Christ, were afterwards seen glittering on the finger of the revolutionary committee-men.

Chaumette, an attorney, was the man who proclaimed atheism, and his example had many imitators. It seemed the wish of that impious being to exile God himself from nature. He it was who imagined those orgies, termed the festivals of reason. One of the most remarkable of these festivals was celebrated in this very church of *St. Eustache.*

Although Mademoiselle Maillard, the singing heroine of the French opera, figured more than once as the goddess of reason, that divinity was generally personified by some shameless female, who, if not a notorious prostitute, was frequently little better. Her throne occupied the place of the altar; her supporters were chiefly drunken soldiers, smoking their pipe; and before her, were a set of half-naked vagabonds, singing and dancing the *carmagnole*.

" In this church," says an eye-witness, " the interior of the choir represented a landscape, decorated with cottages and clumps of trees. In the distance were mysterious bowers, to which narrow paths led, through declivities formed of masses of artificial rock.

" The inside of the church presented the spectacle of a large public-house. Round the choir were arranged tables, loaded with bottles, sausages, pies, pâtés, and other viands. On the altars of the lateral chapels, sacrifices were made to luxury and gluttony; and the consecrated stones bore the disgusting marks of beastly intemperance.

" Guests crowded in at all doors: whoever came partook of this festival: children thrust their hands into the dishes, and helped themselves out of the bottles, as a sign of liberty; while the speedy consequences of this freedom became a matter of amusement to grown persons in a similar state of ebriety. What a deplorable picture of the people, who blindly obeyed the will of a few factious leaders!

" In other churches, balls were given; and, by way of shutting the door in the face of modesty, these were continued during the night, in order that, amidst the confusion of nocturnal revelry, those desires which had been kindled during the day, might be freely gratified under the veil of darkness.

" The processions which accompanied these orgies, were no less attended with every species of atheistical frenzy. After feasting their eyes with the sacrifice of human victims, the Jacobin faction, or their satellites, followed the car of their impure goddess: next came, in another car, a moving orchestra, composed of blind musicians, a too faithful image of that Reason which was the object of their adoration."

The state of France, at that period, proves that religion being detached from social order, there remained a frightful void, which nothing could have filled up but its subsequent restoration. Without religion, men become enemies to each other, criminals by principle, and bold violators of the laws; force is the only curb that can restrain them. The inevitable consequence is, that anarchy and rapine desolate the face of the earth, and reduce it to a heap of misfortune and ruin.

LETTER XXIV.

Paris, November 27, 1801.

When we travel back in idea for the last ten years, and pass in review the internal commotions which have distracted France during that period, and the external struggle she has had to maintain for the security of her independence, we cannot refuse our admiration to the constancy which the French have manifested in forming institutions for the diffusion of knowledge, and repositories of objects tending to the advancement of the arts and sciences. In this respect, if we except the blood-thirsty reign of Robespierre, no clash of political interests, no change in the form or administration of the government, has relaxed their ardour, or slackened their perseverance. Whatever set of men have been in power, the arts and sciences have experienced almost uninterrupted protection.

In the opinion of the French themselves, the GALLERY OF ANTIQUES, in the CENTRAL MUSEUM OF THE ARTS, may claim pre-eminence over every other repository of sculpture; but many persons may, probably, feel a satisfaction more pure and unadulterated in viewing the

MUSEUM OF FRENCH MONUMENTS.

Here, neither do insignia of triumph call to mind the afflicting scenes of war, nor do emblems of conquest strike the eye of the travelled visiter, and damp his enjoyment by blending with it bitter recollections. Vandalism is the only enemy from whose attacks the monuments, here assembled, have been rescued.

This Museum, which has, in fact, been formed out of the wrecks of the revolutionary storm, merits particular attention. Although it was not open to the public, for the first time, till the 15th of Fructidor, year III (2nd of September 1795), its origin may be dated from 1790, when the Constituent Assembly, having decreed the possessions of the Clergy to be national property, charged the *Committee of Alienation* to exert their vigilance for the preservation of all the monuments of the arts, spread throughout the wide extent of the ecclesiastical domains.

The philanthropic LA ROCHEFOUCAULD, (the last Duke of the family), as President of that committee, fixed on a number of artists and literati to select such monuments as the committee were anxious to preserve. The municipality of Paris, being specially entrusted, by the National Assembly, with the execution of this decree, also nominated several literati and artists of acknowledged merit to co-operate with the former in their researches and labours. Of this association was formed a commission, called *Commission des Monumens*. From that epoch, proper places were sought for the reception of the treasures which it was wished to save from destruction. The *Committee of Alienation* appointed the *ci-devant* monastery of the *Petits Augustins* for the monuments of sculpture and pictures, and those of the *Capucins*, *Grands Jesuites*, and *Cordeliers*, for the books and manuscripts.

By these means, the monuments in the suppressed convents and churches were, by degrees, collected in this monastery, which is situated in the *Rue des Petits Augustins*, so named after that order of monks, whose church here was founded, in 1613, by Marguerite de Valois, first wife of Henry IV.

At the same period, ALEXANDRE LENOIR was appointed, by the Constituent Assembly, director of this establishment. As I shall have frequent occasion to mention the name of that estimable artist, I shall here content myself with observing, that the choice did honour to their judgment.

In the mean time, under pretext of destroying every emblem of feudality, the most celebrated master-pieces were consigned to ruin;

but the commission before-mentioned opportunely published instructions respecting the means of preserving the valuable articles which they purposed to assemble.

The National Convention also gave indisputable proof of its regard for the arts, by issuing several decrees in their favour. Its *Committee of Public Instruction* created a commission, composed of distinguished literati and artists of every class, for the purpose of keeping a watchful eye over the preservation of the monuments of the arts. The considerable number of memoirs, reports, and addresses, diffused through the departments by this learned and scientific association, enlightened the people, and arrested the arm of those modern Vandals who took a pleasure in mutilating the most admired statues, tearing or defacing the most valuable pictures, and melting casts of bronze of the most exquisite beauty.

Among the numerous reports to which these acts of blind ignorance gave birth, three published by GRÉGOIRE, ex-bishop of Blois, claim particular distinction, no less on account of the taste and zeal which they exhibit for the advancement of literature and the fine arts, than for the invective with which they abound against the madness of irreligious barbarism. This last stroke, aptly applied, was the means of recovering many articles of value, and of preserving the monuments still remaining in the provinces.

In these eventful times, LENOIR, the Conservator of the rising Museum, collected, through his own indefatigable exertions, a considerable number of mausolea, statues, bas-reliefs, and busts of every age and description. No sooner did a moment of tranquillity appear to be reestablished in this country, than he proposed to the government to place all these monuments in historical and chronological order, by classing them, according to the age in which they had been executed, in particular halls or apartments, and giving to each of these apartments the precise character peculiar to each century. This plan which, in its aggregate, united the history of the art and that of France, by means of her monuments, met with general approbation, and was accordingly adopted by the members of the government.

Thus, throughout this Museum, the architectural decorations of the different apartments are of the age to which the monuments of sculpture, contained in each, belongs; and the light penetrates through windows of stained glass, from the designs of RAPHAEL, PRIMATICCIO, ALBERT DURER, LE SUEUR, &c., the production of the particular century corresponding to that of the sculpture.

Come then, let us visit this Museum, and endeavour to discriminate the objects which may be most interesting both to the artist and historian. We first enter the

ANTI-CHAMBER.

This apartment presents itself to our inquisitive looks, as a Hall of Introduction, which may not be unaptly compared to the preface of a grand work. Here we behold a crowd of monuments, arranged methodically, so as to prepare our eyes for tracing the different ages through which we have to travel.

We first remark those altars, worn by the hand of Time, on which the trading Gauls of the ancient *Lutetia*, now Paris, sacrificed to the gods in the time of Tiberius. Jupiter, Mars, Vulcan, Mercury, Venus, Pan, Castor and Pollux, and the religious ceremonies here sculptured, are sufficient to attest that the Parisians were then idolaters, and followed the religion of the Romans, to whom they were become tributary. The Inscriptions on each of these monuments, which are five in number, leave no doubt as to their authenticity, and the epoch of their erection.

These altars, five in number, are charged with bas-reliefs, and the first of them is inscribed with the following words in Latin.

TIB. CAESARE.
AVG. IOVI OPTVMO
MAXSVMO *(aram)* M.
NAVTAE. PARISIACI
PUBLICE POSIERVNT.

Tiberius Cæsar, having accepted or taken the name of Augustus, the navigators (Nautæ) *belonging to the city of Paris, publicly consecrated this altar to Jupiter the most great and most good.*

In 1711, these monuments were dug up from the choir of the cathedral of *Notre-Dame,* out of the foundations of the ancient church of Paris, constructed by Childebert, on the ruins of a temple, formerly dedicated to Isis, which he caused to be demolished. Near them we see the great goddess of the Germans figure under the name of Nehalennia, in honour of whom that people had erected a great number of monuments, some of which were discovered in the year 1646, when the sea retired from the island of Walcheren.

Capitals, charged with bas-reliefs, taken from a subterraneous basilic, built by Pepin, have likewise been collected, and follow those which I have just mentioned. Next comes the tomb of Clovis, which exhibits that prince lying at length; he is humbling himself before the Almighty, and seems to be asking him forgiveness for his crimes. We likewise see those of CHILDEBERT and of the cruel CHILPERIC. The intaglio, relieved by inlaid pieces of Mosaic, of queen FREDEGOND, has escaped the accidents of twelve centuries. Just Heaven! what powers have disappeared from the face of the earth since that period! And to what reflections does not this image, still existing of that impious woman, give birth in the mind of the philosopher! CHARLEMAGNE, who was buried at Aix-la-Chapelle, seated on a throne of gold, appears here, in a haughty attitude, with his sword in his hand, still to be giving laws to the world!

As might naturally be supposed, most of these figures have suffered much by the rude attacks of Time; but in spite of his indelible impression, the unpolished hand of the sculptor is still distinguishable, and betrays the degraded state of the arts during the darkness of the middle ages. Let us pass into the

HALL OF THE THIRTEENTH CENTURY.

Here we shall remark arches in the Gothic style, supported by thick pillars, according to the architecture of that period. Ornaments, in the form of *culs-de-lampe*, terminate the centre of the arches, which are painted in azure-blue, and charged with stars. When temples were begun to be sheltered or covered, nations painted the inside of the roof in this manner, in order to keep in view the image of the celestial canopy to which they directed all their affections, and to preserve the memory of the ancient custom of offering up sacrifices to the divinity in the open air.

Here the statue of Lewis IX, surnamed the Saint, is placed near that of Philip, one of his sons, and of Charles, his brother, king of Sicily, branded in history, by having, through his oppression, driven his subjects into revolt, and caused the massacre of the French in that island in 1277; a massacre well known by the name of the *Sicilian vespers.*

It seems that it was the fashion, in those days, for kings themselves to be bearers at funerals. We are told by St. Foix, that the body of Lewis, another son of the Saint, who died in 1662, aged 26, and whose cenotaph is here, was first carried to St. Denis, and thence to the abbey of Royaumont, where it was interred. " The greatest lords of the kingdom," says he, " alternately bore the coffin on their shoulders, " and Henry III, king of England, carried it " himself for a considerable time, as feudatory " of the crown."

Philip III, too, above-mentioned, having brought to Paris the remains of his father from Tunis in Africa, carried them barefooted, on his shoulders, to St. Denis. Wherever he rested by the way, towers were erected in commemoration of this act of filial piety; but these have been destroyed since the revolution.

The casements of this hall, in the form of ogives, are ornamented with stained glass of the first epoch of the invention of that art. We now come to the

HALL OF THE FOURTEENTH CENTURY.

This hall shews us the light, yet splendid architecture of the Arabs, introduced into France in consequence of the Crusades. Here are the statues of the kings that successively appeared in this age down to king John, who was taken prisoner by Edward, the black prince, at the battle of Poictiers. They are clad after the manner of their time, and lying at length on a stylobate, strewn with flower-de-luces. Twenty-two knights, each mounted on lions, armed cap-à-pié, represented of the natural size, and coloured, fill ogive niches ornamented with Mosaic designs, relieved with gold, red, and blue.

The tombs of Charles V, surnamed the *Wise*, and of the worthy constable, Du Guesclin, together with that of Sancerre, his faithful friend, rise in the middle of this apartment; which presents to the eye all the magnificence of a Turkish mosque. After having quitted it, what a striking contrast do we not remark on entering the

HALL OF THE FIFTEENTH CENTURY!

Columns, arabesque ceilings charged with gilding, light pieces of sculpture applied on blue and violet grounds, imitating cameo, china, or enamel; every thing excites astonishment, and concurs in calling to mind the first epoch of the regeneration of the arts in this country.

The ideas of the amateur are enlivened in this brilliant apartment: they prepare him for the gratification which he is going to experience at the sight of the beautiful monuments produced by the age, so renowned of Francis I. There, architecture predominates over sculpture; here, sculpture over architecture.

The genius of RAPHAEL paved the way to this impulse of regeneration: he had recently produced the decorations of the Vatican; and the admirable effect of these master-pieces of art, kindled an enthusiasm in the mind of the artists, who travelled. On their return to France, they endeavoured to imitate them: in this attempt, JEAN JUSTE, a sculptor sent to Rome, at the expense of the Cardinal D'AMBOISE, was the most succcessful.

First, we behold the mausoleum of LOUIS D'ORLÉANS, victim of the faction of the Duke of Burgundy, and that of his brother CHARLES, the poet. Near them is that of VALENTINE DE MILAN, the inconsolable wife of the former, who died through grief the year after she lost her husband. As an emblem of her affliction, she took for her device a watering-pot stooped, whence drops kept trickling in the form of tears. Let it not be imagined, however, that it was on account of his constancy that this affectionate woman thus bewailed him till she fell a victim to her sorrow.

LOUIS D'ORLÉANS was a great seducer of ladies of the court, and of the highest rank too, says Brantome. Indeed, historians concur in stating that to a brilliant understanding, he joined the most captivating person. We accordingly find that the Dutchess of Burgundy and several others were by no means cruel to him; and he had been supping tête-à-tête with Queen Isabeau de Baviere, when, in returning home, he was assassinated on the twenty-third of November 1407. His amorous intrigues at last proved fatal to the English, as you will learn from the following story, related by the same author.

One morning, M. d'Orléans having in bed with him a woman of quality, whose husband came to pay him an early visit, he concealed the lady's head, while he exhibited the rest of her person to the contemplation of the unsuspecting intruder, at the same time forbidding him, as he valued his life, to remove the sheet from her face. Now, the cream of the jest was, that, on the following night, the good soul of a husband, as he lay beside his dear, boasted to her that the Duke of Orleans had shewn him the most beautiful woman that he had ever seen: but that for her face he could not tell what to say of it, as it was concealed under the sheet. "From this little intrigue," adds Brantome, " sprang that brave and valiant " bastard of Orleans, Count Dunois, the pillar " of France, and the scourge of the English."

Here we see the statues of CHARLES VI, and of JANE of Burgundy. The former being struck by a *coup de soleil*, became deranged in his intellects and imbecile, after having displayed great genius; he is represented with a pack of cards in his hand to denote that they were first invented for that prince's diversion. The latter was Dutchess of BEAUFORT, wife to the Duke, who commanded the English army against Charles VII, and as brother to our Henry IV, was appointed regent of France, during the minority of his nephew, Henry V.

Next come those of Rénée d'Orléans, grand-daughter of the intrepid Dunois; and of Philippe de Commines, celebrated by his memoirs of the tyrant, Lewis XI, whose statue faces that of Charles VII, his father.

The image of Joan of Arc, whom that king had the baseness to suffer to perish, after she had maintained him on the throne, also figures in this hall with that of Isabeau de Bavière. The shameful death of the Maid of Orleans, who, as every one knows, was, at the instigation of the English, condemned as a witch, and burnt alive at Rouen on the 30th of May 1430, must inspire with indignation every honest Englishman who reflects on this event, which will ever' be a blot in the page of our history. Isabeau affords a striking example of the influence of a queen's morals on the affections of the people. On her first arrival in Paris, she was crowned by angels, and received from the burghers the most magnificent and costly presents. At her death, she was so detested by the nation, that in order to convey her body privately to St. Denis, it was embarked in a little skiff at *Port-Landri*, with directions to the waterman to deliver it to the abbot.

The superb tomb of Lewis XII, placed in the middle of this apartment, displays great magnificence; and his statue, lying at length, which represents him in a state of death, recalls to mind that moment so grievous to the French people, who exclaimed, in following his funeral procession to St. Denis, " Our good king Lewis XII " is dead, and we have lost our father."

The historian delights to record a noble trait of that prince's character. Lewis XII had been taken prisoner at the battle of St. Aubin by Louis de la Trimouille, who, fearing the resentment of the new king, and wishing to excuse himself for his conduct, received this magnanimous reply: " It is not for the king of France to revenge the " quarrels of the duke of Orleans."

The statue of Pierre de Navarre, son of Charles the *Bad*, seems placed here to form in the mind of the spectator a contrast between his father and Lewis XII. The tragical end of Charles is of a nature to fix attention, and affords an excellent subject for a pencil like that of Fuseli.

Charles the *Bad*, having fallen into such a state of decay that he could not make use of his limbs, consulted his physician, who ordered him to be wrapped up from head to foot, in a linen cloth impregnated with brandy, so that he might be inclosed in it to the very neck as in a sack. It was night when this remedy was administered. One of the female attendants of the palace, charged to sew up the cloth that contained the patient, having come to the neck, the fixed point where she was to finish her seam, made a knot according to custom; but as there was still remaining an end of thread, instead of cutting it as usual with scissars, she had recourse to the candle, which immediately set fire to the whole cloth. Being terrified, she ran away, and abandoned the king, who was thus burnt alive in his own palace.

What a picture for the moralist is this assemblage of persons, celebrated either for their errors, crimes, talents, or virtues!

LETTER XXV.

Paris, November 28, 1801.

CONCEIVING how interested you (who are not only a connoisseur, but an F. A. S.) must feel in contemplating the only repository in the world, I believe, which contains such a chronological history of the art of sculpture, I lose no time in conducting you to complete our survey of the MUSEUM OF FRENCH MONUMENTS in the *Rue des Petits Augustins.*

Having examined those of the fifteenth century, during our former visit, we are at length arrived at the age of the Fine Arts in France, and now enter the

HALL OF THE SIXTEENTH CENTURY.

> " But see! each muse in Leo's golden days,
> " Starts from her trance, and trims her wither'd bays;
> " Rome's ancient Genius, o'er its ruins spread,
> " Shakes off the dust, and rears his reverend head;
> " Then Sculpture and her sister arts revive,
> " Stones leap'd to form, and rocks began to live."

These beautiful lines of Pope immediately occur to the mind, on considering that, in Italy, the Great Leo, by the encouragement which he gave to men of talents, had considerably increased the number of master-pieces; when the taste for the Fine Arts, after their previous revival by the Medici, having spread throughout that country, began to dawn in France about the end of the fifteenth century. By progressive steps, the efforts made by the French artists to emulate their masters, attained, towards the middle of the sixteenth century, a perfection which has since fixed the attention of Europe.

On entering this hall, which is consecrated to that period, the amateur finds his genius inflamed. What a deep impression does not the perfection of the numerous monuments which it has produced make on his imagination! First, he admires the beautiful tomb erected to the memory of FRANCIS I, the restorer of literature and the arts; who, by inviting to his court LEONARDO DA VINCI and PRIMATICCIO, and establishing schools and manufactories, consolidated the great work of their regeneration.

" Curse the monks!" exclaimed I, on surveying this magnificent monument, constructed in 1550, from the designs of the celebrated PHILIBERT DE L'ORME. " Who cannot but regret," continued I to myself, " that so gallant a knight as Francis I.
" should fall a victim to that baneful disease
" which strikes at the very sources of genera-
" tion? Who cannot but feel indignant that so
" generous a prince, whose first maxim was, that
" *true magnanimity consisted in the forgiveness of*
" *injuries, and pusillanimity in the prosecution of*
" *revenge,* should owe his death to the diabolical
" machinations of a filthy friar?" Yet, so it was; the circumstances are as follows:

Francis I. was smitten by the charms of the wife of one Lunel, a dealer in iron. A Spanish chaplain, belonging to the army of the Emperor Charles V, passing through Paris in order to repair to Flanders, threw himself in this man's way, and worked on his mind till he had made him a complete fanatic: " Your king," said the friar, " protects Lutheranism in Germany, and

" will soon introduce it into France. Be re-
" venged on him and your wife, by serving re-
" ligion. Communicate to him that disease for
" which no certain remedy is yet known."—
" And how am I to give it to him?" replied Lunel;
" neither I nor my wife have it."—" But I have,"
rejoined the monk: " I hold up my hand and
" swear it. Introduce me only for one half-hour
" by night, into your place, by the side of your
" faithless fair, and I will answer for the rest."

The priest having prevailed on Lunel to consent to his scheme, went to a place where he was sure to catch the infection, and, by means of Lunel's wife, he communicated it to the king. Being previously in possession of a secret remedy, the monk cured himself in a short time; the poor woman died at the expiration of a month; and Francis I, after having languished for three or four years, at length, in 1547, sunk under the weight of a disorder then generally considered as incurable.

The tomb of the VALOIS, erected in honour of that family, by Catherine de Medicis, soon after the death of Henry II, is one of the master-pieces of GERMAIN PILON. In the execution of this beautiful monument, that famous artist has found means to combine the correctness of style of Michael Angelo with the grace of Primaticcio. To the countenance of HENRY and CATHERINE, who are represented in a state of death, lying as on a bed, he has imparted an expression of sensibility truly affecting.

Next comes the tomb of DIANE DE POITIERS, that celebrated beauty, who displayed equal judgment in the management of State affairs and in the delicacy of her attachments; who at the age of 40, captivated king Henry II, when only 18; and, who, though near 60 at the death of that prince, had never ceased to preserve the same empire over his heart. At the age of fourteen, she was married to Louis de Brézé, grand seneschal of Normandy, and died in April 1566, aged 66.

Brantome, who saw her not long before her death, when she had just recovered from the confinement of a broken leg, and had experienced troubles sufficient to lessen her charms, thus expresses himself: " Six months ago, when I met " her, she was still so beautiful that I know not " any heart of adamant which would not have " been moved at the sight of her."—To give you a perfect idea of her person, take this laconic description, which is not one of fancy, but collected from the best historians.

Her jet black hair formed a striking contrast to her lily complexion. On her cheeks faintly blushed the budding rose. Her teeth vied with ivory itself in whiteness: in a word, her form was as elegant as her deportment was graceful.

By way of lesson to the belles of the present day, let them be told that DIANE DE POITIERS was never ill, nor affected indisposition. In the severity of the winter, she daily washed her face with spring-water, and never had recourse to cosmetics.—— " What pity," says Brantome, " that " earth should cover so beautiful a woman!"

No man, indeed, who sympathizes with the foibles of human nature, can contemplate the tomb of DIANE DE POITIERS, and reflect on her numerous virtues and attractions, without adopting the sentiments of Brantome, and feeling his breast glow with admiration.

This extraordinary woman afforded the most signal protection to literati and men of genius, and was, in fact, no less distinguished for the qualities of her heart than for the beauty of her person. " She was extremely good-humoured, " charitable, and humane," continues Brantome. " The people of France ought to pray to God " that the female favourite of every chief magis- " trate of their country may resemble this amiable " frail one."

As a proof of the elevation of her sentiments, I shall conclude by quoting to you the spirited reply DIANE made to Henry II, who, by dint of royal authority, wished to legitimate a daughter he had by her: " I am of a birth," said she, " to " have had lawful children by you. I have been

" your mistress, because I loved you. I will
" never suffer a decree to declare me your con-
" cubine."

The beautiful group of the modest Graces, and that representing Diana, accompanied by her dogs Procion and Syrius, sculptured by Jean Gougeon, to serve as the decoration of a fountain in the park of Diane de Poitiers at Anet, attracts the attention of the connoisseur.

The tomb of Gougeon, composed of his own works, and erected to the memory of that great artist, through gratitude, is, undoubtedly, a homage which he justly deserved. This French Phidias was a Calvinist, and one of the numerous victims of St. Bartholomew's day, being shot on his scaffold, as he was at work on the *Louvre*, the 24th of August 1572. Here too we behold the statues of Birague and of the Gondi, those atrocious wretches who, together with Catherine de Medicis, plotted that infamous massacre; while Charles IX, no less criminal, here exhibits on his features the stings of a guilty conscience.

The man that has a taste for learning, gladly turns his eye from this horde of miscreants, to fix it on the statue of Claude-Catherine de Clermont-Tonnerre, who was so conversant in the dead languages as to bear away the palm from Birague and Chiveray, in a speech which she composed and spoke in Latin, at twenty-four hours' notice, in answer to the ambassadors who tendered the crown of Poland to Charles IX.

If the friend of the arts examine the beautiful portico erected by Philibert de l'Orme, on the banks of the Eure, for Diane de Poitiers, composed of the three orders of architecture, placed the one above the other, and forming altogether an elevation of sixty feet, he will be amazed to learn that this superb monument constructed at Anet, twenty leagues distant from Paris, was removed thence, and re-established in this Museum, by the indefatigable conservator, LENOIR.

On leaving the apartment containing the master-pieces brought to light by Francis I, the next we reach is the

HALL OF THE SEVENTEENTH CENTURY.

What a crowd of celebrated men contained in the temple consecrated to virtue, courage, and talents!

There, I behold TURENNE, CONDÉ, MONTAUSIER, COLBERT, MOLIÈRE, CORNEILLE, LA FONTAINE, RACINE, FÉNÉLON, and BOILEAU. The great LEWIS XIV, placed in the middle of this hall, seems to become still greater near those immortal geniuses.

Farther on, we see the statue of the implacable RICHELIEU, represented expiring in the arms of Religion, while Science is weeping at his feet. Ye Gods! what a prostitution of talent! This is the master-piece of GIRARDON; but, in point of execution, many connoisseurs prefer the mausoleum of the crafty MAZARIN, whom COYZEVOX has pourtrayed in a supplicating posture.

LEWIS XIII, surnamed the *Just*, less great than his illustrious subject, DE THOU, casts down his eyes in the presence of his ministers.

The mausolea of LE BRUN, LULLI, and JÉROME BIGNON, the honour, the love, and the example of his age, terminate the series of monuments of that epoch, still more remarkable for its literati than its artists. We at last come to the

HALL OF THE EIGHTEENTH CENTURY.

Here we admire the statues of MONTESQUIEU, FONTENELLE, VOLTAIRE, ROUSSEAU, HELVÉTIUS, CRÉBILLON, PIRON, &c. &c. The tombs of the learned MAUPERTUIS and CAYLUS, and also that of Marshal D'HARCOURT, give a perfect idea of the state of degradation into which the art of design had fallen at the beginning of this century; but the new productions which decorate the extremity of this spacious hall are sufficient to prove to what degree the absolute will of a great genius can influence the progress of the arts, as well as of the sciences. VIEN and DAVID appeared, and the art was regenerated.

Here, too, we find a statue, as large as life, representing Christ leaning on a pillar, executed by MICHAEL ANGELO STODTZ. I notice this statue merely to observe, that the original, from which it is taken, is to be seen at Rome, in the *Chiesa della Minerva* where it is held in such extraordinary veneration, that the great toe-nail of the right foot having been entirely worn away by the repeated kisses of the faithful, one of silver had been substituted. At length this second nail having been likewise worn away, a third was placed, of copper, which is already somewhat worn. It was sculptured by MICHAEL ANGELO BUONAROTI.

We experience an emotion of regret at the aspect of the handsome monument by MICHALLON, on learning that it was erected to the memory of young DROUAIS, a skilful and amiable artist, stopped by death, in 1788, during his brilliant career, at the early age of 24. He has left behind him three historical pictures, which are so many master-pieces.

The beautiful statue of the youthful Cyparissus, by CHAUDET, the most eminent French sculptor, reminds us of the full and elegant form of the fine Greek Bacchus, which decorates the peristyle of the antichamber or Hall of Introduction.

Thus the amateur and the student will find, in this Museum, an uninterrupted chronology of monuments, both antique and modern, beginning by those of ancient Greece, whose date goes back to two thousand five hundred years before our era, to examine those of the Romans, of the Lower Empire, of the Gauls, and thence pass to the first epoch of the French monarchy, and at length follow all the gradations through which the art has passed from its cradle to its decrepitude. The whole of this grand establishment is terminated by a spacious garden, which is converted into an

ELYSIUM.

There, on a verdant lawn, amid firs, cypresses, poplars, and weeping willows, repose the ashes of the illustrious poets, MOLIÈRE, LA FONTAINE, BOILEAU, &c.; of the learned DESCARTES, MABILLON, MONTFAUCON, &c., inclosed in sarcophagi; there, they still receive the homage which mankind owe to talents and virtue.

But hold! mark the sepulchre of the learned and tender HÉLOÏSE. Her remains, though formerly conjoined to those of her lover, were subsequently separated, and after a lapse of three hundred years, they are now reassembled.

> Here one kind grave unites their hapless name,
> And grafts her love immortal on his fame.

With a smile seated on her lips, Héloïse seems to be sighing for the object of her glowing affection: while the unfortunate Abélard, coldly reclined, is still commenting on the Trinity. The *Paraclete*, having been sold and demolished, Lenoir, with all the sensibility of an admirer of genius, withdrew the bones of Abélard and Héloïse from that monastery, and placed them here in a sepulchral chapel, partly constructed from the remains of their ancient habitation.

Such is the Museum of French Monuments. When completed, for some valuable specimens of the arts still remain to be added, it will be one of the most interesting establishments in Paris, and perhaps in Europe, especially if considered in regard to the improvement of modern sculpture, and, I may add, architecture. No building can be better adapted than a monastery for an establishment of this nature. The solemn gloom of cloisters suits the temper of the mind, when we reflect on the mortality incident to a succession of ages, and the melancholy which it inspires, is in perfect unison with our feelings, when we contemplate the sepulchral monuments that recall to our memory the actions of the illustrious departed.

This Museum is very extensive, the three courts and large garden, which at present compose the whole of its premises, occupying a space of three thousand seven hundred and sixty-two toises. LENOIR, however, has recently presented to the First Consul a plan for enlarging it, without any additional expense of building, by adding to it the neighbouring *Hôtel de Bouillon*. He proposes that there should be a new entrance by the quay, exhibiting a spacious court, decorated with statues, erected in regular order; and that the apartments on the ground-floor should be appropriated as follows:

1. To a collection of portraits of all the celebrated men of France.
2. To a chronological series of armour of all ages.
3. To a complete collection of French medals.
4. To a library, solely formed of the books necessary for obtaining a knowledge of the monuments contained in this Museum.

When I consider the mutilated state in which most of these monuments were found at the first formation of this interesting establishment, and view the perfection in which they now appear; when I remark the taste and judgment displayed in the distribution and interior arrangement of the different apartments of this rich museum; when I learn, from the printed documents on the subject, the strict economy which has been observed in the acquisition or restoration of a great number of monuments, the more valuable as they illustrate the history of the arts; I confess that I find myself at a loss which most to admire in the Conservator, his courage, zeal, perseverance, or discrimination. Indeed, nothing but an assemblage of those qualities could have overcome the difficulties and obstacles which he has surmounted.

I shall add that LENOIR's obliging disposition and amenity of manners equally entitle him to the gratitude and esteem of the connoisseur, the student, or the inquisitive stranger.

LETTER XXVI.

Paris, December 1, 1801.

I WAS highly gratified the other day on finding myself in company with some of those men whom (to borrow Lord Thurlow's expression, in speaking of Warren Hastings,) I have known only as I know Alexander, by the greatness of their exploits; men whose names will be transmitted to posterity, and shine with distinguished lustre in the military annals of France.

General A———y had already invited me to dine with him, in order to meet General B———r; but, on the day fixed, the latter, as minister for the war department, being under the necessity of entertaining Lord Cornwallis, the party was postponed till the 8th of Frimaire, (29th of November), when, in addition to General B———r, General A———y had assembled at his table several men of note. Among others, were General M———rd, who commanded the right wing of the army of Naples under Macdonald, in which he distinguished himself as a brave soldier; and D———ttes, physician in chief to the army of the East. This officer of health, as medical men are here denominated, is lately returned from Egypt, where his skill and attention to his professional duties gained him universal admiration.

In society so agreeable, time passed away rapidly till General B———r arrived. It was late, that is about seven o'clock, though the invitation expressed five precisely, as the hour of dinner. But, in Paris, a minister is always supposed to be detained on official business of a nature paramount to every other consideraton. On my being introduced to General B———r, he immediately entered into conversation with me concerning Lord Cornwallis, whom he had known in the American war, having served in the staff of Rochambeau at the siege of Yorktown. As far back as that period, B———r signalized himself by his skill in military science. It was impossible to contemplate these distinguished officers without calling to mind how greatly their country was indebted to the exertion of their talents on various important occasions. These recollections led me to admire that wisdom which had placed them in stations for which they had proved themselves so eminently qualified. In England, places are generally sought for men; in France, men are sought for places.

At seven, dinner was announced, and an excellent one it was, both in quality and quantity. *Presto* was the word, and all the guests seemed habituated to expedition. The difference between the duration of such a repast at this day, and what it was before the revolution, shews how constantly men become the slaves of fashion. Had BONAPARTE resembled Lucullus in being addicted to the pleasures of the festive board, I make no doubt that it would have been the height of *ton* to sit quietly two or three hours after dinner. But the Chief Consul is said to be temperate almost to abstemiousness; he rises from table in less than half an hour; and that mode is now almost universal in Paris, especially among the great men in office. Two elegant courses and a desert were presently dispatched; the whole time employed in eating I know not how many good dishes, and drinking a variety of choice wines, not exceeding thirty-five minutes. At the end of the repast, coffee was presented to the company in an adjoining room, after which the opera of *Tarare* was the attraction of the evening.

I have already mentioned to you that General A———y had put into my hand *L'Histoire du Canal du Midi*, written by himself. From a perusal of this interesting work, it appears that one of his ancestors[*] was the first who conceived the idea of that canal, which was not only planned by him, but entirely completed under his immediate direction. Having communicated his plan to Riquet, the latter submitted it to Colbert, and, on its being approved by Lewis XIV, became *contractor* for all the works of that celebrated undertaking, which he did not live to see finished. Riquet, however, not content with having derived from the undertaking every advantage of honour and

[*] FRANÇOIS ANDREOSSY; who was the great great grandfather of the present French ambassador at our court.

emolument, greedily snatched from the original projector the meed of fame, so dearly earned by the unremitting labour of thirty successive years. These facts are set forth in the clearest light in the above-mentioned work, in which I was carefully examining General A———y's plans for the improvement of this famous canal, when I was most agreeably interrupted.

I had expressed to the General a wish to know the nature of the establishment of which he is the director, at the same time apprizing him that this wish did not extend to any thing that could not with propriety be made public. He obligingly promised that I should be gratified, and this morning I received from him a very friendly letter, accompanied by the following account of the

DÉPÔT DE LA GUERRE.

The general *Dépôt* or repository of maps and plans of war, &c, &c, was established by Louvois, in 1688. This was the celebrated period when France, having attained the highest degree of splendour, secured her glory by the results of an administration enlightened in all its branches.

At the beginning of its institution, the *Dépôt de la guerre* was no more than archives, where were collected, and preserved with order, the memoirs of the generals, their correspondence, the accounts yet imperfect, and the traces of anterior military operations.

The numerous resources afforded by this collection alone, the assistance and advantages derived from it on every occasion, when it was necessary to investigate a military system, or determine an important operation, suggested the idea of assembling it under a form and classification more methodical. Greater attention and exactness were exerted in enriching the *Dépôt* with every thing that might complete the theoretical works and practical elucidations of all the branches of the military art.

Marshal DE MAILLEBOIS, who was appointed director of this establishment in 1730, was one of the first authors of the present existing order. The classification at first consisted only in forming registers of the correspondence of the generals, according to date, distinguishing it by *different wars*. It was divided into two parts, the former containing the letters of the generals; and the latter, the minutes or originals of the answers of the king and his ministers. To each volume was added a summary of the contents, and, in regular succession, the journal of the military operations of the year. These volumes, to the number of upwards of two thousand seven hundred, contain documents from the eleventh century to the close of the last American war; but the series is perfect only from the year 1631. This was a valuable mine for a historiographer to explore; and, indeed, it is well known that the *Memoirs of Turenne and of Condé*, the *History of the war of* 1741, and part of the fragments of the *Essay on the Manners and History of Nations*, by Voltaire, were compiled and digested from the original letters and memoirs preserved in the *Dépôt de la guerre*.

Geographical engineers did not then exist as a corps. Topography was practised by insulated officers, impelled thereto by the rather superficial study of the mathematics and a taste for drawing; because it was for them a mean of obtaining more advantageous employments in the staffs of the armies: but the want of a central point, the difference of systems and methods, not admitting of directing the operations to one same principle, as well as to one same object, topography, little encouraged, was making but a slow progress, when M. De Choiseuil established, as a particular corps, the officers who had applied themselves to the practice of that science. The *Dépôt* was charged to direct and assemble the labours of the new corps. This authority doubled the utility of the

Dépôt: its results had the most powerful influence during the war from 1757 to 1763.

Lieutenant-General DE VAULT, who had succeeded Marshal DE MAILLEBOIS as director of the *Dépôt de la guerre*, conceived, and executed a plan, destined to render still more familiar and secure the numerous documents collected in this establishment. He first retrenched from the *Military Correspondences and Memoirs* all tedious repetitions and unnecessary details; he then classed the remainder under the head of a different army or operation, without subjecting himself to any other order than a simple chronology; but he caused each volume to be preceded by a very succinct, historical summary, in order to enable the reader to seize the essence of the original memoirs and documents, the text of which was faithfully copied in the body of each volume. In this manner did he arrange all the military events from the German war in 1677 to the peace of 1763. This analysis forms one hundred and twenty-five volumes.

It is easy to conceive how much more intetesting these historical volumes became by the addition, which took place about the same epoch, of the labours of the geographical engineers employed in the armies. The military men having it at the same time in his power to follow the combinations of the generals with the execution of their plans, imbibes, without difficulty, the principles followed by great captains, or improves himself from the exact account of the errors and faults which it is so natural to commit on critical occasions.

When all the establishments of the old *régime* were tottering, or threatened by the revolutionary storm, measures were suggested for preserving the *Dépôt de la guerre*, and, towards the end of 1791, it was transferred from Versailles to Paris. Presently the new system of government, the war declared against the emperor, and the foreseen conflagration of Europe, concurred to give a new importance to this establishment. Alone, amidst the general overthrow, it had preserved a valuable collection of the military and topographical labours of the monarchy, of manuscripts of the greatest importance, and a body of information of every kind respecting the resources, and the country, of the powers already hostile, or on the point of becoming so. All the utility which might result from the *Dépôt* was then felt, and it was thought necessary to give it a new organization.[*]

---

[*] On the 25th of April, 1792, was published a regulation, decreed by the king, respecting the general direction of the

The *Dépôt de la guerre*, however, would have attained but imperfectly the object of its institution, had there not been added to its topographical treasure, the richest, as well as the finest, collection in Europe of every geographical work held in any estimation. The first epochs of the revolution greatly facilitated the increase of its riches of that description. The general impulse, imprinted on the mind of the French nation, prompted every will towards useful sacrifices. Private cabinets in possession of the scarcest maps, gave them up to the government. The suppression of the monasteries and abbeys caused to flow to the centre the geographical riches which they preserved in an obscurity hurtful to the progress of that important science: and thus the *Dépôt de la guerre* obtained one of the richest collections in Europe.* The government, besides, completed it by the delivery of the great map of France by Cassini, begun in 1750, together with all the materials forming the elements of that grand work. It is painful to add that not long before that period (in 1791) the corps of

Dépôt de la guerre. The annual expense of the establishment, at that time amounted to 68,000 francs, but the geographical and historical departments were not filled. *Note of the Author.*

* An *Agence des cartes* was appointed, by the National Assembly, to class these materials, and arrange them in useful order.

geographical engineers, which alone could give utility to such valuable materials had been suppressed.*

In the mean time, the sudden changes in the administrative system had dispersed the learned societies employed in astronomy, or the mathematical sciences. The *National Observatory* was disused. The celebrated astronomers attached to it had no rallying point: they could not devote themselves to their labours but amidst the greatest difficulties; the salary allowed to them was not paid; the numerous observations, continued for two centuries, were on the point of being interrupted.

The *Dépôt de la guerre* then became the asylum of those estimable men. This establishment excited and obtained the reverification of the measure of an arc of the meridian, in order to serve as a basis for the uniformity of the weights and measures which the government wished to establish.

MÉCHAIN, DELAMBRE, NOUET, TRANCHOT,

---

* At the juncture alluded to (1793), the want of geographical engineers having been felt as soon as the armies took the field, three brigades were formed, each consisting of twelve persons. The composition of the *Dépôt de la guerre*, was increased in proportion to its importance: intelligent officers were placed there; and no less than thirty-eight persons were employed in the interior labour, that is, in drawing plans of campaigns, sieges, &c. *Note of the Author.*

and PERNY were dispatched to different places from Barcelona to Dunkirk. After having established at each extremity of this line a base, measured with the greatest exactness, they were afterwards to advance their triangles, in order to ascend to the middle point of the line. This operation, which has served for rectifying a few errors that the want of perfection in the instruments had occasioned to be introduced into the measure of the meridian of CASSINI, may be reckoned one of the most celebrated works which have distinguished the close of the eighteenth century.

The establishment of the system of administration conformably to the constitution of the year III (1795) separated the various elements which the *Dépôt de la guerre* had found means to preserve. The *Board of Longitude* was established; the *National Institute* was formed to supply the place of the *Academy of Sciences, &c.* The *Dépôt de la guerre* was restored solely to its ancient prerogatives. Two years before, it had been under the necessity of forming new geographical engineers and it succeeded in carrying the number sufficiently high to suffice for the wants of the *fourteen* armies which France had afterwards on foot*. These officers being

---

* That tempestuous period having dispersed the then director and his assistants, the *Dépôt de la guerre* remained, for

employed in the service of the staffs, no important work was undertaken. But, since the 18th of Brumaire, year VIII, (9th of November, 1799) the Consuls of the Republic have bestowed particular attention on geographical and topographical operations. The new limits of the French territory require that the map of it should be continued; and the new political system, resulting from the general pacification, renders necessary the exact knowledge of the states of the allies of the Republic.

The *Dépôt de la guerre* forms various sections of geographers, who are at present employed in constructing accurate maps of the four united departments, Piedmont, Savoy, Helvetia, and the part of Italy comprised between the Adige and the Adda. One section, in conjunction with the Bavarian engineers, is constructing a topographical map of Bavaria: another section is carrying into execution the military surveys, and other topographical labours, ordered by General Mo-

---

some time, without officers capable of conducting it in a manner useful to the country. In the mean while, wants were increasing, and military operations daily becoming more important, when, in 1793, CARNOT, then a member of the Committee of Public Welfare, formed a private cabinet of topography, the elements of which he drew from the *Dépôt de la guerre*. This was a first impulse given to these valuable collections. *Note of the Author.*

reau for the purpose of forming a map of Suabia.

The *Dépôt* has just published an excellent map of the Tyrol, reduced from that of Paysan, and to which have been added the observations made by Chevaliers Dupay and La Lucerne. It has caused to be resumed the continuation of the superb map of the environs of Versailles, called *La carte des chasses*, a master-piece of topography and execution in all the arts relating to that science. Since the year V (1795), it has also formed a library composed of upwards of eight thousand volumes or manuscripts, the most rare, as well as the most esteemed, respecting every branch of the military art in general.

Although, in the preceding account, General A————y, with that modesty which is the characteristic of a superior mind, has been totally silent respecting his own indefatigable exertions, I have learned from the best authority, that France is soon likely to derive very considerable advantages from the activity and talent introduced by him, as director, into every branch of the *Dépôt de la guerre*, and of which he has afforded in his own person an illustrious example.

In giving an impulse to the interior labours of the *Dépôt*, the sole object of General A————y is to make this establishment lose its *paralyzing* destination of archives, in which, from time to time, literati might come to collect information concerning some periods of national or foreign history. He is of opinion that these materials ought to be drawn from oblivion, and brought into action by those very persons who, having the experience of war, are better enabled than any others to arrange its elements. Instruction and method being the foundations of a good administration, of the application of an art and of a science, as well as of their improvement, he has conceived the idea of uniting in a classical work the exposition of the knowledge necessary for the direction of the *Dépôt*, for geographical engineers, staff-officers, military men in general, and historians. This, then, is the object of the *Mémomorial du Dépôt de la guerre*, a periodical work, now in hand, which will become the guide of every establishment of this nature*, by directing with method the various labours used in the application of mathematical and physical sciences to topography, and to that art which, of all others, has the greatest influence on the destiny of empires: I mean the art military. The improve-

---

* Prince Charles is employed at Vienna in forming a collection of books, maps, and military memoirs for the purpose of establishing a *Dépôt* for the Instruction of the staff-officers of the Austrian army. Spain has also begun to organize a system of military topography in imitation of that of France. Portugal follows the example. What are we doing in England?

ments of which it is still susceptible will be pointed out in the *Mémorial*, and every new idea proposed on the subject will there be critically investigated.

In transcribing General A———y's sketch of this extremely-interesting establishment, I cannot but reflect on the striking contrast that it presents, in point of geographical riches, even half a century ago, to the disgraceful poverty, in that line, which, about the same period, prevailed in England, and was severely felt in the planning of our military expeditions.

I remember to have been told by the late Lord Howe, that, when he was captain of the Magnanime at Plymouth, and was sent for express to London, in the year 1757, in order to command the naval part of an expedition to the coast of France, George II, and the whole cabinet council, seemed very much astonished at his requiring the production of a map of that part of the enemy's coast against which the expedition was intended. Neither in the apartment where the council sat, nor in any adjoining one, was any such document; even in the Admiralty-office no other than an indifferent map of the coast could be found: as for the adjacent country, it was so little known in England, that, when the British troops landed, their commander was ignorant of the distance of the neighbouring villages.

Of late years, indeed, we have ordered these matters better; but, to judge from circumstances, it should seem that we are still extremely deficient in geographical and topographical knowledge; though we are not quite so ill informed as in the time of a certain duke, who, when First Lord of the Treasury, asked in what part of Germany was the Ohio?

P. S. In order to give you, at one view, a complete idea of the collections of the *Dépôt de la guerre*, and of what they have furnished during the war for the service of the government and of the armies, I shall end my letter by stating that, independently of eight thousand chosen volumes, among which is a valuable collection of atlases, of two thousand seven hundred volumes of old archives, and of upwards of nine hundred *cartons* or pasteboard boxes of modern original documents, the *Dépôt* possesses one hundred and thirty-one volumes and seventy-eight *cartons* of descriptive memoirs, composed at least of fifty memoirs each, four thousand seven hundred engraved maps, of each of which there are from two to twenty-five copies, exclusively of those printed at the *Dépôt*, and upwards of seven thousand four hundred valuable manuscript maps, plans, or drawings of marches, battles, sieges, &c.

By order of the government, it has furnished,

in the course of the war, seven thousand two hundred and seventy-eight engraved maps, two hundred and seven manuscript maps or plans, sixty-one atlases of various parts of the globe, and upwards of six hundred descriptive memoirs.

LETTER XXVII.

Paris, December 3, 1801.

In this season, when the blasts of November have entirely stripped the trees of their few remaining leaves, and Winter has assumed his hoary reign, the garden of the *Tuileries*, loses much of the gaiety of its attractions. Besides, to frequent that walk at present, is like visiting daily one of our theatres, you meet the same faces so often, that the scene soon becomes monotonous. As well for the sake of variety as exercise, I therefore now and then direct my steps along the

BOULEVARDS.

This is the name given to the promenades with which Paris is, in part, surrounded for an extent of six thousand and eighty-four toises.

They are distinguished by the names of the *Old* and the *New*. The *Old*, or *North Boule-*

vards, commonly called the *Grands Boulevards*, were begun in 1536, and, when faced with ditches, which were to have been dug, they were intended to serve as fortifications against the English who were ravaging Picardy, and threatening the capital. Thence, probably, the etymology of their name; *Boulevard* signifying, as every one knows, a bulwark.

However this may be, the extent of these Old Boulevards is two thousand four hundred toises from the *Rue de la Concorde* to the *Place de la Liberté*, formerly the site of the Bastille. They were first planted in 1660, and are formed into three alleys by four rows of trees: the middle alley is appropriated to carriages and persons on horseback, and the two lateral ones are for foot-passengers.

Here, on each side, is assembled every thing that ingenuity can imagine for the diversion of the idle stroller, or the recreation of the man of business. Places of public entertainment, ambulating musicians, exhibitions of different kinds, temples consecrated to love or pleasure, Vauxhalls, ball-rooms, magnificent hotels, and other tasteful buildings, &c. Even the coffee-houses and taverns here have their shady bowers, and an agreeable orchestra. Thus, you may always dine in Paris with a band of music to entertain you, without additional expense.

The *New* Boulevards, situated to the south, were finished in 1761. They are three thousand six hundred and eighty-three toises in extent from the *Observatoire* to the *Hôtel des Invalides*. Although laid out much in the same manner as the *Old*, there is little resemblance between them; each having a very distinct appearance.

On the *New* Boulevards, the alleys are both longer and wider, and the trees are likewise of better growth. There, the prospect is rural; and the air pure; while cultivated fields, with growing corn, present themselves to the eye. Towards the town, however, stand several pretty houses; little theatres even were built, but did not succeed. This was not their latitude. But some skittle-grounds and tea-gardens, lately opened, and provided with swings, &c. have attracted much company of a certain class in the summer.

In this quarter, you seldom meet with a carriage, scarcely ever with persons sprucely dressed, but frequently with honest citizens, accompanied by their whole family, as plain in their garb as in their manners. Lovers too with their mistresses, who seek solitude, visit this retired walk; and now and then a poor poet comes hither, not to sharpen his appetite, but to arrange his numbers.

Before the revolution, the *Old* Boulevards, from the *Porte St. Martin* to the *Théâtre*

Favart, was the rendezvous of the *élegantes*, who, on Sundays and Thursdays, used to parade there slowly, backward and forward, in their carriages, as our belles do in Hyde Park; with this difference, that, if their admirers did not accompany them, they generally followed them to interchange significant glances, or indulge in amorous parley. I understand that the summer lounge of the modern *élegantes* has, of late years, been from the corner of the *Rue Grange Batelière* to that of the *Rue Mont-Blanc*, where the ladies took their seats. This attracting the *muscadins* in great numbers, not long since obtained for that part of the Boulevard the appellation of *Petit Coblentz*.

Nearly about the middle of the North Boulevard stand two edifices, which owe their erection to the vanity of Lewis XIV. In the gratification of that passion did the *Grand Monarque* console himself for his numerous defeats and disappointments; and the age in which he lived being fertile in great men, owing, undoubtedly, to the encouragement he afforded them, his display of it was well seconded by their superior talents. Previously to his reign, Paris had several gates, but some of these being taken down, arcs of triumph, in imitation of those of the Romans, were erected in their stead by *Louis le Grand*, in commemoration of his exploits. And this too, at a time when the allies might, in good earnest, have marched to Paris, had they not, by delay, given Marshal Villars an opportunity of turning the tide of their victories on the plain of Denain. Such was the origin of the

PORTE SAINT DENIS.

The magnificence of its architecture classes it among the first public monuments in Paris. It consists of a triumphal arch, insulated in the manner of those of the ancients: it is seventy-two feet in diameter as well as in elevation, and was executed in 1672, by BULLET from the designs of BLONDEL.

On each side of the principal entrance rise two sculptured pyramids, charged with trophies of arms, both towards the faubourg, and towards the city. Underneath each of these pyramids is a small collateral passage for persons on foot. The arch is ornamented with two bas-reliefs: the one facing the city represents the passage of the Rhine; and the other, the capture of Maestricht.

On the frieze on both sides LUDOVICO MAGNO was formerly to be read, in large characters of gilt bronze. This inscription is removed, and to it are substituted the word *Liberté, Égalité, Fraternité.*

On arriving from Calais, you enter Paris by the *Porte St. Denis*. It was also by the *Porte St. Denis* that kings and queens made their public entry. On these occasions, the houses in all the streets through which they passed, were decorated with silk hangings and tapestry, as far as the cathedral of *Notre-Dame*. Scented waters perfumed the air in the form of *jets d'eau*; while wine and milk flowed from the different public fountains.

Froissard relates that, on the entrance of Isabeau de Bavière, there was in the *Rue St. Denis* a representation of a clouded heaven, thickly sown with stars, whence descended two angels who gently placed on her head a very rich crown of gold, set with precious stones, at the same time singing verses in her praise.

It was on this occasion that Charles VI, anxious for a sight of his intended bride, took a fancy to mix in the crowd, mounted on horseback behind Savoisi, his favourite. Pushing forward in order to approach her, he received from the serjeants posted to keep off the populace several sharp blows on the shoulders, which occasioned great mirth in the evening, when the circumstance was related before the queen and her ladies.

Proceeding along the Boulevard towards the

east, at a short distance from the *Porte St. Denis*, you arrive at the

PORTE SAINT MARTIN.

Although this triumphal arch cannot be compared to the preceding in magnificence, it was nevertheless executed by the same artists; having been erected in 1674. It is pierced with three openings, the centre one of which is eighteen feet wide, and the two others nine. The whole structure, which is fifty-four feet both in height and breadth, is rusticated, and in the spandles of the arch are four bas-reliefs; the two towards the city represent the capture of Besançon, and the rupture of the triple alliance; and those towards the faubourg, the capture of Lomberg, and the defeat of the Germans under the emblem of an eagle repulsed by the god of war. These bas-reliefs are crowned by an entablature of the Doric order, surmounted by an attic. The *Porte St. Martin* is the grand entrance into Paris from all parts of Flanders.

At the west extremity of this *North* Boulevard, facing the *Rue de la Concorde*, stands an unfinished church, called *La Magdeleine*, whose cemetery received not only the bodies of Lewis XVI, his consort, and his sister, but of the greater part of the victims that perished by the guillotine.

In the space comprised between *La Magdeleine* and the *Vieille Rue du Temple,* I speak within compass when I say that there are sometimes to be seen fifty ambulating conjurers of both sexes. They all vary the form of their art. Some have tables, surmounted by flags, bearing mysterious devices; some have wheels, with compartments adapted to every age and profession——One has a robe charged with hieroglyphics, and tells you your fortune through a long tube which conveys the sound to your ear; the other makes you choose, in a parcel, a square piece of white paper, which becomes covered with characters at the moment when it is thrown into a jug that appears empty. The secret of this is as follows:

The jug contains a little sulphuret of potash, and the words are written with acetite of lead. The action of the exterior air, on the sulphuret of potash, disengages from it sulphurated hydrogen gas, which, acting on the oxyd of lead, brings to view the characters that before were invisible.

Here, the philosophic Parisians stop before the moveable stall of an astrologer, who has surmounted it with an owl, as an emblem of his magic wisdom. Many of them take this animal for a curiosity, imported from foreign countries, for they are seldom able to distinguish a bat from a swallow.

"Does that bird come from China, my dear?" says a lusty dame to her elderly husband, a shopkeeper of the *Rue St. Denis.*—" I don't know, my love," replies the other.—" What eyes it has got," continues she; " it must see a great deal better than we." " No," cries a countryman standing by; " though its eyes are so big, it can't, in broad day, tell a cow from a calf."

The lady continues her survey of the scientific repository; and the conjurer, with an air of importance, proposes to her to draw, for two *sous*, a motto from Merlin's wheel. " Take one, my dear," says the husband; " I wish to know whether you love me." The wife blushes and hesitates; the husband insists; she refuses, and is desirous of continuing her walk, saying that it is all foolishness.—" What if it is?" rejoins the husband, " I've paid, so take a motto to please me." For this once, the lady is quite at a nonplus; she at last consents, and, with a trembling hand, draws a card from the magic wheel: the husband unrolls it with eagerness and confidence, and reads these words; " *My young lover is and will be constant.*"—" What the devil does this mean?" exclaims the old husband, quite disconcerted.—" 'Tis a mistake," says the conjurer;

" the lady put her hand into the wrong box; she
" drew the motto from the wheel for *young*
" *girls*, instead of that for *married women*. Let
" *Madame* draw again, she shall pay nothing
" more."—" No, Mr. Conjurer," replies the
shopkeeper, " that's enough. I've no faith in
" such nonsense; but another time, madam, take
" care that you don't put your hand into the
" wrong box." The fat lady, with her face as
red as fire, follows her husband, who walks off
grumbling, and it is easy to see, by their gestures,
that the fatal motto has sown discord in the family, and confirmed the shopkeeper's suspicions.

Independently of these divers into futurity, the
corners of streets and walls of public squares, are
covered with hand-bills announcing books containing secrets, sympathetic calculations of numbers in the lottery, the explanation of dreams in
regard to those numbers, together with the different manners of telling fortunes, and interpreting
prognostics.

At all times, the marvellous has prevailed
over simple truth, and the Cumæan Sibyl attracted the inquisitive in greater crowds than
Socrates, Plato, or any philosopher, had pupils
in the whole course of their existence.

In Paris, the sciences are really making a rapid
progress, notwithstanding the fooleries of the

pseudo-philosophers, who parade the streets, and here, on the *Boulevards*, as well as in other parts of the town, exhibit lessons of physics.

One has an electrifying machine, and phials filled with phosphorus: for two *sous*, he gives you a slight shock, and makes you a present of a small phial.

Farther on, you meet with a *camera obscura*, whose effect surprises the spectators the more, as the objects represented within it have the motion which they do not find in common optics.

There, you see a double refracting telescope: for two *sous*, you enjoy its effect. At either end, you place any object whatever, and though a hat, a board, or a child be introduced between the two glasses, the object placed appears not, on that account, the less clear and distinct to the eye of the person looking through the opposite glass. *Pierre* has seen, and cannot believe his eyes: *Jacques* wishes to see, and, on seeing, is in ecstacy: next comes *Fanchon*, who remains stupified. Enthusiasm becomes general, and the witnesses of their delirium are ready to go mad at not having two *sous* in their pocket.

Another fellow, in short, has a microscope, of which he extols the beauty, and, above all, the effects: he will not describe the causes which produce them, because he is unacquainted with them; but, provided he adapts his lessons to the understanding of those who listen to him, this is all he wants. Sometimes he may be heard to say to the people about him: " Gentlemen, give me a creeping insect, and " for one *sou*, I will shew it to you as big as " my fist." Sometimes too, unfortunately for him, the insect which he requires is more easily found among part of his auditors, than the money.

P. S.—For the preceding account of the Parisian conjurers I am indebted to M. Pujoulx.

LETTER XXVIII.

Paris, December 4, 1802.

IN one of your former letters you questioned me on a subject, which, though it had not escaped my notice, I was desirous to avoid, till I should be able to obtain on it some precise information. This I have done; and I hasten to present you with the following sketch, which will afford you a tolerably-correct idea of the

FRENCH FUNDS,
AND
NATIONAL DEBT.

The booked or consolidated debt is called

TIERS CONSOLIDÉ,

from its being the consolidated third of the national debt, of which the remaining two-thirds were reimbursed in *Bons de deux Tiers* in 1797 and 98. It bears interest at five per Cent. payable half yearly at the *Banque de France*. The payment of the interest is at present six months in arrear. But the intention of the government is, by paying off in specie the interest of one whole year, to pay in future as soon as due.

The days of payment are the 1st of Germinal (23d of March) and the 1st of Vendémiaire (23d of September).

This stock purchased at the present price of from 55 to 60 would produce from eight to nine per cent. The general opinion is, that it will rise to 80; and as it is the chief stock, and the standard of the national credit, it is the interest, and must be the constant object of the government to keep up its price.

There is a *Caisse d'amortissement* or Sinking

Fund, for the special purpose of paying off this stock, the effect of which, though not exactly known, must shortly be very considerable. The *Tiers Consolidé* is saleable and transferrable at a moment's warning, and at a trifling expense. It is not subject to taxation, nor open to attachments, either on the principal or interest.

For purchasing, no sort of formality is required; but for receiving interest, or selling, it is necessary to produce a power of attorney. An established rule is, that the seller always retains his right to half a year's interest at the succeeding stated period of payment, so that he who purchases in the interval between March and September, is entitled to the interest commencing from the 23d of the latter month only; and he who buys between September and March, receives not his first dividend till the 23d of the following September.

TIERS PROVISOIRE.

This is the debt, yet unbooked, which is composed of the provisional claims of the creditors of the emigrants, the contractors, and various other holders of claims on the government.

The *Tiers Provisoire* is to be booked before the 1st of Vendémiaire, year XII of the Republic (23d of September, 1803), and will from that day bear interest of five per cent; so that, setting aside the danger of any retrospect in the interval, and that of any other change, it is at the present price, of from 45 to 50, cheaper than the *Tiers Consolidé*, to which, in about eighteen months, it will, in every respect, be assimilated.

BONS DE DEUX TIERS,

Is paper issued for the purpose of reimbursing the reduced two-thirds of the National Debt, and in the origin rendered applicable to the purchase of national houses and estates in the French Colonies, since ordered to be funded at five per cent; so that the price of this species of paper is entirely subordinate to that of the *Tiers Consolidé*, and supposing that to be 60 francs per cent, the *Bon de deux Tiers* would be worth 3 francs. There are no hopes, however distant, that the government will ever restore the *Bons de deux Tiers* to their original value.

BONS DE TROIS QUARTS,

So called from having been issued for the purpose of reimbursing the three-fourths of the interest of the fifth and sixth years of the Republic (1797 to 1798). They are, in all respects, assimilated to the preceding stock.

COUPONS D'EMPRUNT FORCÉ.

These are the receipts given by the government to the persons who contributed to the various forced loans. This paper is likewise assimilated to the two last-mentioned species, with this difference, that it is generally considered as a less sacred claim, and is therefore liquidated with greater difficulty. The holders of these three claims are hastening the liquidation and consolidation of them, and they are evidently right in so doing.

QUARTS AU NOM ET QUART NUMÉRAIRE.

This paper is thus denominated from its having been issued for the purpose of reimbursing the fourth of the dividend of the fifth and sixth years of the Republic (1797 to 1798). It is generally thought that this very sacred claim on the government will be funded *in toto*.

RACHATS DE RENTE,

Is the name given to the redemption of perpetual annuities due by individuals to the government, on a privileged mortgage on landed estates; the said annuities having been issued by the government in times of great distress, for the purpose of supplying immediate and urgent events.

This paper is not only a mere government security, but is also specially mortgaged on the estates of the person who owes the annuity to the government, and who is, at any time, at liberty to redeem it at from twenty to twenty-five years purchase. Claims of this description, mortgaged on most desirable estates near the metropolis, might be obtained for less than 60 per cent; which, at the interest of five per cent, and with the additional advantage, in some instances, of the arrears of one or two years, would produce between eight and nine per cent.

Next to the *Tiers Consolidé, Rachats de Rente* are particularly worthy of attention; indeed, this debt is of so secure and sacred a nature, that the government has appropriated a considerable part of it to the special purpose and service of the hospitals and schools; two species of institutions which ought ever to be sheltered from all vicissitudes, and which, whatever may be the form or character of the government, must be supported and respected.

ACTIONS DE LA BANQUE DE FRANCE.

These are shares in the National Bank of France, which are limited to the number of thirty thousand, and were originally worth one thousand francs each; they therefore form a capital of 30,000,000 francs, or £1,250,000 sterling, and afford as follows:

1. A dividend which at present, and since the foundation, has averaged from eight to ten per cent, arising from the profits on discount.
2. A profit of from four to five per cent more on the discount of paper, which every holder of an *action* or share effects at the Bank, at the rate of one-half per cent per month, or six per cent for the whole year.

The present price of an *action* is about twelve hundred francs, which may be considered as producing:

    80 francs; dividend paid by the Bank on each share.
    30 francs; certain profits according to the present discount of bills.
  110 francs; per share $10\tfrac{10}{11}$ per cent.

Actions de la Banque de France, though subject, in common with all stocks, to the influence of the government, are, however, far more independent of it than any other, and are the more secure, as the National Bank is not only composed of all the first bankers, but also supported by the principal merchants in the country. This investment is at present very beneficial, and certainly promises great eventual advantages. The dividends are paid in two half-yearly instalments.

ACTIONS DE LA CAISSE DE COMMERCE,
ET
ACTIONS DU COMPTOIR COMMERCIAL.

The *Caisse de Commerce* and the *Comptoir Commercial* are two establishments on the same plan, and affording, as nearly as possible, the same advantages as the *Banque de France*: the only difference is as follows:

1. These last two are, as far as any commercial establishment can be, independent of the government, and are more so than the *Banque de France*, as the *actions* or shares are not considered as being a public fund.
2. The *Actions de la Caisse de Commerce* limited in number to two thousand four hundred, originally cost 5000 francs, and are now worth 6000. The holder of each *action* moreover, signs circulating notes to the amount of five thousand francs, which form the paper currency of the Bank, and for the payment of which the said holder would be responsible, were the Bank to stop payment.
3. The *Actions du Comptoir Commercial* are still issued by the administrators of the establishment. The number of *actions* is not as yet li-

mited: the price of each *action* is fifteen hundred francs (*circa* £60 sterling), and the plan and advantages are almost entirely similar to those of the two last-mentioned institutions.

The *Banque de France*, the *Caisse de Commerce*, and the *Comptoir Commercial*, discount three times aweek. The first, the paper of the banking-houses and the principal commercial houses holding bank-stock; the second, the paper of the wholesale merchants of every class; and the third, the paper of retailers of all descriptions; and in a circulation which amounts to 100 millions of francs (*circa* 4 millions sterling) per month, there have not, it is said, been seen, in the course of the last month, protests to the amount of 20,000 francs.

BONS DE L'AN VII ET DE L'AN VIII,

Is a denomination applied to paper, issued for the purpose of paying the dividend of the debt during the seventh and eighth years of the Republic.

These *Bons* are no further deserving of notice than as they still form a part of the floating debt, and are an article of the supposed liquidation at the conclusion of the present summary. It is therefore unnecessary to say more of them.

ARRÉRAGES DES ANNÉES V ET VI.

These are the arrears due to such holders of stock as, during the fifth and sixth years of the Republic, had not their dividend paid in *Bons de trois Quarts* and *Quart Numéraire*, mentioned in Art. IV and VI of this sketch. I also notice them as forming an essential part of the above-mentioned supposed liquidation, at the end of the sketch, and shall only add that it is the general opinion that they will be funded.

To the preceding principal investments and claims on the government, might be added the following:

Coupes de Bois.
Cédules Hypothécaires.
Rescriptions de Domaines Nationaux.
Actions de la Caisse des Rentiers.
Actions des Indes.
Bons de Moines et Réligieuses.
Obligations de Receveur.

However, they are almost entirely unworthy of attention, and afford but occasionally openings for speculation. Of the last, *(Obligations de Receveur)* it may be necessary to observe that they are monthly acceptances issued by the Receivers-General of all the departments, which the government has given to the five bankers, charged with supplying money for the current

A SKETCH OF PARIS. 325

service, as security for their advances, and which are commonly discounted at from $\frac{7}{4}$ to one per cent per month.

I shall terminate this concise, though accurate sketch of the French funds by a general statement of the National Debt, and by an account of an annuity supposed to be held by a foreigner before the revolution, and which, to become *Tiers Consolidé*, must undergo the regular process of reduction and liquidation.

National Debt.

	Francs.
Consolidated Stock *(Tiers Consolidé)*	38,750,000
Floating Debt, to be consolidated, about	23,000,000
Life Annuities	20,000,000
Ecclesiastical, Military, and other Pensions	19,000,000
	100,750,000

The value of a *franc* is something more than 10*d.* English money: according to which calculation, the National Debt of France is in round numbers no more than } £4,000,000

Supposed liquidation of an annuity of £100. sterling, or 2,400 *livres tournois* held by a foreigner before the war and yet unliquidated.

	Francs.
Original Annuity	2,400
Tiers Consolidé	} 2,400
Bons de deux Tiers	

The actual value of the whole, including the arreared dividends up to the present day is as follows:

	Francs.
Tiers Consolidé as above, 800 francs sold at 60 francs	9,600
Bons de deux Tiers, ditto 1600 .... at 3	48

Arrears from the first year of the Republic to the fifth ditto (23d of September, 1792 to the 23d of September, 1797) are to be paid in Assignats, and are of no value.

Arrears of the fifth and sixth years supposed to be liquidated so as to afford 25 per cent of their nominal value, about	600
Arrears in *Bons* for the year VII, valued at 50 per cent loss........................	400
Arrears of the year VIII, due in *Bons*, valued at 25 per cent loss.....................	600
Arrears of the year IX, due in specie	800
Arrears of the year X, of which three months are nearly elapsed.....................	200
Total of the principal and interest of an original annuity of 2,400 livres, reduced (according to law) to 800.......................	12,248
Or in sterling, *circa*	£500

I had almost forgot that you have asked me more than once for an explanation of the exact value of a modern *franc*. The following you may depend on as correct.

The *unité monétaire* is a piece of silver of the weight of five *grammes*, containing a tenth of alloy and nine tenths of pure silver. It is called *Franc*, and is subdivided into *Décimes*, and *Centimes:* its value is to that of the old *livre tournois* in the proportion of 81 to 80.

	Value in livres tournois.		
	liv.	sous.	deniers.
Franc............	1	0	3
Décime..........		2	0.3
Centime.........			2.43

LETTER XXIX.

Paris, December 7, 1801.

At the grand monthly parade of the 15th of last Brumaire, I had seen the First Consul chiefly on horseback: on which account, I determined to avail myself of that of the 15th of the present month of Frimaire, in order to obtain a nearer view of his person. On these occasions, none but officers in complete uniform are admitted into the palace of the *Tuileries*, unless provided with tickets, which are distributed to a certain number at the discretion of the governor. General A———y sent me tickets by ten o'clock this morning, and about half after eleven, I repaired to the palace.

On reaching the vestibule from the garden of the *Tuileries*, you ascend the grand stair-case to the left, which conducts you to the guard-room above it in the centre pavilion. Hence you enter the apartments of the Chief Consul.

On the days of the grand parade, the first room is destined for officers as low as the rank of captain, and persons admitted with tickets; the second, for field-officers; the third, for generals; and the fourth, for councellors of state, and the diplomatic corps. To the east, the windows of these apartments command the court-yard where the troops are assembled; while to the west, they afford a fine view of the garden of the *Tuileries* and the avenue leading to the *Barrière de Chaillot*. In the first-room, those windows which overlook the parade were occupied by persons standing five or six in depth, some of whom, as I was informed, had been patient enough to retain their places for the space of two or three hours, and among them were a few ladies. Here, a sort of lane was formed from door to door by some grenadiers of the consular guard. I found both sides of this lane so much crowded, that I readily accepted the invitation of a *chef de brigade* of my acquaintance to accompany him into the second room; this, he observed, was no more than a privilege to which I was entitled. This room was also crowded; but it exhibited a most brilliant *coup d'œil* from the great variety and richness of the uniforms of the field-officers here assembled, by which mine was entirely eclipsed. The lace and embroidery is not merely confined to the coats, jackets, and pantaloons, but extends to the sword belts, and even to the boots, which are universally worn by the military. Indeed, all the foreign ambassadors admit that none of the levees of the European courts can vie in splendour with those of the Chief Consul.

My first care on entering this room, was to place myself in a situation which might afford me an uninterrupted view of BONAPARTE. About twenty-five minutes past twelve, his sortie was announced by a *huissier*. Immediately after, he came out of the inner apartment, attended by several officers of rank, and, traversing all the other rooms with a quick step, proceeded, uncovered, to the parade, the order of which I have described to you in a former letter. On the present occasion, however, it lasted longer on account of the distribution of arms of honour, which the First Consul presents with his own hand to those heroes who have signalized themselves in fighting their country's battles.

This part of the ceremony, which was all that I saw of the parade yesterday, naturally revived in my mind the following question, so often agitated: "Are the military successes of the French the consequences of a new system of operations and new tactics, or merely the effect of the blind courage of a mass of men, led on by chiefs whose resolutions were decided by presence of mind alone and circumstances?"

The latter method of explaining their victories has been frequently adopted, and the French generals have been reproached with lavishing the lives of thousands for the sake of gaining unimportant advantages, or repairing inconsiderable faults.

Sometimes, indeed, it should seem that a murderous obstinacy has obtained them successes to which prudence had not paved the way; but, certainly, the French can boast, too, of memorable days when talent had traced the road to courage, when vast plans combined with judgment, have been followed with perseverance, when resources have been found in those awful moments in which Victory, hovering over a field of carnage, leaves the issue of the conflict doubtful, till a sudden thought, a ray of genius, inclines her in favour of the general, thus inspired, and then art may be said to triumph over art, and valour over valour.

And whence came most of these generals who have shewn this inspiration, if I may so term it?

Some, as is well known, emerged from the schools of jurisprudence; some, from the studies of the arts; and others, from the counting-houses of commerce, as well as from the lowest ranks of the army. Previously to the revolution, it was not admitted, in this country at least, that such sources could furnish men fit to be one day the arbiters of battles and of the fate of empires. Till that period, all those Frenchmen who had distinguished themselves in the field, had devoted themselves from their infancy to the profession of arms, were born near the throne of which they constituted the lustre, or in that cast who arrogated to themselves the exclusive right of defending their country. The glory of the soldier was not considered; and a private must have been more than a hero to be as much remarked as a second lieutenant.

Men of reflection, seeing the old tactics fail against successful essays, against enthusiasm whose effects are incalculable, studied whether new ideas did not direct some new means; for it would have been no less absurd to grant all to valour than to attribute all to art. But to return to the main subject of my letter.

In about three quarters of an hour, BONAPARTE came back from the parade, with the same suite as before, that is, preceded by his aides-de-camp, and followed by the generals and field-officers of the consular guard, the governor of the palace, the general commanding the first military division, and him at the head of the garrison of Paris. For my part, I scarcely saw any one but himself; Bonaparte alone absorbed my whole attention.

A circumstance occurred which gave me an opportunity of observing the Chief Consul with critical minuteness. I had left the second room, and taken my station in front of the row of gazers, close to the folding-doors which opened into the first room, in order to see him receive petitions and memorials. There was no occasion for Bonaparte to cast his eyes from side to side, like the *Grand Monarque* coming from mass, by way of inviting petitioners to approach him. They presented themselves in such numbers that, after he put his hat under his arm, both his hands were full in a moment. To enable him to receive other petitions, he was under the necessity of delivering the first two handfuls to his aides-decamp. I should like to learn what becomes of all these papers, and whether he locks them up in a little desk of which he alone has the key, as was the practice of Lewis XIV.

When Bonaparte approached the door of the second room, he was effectually impeded in his progress by a lady, dressed in white, who, throwing herself at his feet, gracefully presented to him a memorial, which he received with much apparent courtesy; but still seemed, by his manner, desirous to pass forward. However, the crowd was so considerable and so intent on viewing this scene, that the grenadiers, posted near the spot where it took place, were obliged to use some degree of violence before they could succeed in clearing a passage.

Of all the portraits which you and I have seen of BONAPARTE in England, that painted by Masquerier, and exhibited in Piccadilly, presents the greatest resemblance. But for his side-face, you may, for twelve *sous*, here procure a perfect likeness of it at almost every stall in the street. In short, his features are such as may, in my opinion, be easily copied by any artist of moderate abilities. However incompetent I may be to the task, I shall, as you desire it, attempt to *sketch* his person; though I doubt not that any French *commis*, in the habit of describing people by words, might do it greater justice.

BONAPARTE is rather below the middle size, somewhat inclined to stoop, and thin in person; but, though of a slight make, he appears to be muscular, and capable of fatigue; his forehead is broad, and shaded by dark brown hair, which is cut short behind; his eyes, of the same colour, are full, quick, and prominent;

his nose is aquiline; his chin, protuberant and pointed; his complexion, of a yellow hue; and his cheeks, hollow. His countenance, which is of a melancholy cast, expresses much sagacity and reflection: his manner is grave and deliberate, but at the same time open. On the whole, his aspect announces him to be of a temperate and phlegmatic disposition; but warm and tenacious in the pursuit of his object, and impatient of contradiction. Such, at least, is the judgment which I should form of BONAPARTE from his external appearance.

While I was surveying this man of universal talent, my fancy was not idle. First, I beheld him, flushed with ardour, directing the assault of the *tête-de-pont* at *Lodi*; next dictating a proclamation to the Beys at *Cairo*, and styling himself the friend of the faithful; then combating the ebullition of his rage on being foiled in the storming of *Acre*. I afterwards imagined I saw him like another CROMWELL, expelling the Council of Five Hundred at *St. Cloud*, and seizing on the reins of government: when established in power, I viewed him, like HANNIBAL, crossing the *Alps*, and forcing victory to yield to him the hard-contested palm at *Marengo*; lastly, he appeared to my imagination in the act of giving the fraternal embrace to Caprara, the Pope's legate, and at the same time holding out to the see of Rome the re-establishment of catholicism in France.

Voltaire says that "no man ever was a hero in the eyes of his *valet-de-chambre.*" I am curious to know whether the valet of the First Consul be an exception to this maxim. As to Bonaparte's public character, numerous, indeed, are the constructions put on it by the voice of rumour: some ascribe to him one great man of antiquity as a model; some, another; but many compare him, in certain respects, to Julius Cæsar. Now, as imitators generally succeed better in copying the failings than the good qualities of their archetypes, let us hope, supposing this comparison to be a just one, that the Chief Consul will, in one particular, never lose sight of the generous clemency of that illustrious Roman—who, if any spoke bitterly against him, deemed it sufficient to complain of the circumstance publicly, in order to prevent them from persevering in the use of such language. " *Acerbè loquentibus satis habuit pro* "' *concione denunciare, ne perseverarent.*"

"The character of a great man," says a French political writer, who denies the justness of this comparison, " like the celebrated picture of " Zeuxis, can be formed only of a multitude of " imitations, and it is as little possible for the

" observer to find for him a single model in his-
" tory, as it was for the painter of Heraclea to
" discover in nature that of the ideal beauty he
" was desirous of representing *."—" The French
" revolution," observes the same author, a little
farther on, " has, perhaps, produced more than
" one CÆSAR, or one CROMWELL; but they have
" disappeared before they have had it in their
" power to give full scope to their ambition †."
Time will decide on the truth and impartiality
of these observations of M. HAUTERIVE.

As at the last monthly parade, BONAPARTE was
habited in the consular dress, that is, a coat of
scarlet velvet, embroidered with gold: he wore
jockey boots, carelessly drawn over white cotton
pantaloons, and held in his hand a cocked hat,
with the national cockade only. I say only,
because all the generals wear hats trimmed with
a splendid lace, and decorated with a large,
branching, tricoloured feather.

After the parade, the following, I understand, is
the *étiquette* usually observed in the palace. The
Chief Consul first gives audience to the general-
officers, next to the field-officers, to those belonging to the garrison, and to a few petitioners.
He then returns to the fourth apartment, where

---

* *De l'État de la France, à la fin de l'an VIII.* page 270.
† *Ibid.* page 274.

the counsellors of state assemble. Being arrived there, notice is sent to the diplomatic corps, who meet in a room on the ground-floor of the palace, called *La Salle des Ambassadeurs.* They immediately repair to the levee-room, and, after paying their personal respects to the First Consul, they each introduce to him such persons, belonging to their respective nations, as they may think proper. Several were this day presented by the Imperial, Russian, and Danish ambassadors: the British minister, Mr. Jackson, has not yet presented any of his countrymen, nor will he, in all probability, as he is merely a *locum tenens.* After the levée, the Chief Consul generally gives a dinner of from one hundred and fifty to two hundred covers, to which all those who have received arms of honour, are invited.

Before I left the palace, I observed the lady above-mentioned, who had presented the memorial, seated in one corner of the room, all in tears, and betraying every mark of anxious grief: she was pale, and with her hair dishevelled; but, though by no means handsome, her distressed situation excited a lively interest in her favour. On inquiry, I was informed that it was Madame Bourmont, the wife of a Vendean chief, condemned to perpetual imprisonment for a breach of the convention into which he had jointly entered with the agents of the French government.

Having now accomplished my object, when the crowd was somewhat dispersed, I retired to enjoy the fine weather by a walk in the

CHAMPS ELYSÉES.

After traversing the garden of the *Tuileries* and the *Place de la Concorde*, from east to west, you arrive at this fashionable summer promenade. It is planted with trees in quincunx; and although, in particular points of view, this gives it a symmetrical air; yet, in others, the hand of art is sufficiently concealed to deceive the eye by a representation of the irregular beauties of nature. The French, in general, admire the plan of the garden of the *Tuileries*, and think the distribution tasteful; but, when the trees are in leaf, all prefer the *Champs Elysées*, as being more rural and more inviting. This spot, which is very extensive, as you may see by the Plan of Paris, has frequently been chosen for the scene of national fêtes, for which it is, in many respects, better calculated than the *Champ de Mars*. However, from its proximity to the great road, the foliage is imbrowned by the dust, and an idea of aridity intrudes itself on the imagination from the total absence of water. The sight of that refreshing element recreates the mind, and communicates a powerful attraction even to a wilderness.

In fact, at this season of the year, the *Champs Elysées* resemble a desert; but, in summer, they present one of the most agreeable scenes that can be imagined. In temporary buildings, of a tasteful construction, you then find here *restaurateurs*, &c, where all sorts of refreshments may be procured, and rooms where " the merry dance" is kept up with no common spirit. Swings and roundabouts are also erected, as well as different machines for exercising the address of those who are fond of running at a ring, and other sports. Between the road leading to *l'Étoile*, the *Bois de Boulogne*, &c, and that which skirts the Seine, formerly called the *Cours de la Reine*, is a large piece of turf, where, in fine weather, and especially on Sundays, the Parisian youths amuse themselves at foot-ball, prison-bars, and long tennis. Here, too, boys and girls assemble, and improve their growth and vigour by dancing, and a variety of healthful diversions; while their relations and friends, seated on the grass, enjoy this interesting sight, and form around each group a circle which is presently increased by numbers of admiring spectators.

Under the shade of the trees, on the right hand, as you face the west, an immense concourse of both sexes and all ages is at the same time collected. Those who prefer sitting to walking occupy three long rows of chairs, set out for hire, three deep on each side, and forming a lane through which the great body of walkers parade. This promenade may then be said to deserve the appellation of *Elysian Fields,* from the number of handsome women who resort hither. The variety of their dresses and figures, the satisfaction which they express in seeing and being seen, their anxious desire to please, which constitutes their happiness and that of our sex, the triumph which animates the countenance of those who eclipse their rivals; all this forms a diversified and amusing picture, which fixes attention, and gives birth to a thousand ideas respecting the art and coquetry of women, as well as what beauty loses or gains by adopting the ever-varying caprices of fashion. Here, on a fine summer's evening, are now to be seen, I am told, females displaying almost as much luxury of dress as used to be exhibited in the days of the monarchy. The essential difference is that the road in the centre is not now, as in those times, covered with brilliant equipages; though every day seems to produce an augmentation of the number of private carriages.

At the entrance of the *Champs Elysées* are placed the famous groups of Numidian horses, held in by their vigorous and masterly conductors, two *chefs d'œuvre* of modern art, copied from the group of *Monte-Cavallo* at Rome. By order of the Directory, these statues were brought from *Marly*, where they ornamented the terrace. They are each of them cut out of a block of the most faultless Carrara marble. On the pedestal on which they stood at that once-royal residence, was engraved the name of Costou, 1745, without any surname: but, as there were two brothers of that name, *Nicolas* and *Guillaume*, natives of Lyons, and both excellent sculptors, it is become a matter of doubt by which of them these master-pieces were executed; though the one died in 1733, and the other in 1746. It is conjectured, however, that fraternal friendship induced them to share the fame arising from these capital productions, and that they worked at them in common till death left the survivor the task of finishing their joint labour.

To whichever of the two the merit of the execution may be due, it is certain that the fiery, ungovernable spirit of the horses, as well as the exertion of vigour, and the triumph of strength in their conductors, is very happily expressed. The subject has frequently afforded a comparison to politicians. " These statues," say some observers, " appear to be the emblem " of the French people, over whom it is ne- " cessary to keep a tight hand."—" It is to be

" apprehended," add others, " that the reins,
" which the conductors hold with so powerful
" an arm, are too weak to check these un-
" governable animals."

LETTER XXX.

Paris, December 8, 1801.

You desire that I will favour you with a particular account of the means employed to transfer from pannel to canvas those celebrated pictures which I mentioned in my letter of the 13th ult°. Like many other things that appear simple on being known, so is this process; but it is not, on that account, the less ingenious and difficult in execution.

Such is the great disadvantage of the art of painting that, while other productions of genius may survive the revolution of ages, the creations of the pencil are intrusted to perishable wood or canvas. From the effect of heat, humidity, various exhalations to which they may be carelessly exposed, and even an unperceived neglect in the priming of the pannel or cloth, master-pieces are in danger of disappearing for ever. Happy, then, is it for the arts that this invaluable discovery has been lately brought to so great a degree of perfection, and that the restoration of several capital pictures having been confided to men no less skilful than enlightened, they have thus succeeded in rescuing them from approaching and inevitable destruction.

Of all the fruits of the French conquests, not a painting was brought from Lombardy, Rome, Florence, or Venice, that was not covered with an accumulation of filth, occasioned by the smoke of the wax-tapers and incense used in the ceremonies of the catholic religion. It was therefore necessary to clean and repair them; for to bring them to France, without rendering them fit to be exhibited, would have answered no better purpose than to have left them in Italy. One of those which particularly fixed the attention of the Administration of the CENTRAL MUSEUM OF THE ARTS, was the famous picture by RAPHAEL, taken from the *Chiesa delle Contesse* at Foligno, and thence distinguished by the appellation of the

MADONNA DI FOLIGNO.

This *chef d'œuvre* was in such a lamentable state of decay, that the French commissioners who selected it, were under the necessity of pasting paper over it in order to prevent the scales, which curled up on many parts of its surface, from falling off during its conveyance to to Paris. In short, had not the saving hand of art interposed, this, and other monuments of the transcendent powers of the Italian school, marked by the corroding tooth of Time, would soon have entirely perished.

As this picture could not be exhibited in its injured state, the Administration of the Museum determined that it should be repaired. They accordingly requested the Minister of the Interior to cause this important operation to be attended by Commissioners chosen from the National Institute. The Class of Physical and Mathematical Sciences of that learned Society appointed to this task, GUYTON and BERTHOLLET, chymists, and the Class of Literature and Fine Arts named VINCENT and TAUNAY, painters.

These Commissioners, in concert with the Administration, having ascertained the state of the picture, it was unanimously agreed that the only mean of saving it would be to remove it from the worm-eaten pannel on which it was painted. It was, besides, necessary to ascertain the safety of the process, in order that, without exciting the apprehensions of the lovers of the arts, it might be applied to other pictures which required it.

The Report of the four Commissioners before-named, respecting the restoration of the

Madonna di Foligno, has been adopted by the Classes to which they respectively belong, and is to be made to the National Institute at their next public sitting on the 15th of Nivose (5th of January, 1802).

In order to make you perfectly acquainted with the whole of the process, I shall transcribe, for your satisfaction, that part of the Report immediately connected with the art of restoring damaged or decayed paintings. This labour, and the success by which it was attended, are really a memorial of what the genius and industry of the French can achieve. To all those who, like you, possess valuable collections, such information cannot but be particularly interesting.

" The desire of repairing the outrages of time has unfortunately accelerated the decay of several pictures by coarse repainting and bad varnish, by which much of the original work has been covered. Other motives, too, have conspired against the purity of the most beautiful compositions: a prelate has been seen to cause a discordant head of hair to conceal the charms of a Magdalen."

" Nevertheless, efficacious means of restoration have been discovered: a painting, the convass of which is decayed, or the pannel worm-eaten, is transferred to a fresh cloth; the profane touches of a foreign pencil are made to disappear; the effaced strokes are reinserted with scrupulous nicety; and life is restored to a picture which was disfigured, or drawing near to its end. This art has made great progress, especially in Paris, and experienced recent improvement under the superintendance of the Administration of the Museum; but it is only with a religious respect that any one can venture on an operation which may always give rise to a fear of some change in the drawing or colouring, above all when the question is to restore a picture by RAPHAEL."*

" The restoration may be divided into two parts; the one, which is composed of mechanical operations, whose object is to detach the painting from the ground on which it is fixed, in order to transfer it to a fresh one; the other, which consists in cleaning the surface of the painting from every thing that can tarnish it, in restoring the true colouring to the picture, and in repairing the parts destroyed, by tints skilfully blended with the primitive touches. Thence the distinctive division of the mecha-

---

* It may not be amiss to observe that RAPHAEL employed the *impasto* colour but in few of his pictures, of which the *Transfiguration* is one wherein it is the most conspicuous: his other productions are painted with great transparency, the colours being laid on a white ground; which rendered still more difficult the operation above-mentioned. *Note of the Author.*

nical operations, and of the art of painting, which will be the object of the two parts of this Report. The former particularly engaged the attention of the Commissioners of the *Class of Sciences*; and the latter, which required the habit of handling a scientific pencil, fell to the share of the Commissioners of the *Class of Fine Arts*."

FIRST PART.

" Although the mechanical labour is subdivided into several operations, it was wholly intrusted to Citizen HACQUINS, on whose intelligence, address, and skill, it is our duty to bestow every commendation."

" The picture represents the Virgin Mary, the infant Jesus, St. John, and several other figures of different sizes. It was painted on a pannel of $1\frac{1}{4}$ inches in thickness: a crack extended from its circumference to the left foot of the infant Jesus: it was $4\frac{1}{2}$ lines wide at its upper part, and diminished progressively to the under: from this crack to the right hand border, the surface formed a curve whose greatest bend was 2 inches $5\frac{1}{2}$ lines, and from the crack to the other border, another curve bending 2 inches. The picture was scaling off in several places, and a great number of scales had already detached themselves; the painting was, besides, worm-eaten in many parts."

"It was first necessary to render the surface even: to effect this, a gauze was pasted on the painting, and the picture was turned on its face. After that, Citizen Hacquins made, in the thickness of the wood, several grooves at some distance from each other, and extending from the upper extremity of the bend to the place where the pannel presented a more level surface. Into these grooves he introduced little wooden wedges; he then covered the whole surface with wet cloths, which he took care to remoisten. The action of the wedges, which swelled by the moisture against the softened pannel, compelled the latter to resume its primitive form: both edges of the crack before-mentioned being brought together, the artist had recourse to glue, in order to unite the two separated parts. During the desiccation, he laid oak bars across the picture, for the purpose of keeping the pannel in the form which he wished it to assume."

"The desiccation being effected slowly, the artist applied a second gauze on the first, then successively two thicknesses of grey blotting paper."

"This preparation (which the French artists call *cartonnage*) being dry, he laid the picture with its face downward on a table, to which he carefully confined it; he next proceeded to the separation of the wood on which the painting was fixed."

"The first operation was executed by means of two saws, one of which acted perpendicularly; and the other, horizontally: the work of the two saws being terminated, the pannel was found to be reduced to the thickness of $4\frac{1}{4}$ lines. The artist then made use of a plane of a convex form on its breadth: with this instrument he planed the pannel in an oblique direction, in order to take off very short shavings, and to avoid the grain of the wood: by these means he reduced the pannel to $\frac{2}{3}$ of a line in thickness. He then took a flat plane with a toothed iron, whose effect is much like that of a rasp which reduces wood into dust: in this manner he contrived to leave the pannel no thicker than a sheet of paper."

"In that state, the wood was successively moistened with clear water, in small compartments, which disposed it to detach itself: then the artist separated it with the rounded point of a knife-blade."

"The picture, thus deprived of all the wood, presented to the eye every symptom of the injury which it had sustained. It had formerly been repaired; and, in order to fasten again the parts which threatened to fall off, recourse had been had to oils and varnishes. But those ingredients passing through the intervals left by such parts of the picture as were reduced to curling scales, had been extended in the impression to the paste, on which the painting rested, and had rendered the real restoration more difficult, without producing the advantageous effect which had thence been expected."

"The same process would not serve for separating the parts of the impression which had been indurated by varnishes, and those where the paste had remained unmixed: it was necessary to moisten the former for some time in small compartments: when they were become sufficiently softened, the artist separated them with the blade of his knife: the others were more easily separated by moistening them with a flannel, and rubbing them slightly. It required all the address and patience of Citizen HACQUINS to leave nothing foreign to the work of the original painter: at length the outline of RAPHAEL was wholly exposed to view, and left by itself."

"In order to restore a little suppleness to the painting, which was too much dried, it was rubbed all over with carded cotton imbibed with oil, and wiped with old muslin: then white lead, ground with oil, was substituted in the room of the impression made by paste, and fixed by means of a soft brush."

" After being left to dry for three months, a gauze was glued on the impression made by oil; and on the latter, a fine canvas."

" When this canvas was dry, the picture was detached from the table, and turned, in order to remove the *cartonnage* from it with water; this operation being effected, the next proceeding was to get rid of the appearance of the inequalities of the surface arising from the curling up of its parts: for that purpose, the artist successively applied on the inequalities, flour-paste diluted. Then having put a greasy paper on the moistened part, he laid a hot iron on the parts curled up, which became level: but it was not till after he had employed the most unequivocal signs to ascertan the suitable degree of heat, that he ventured to come near the painting with the iron."

" It has been seen that the painting, disengaged from its impression made by paste and from every foreign substance, had been fixed on an impression made by oil, and that a level form had been given to the uneven parts of its surface. This master-piece was still to be solidly applied on a new ground: for that, it was necessary to paste paper over it again, detach it from the temporary gauze which had been put on the impression, add a new coat of oxyde of lead and oil, apply to it a gauze rendered very supple, and on the latter, in like manner done over with a preparation of lead, a raw cloth, woven all in one piece, and impregnated, on its exterior surface, with a resinous substance, which was to confine it to a similar canvass fixed on the stretching-frame. This last operation required that the body of the picture, disengaged from its *cartonnage,* or paper facing, and furnished with a new ground, should be exactly applied to the cloth done over with resinous substances, at the same time avoiding every thing that might hurt it by a too strong or unequal extension, and yet compelling every part of its vast extent to adhere to the cloth strained on the stretching-frame. It is by all these proceedings that the picture has been incorporated with a ground more durable than the original one, and guarded against the accidents which had produced the injuries. It was then subjected to restoration, which is the object of the second part of this Report."

" We have been obliged to confine ourselves to pointing out the successive operations, the numerous details of which we have attended; we have endeavoured to give an idea of this interesting art, by which the productions of the pencil may be indefinitely perpetuated, in order only to state the grounds of the confidence that it has appeared to us to merit."

Second Part.

"After having given an account of the mechanical operations, employed with so much success in the first part of the restoration of the picture by RAPHAEL, it remains for us to speak of the second, the restoration of the painting, termed by the French artists *restauration pittoresque*. This part is no less interesting than the former. We are indebted to it for the reparation of the ravages of time and of the ignorance of men, who, from their unskilfulness, had still added to the injury which this master-piece had already suffered.

"This essential part of the restoration of works of painting, requires, in those who are charged with it, a very delicate eye, in order to know how to accord the new tints with the old, a profound knowledge of the proceedings employed by masters, and a long experience, in order to foresee, in the choice and use of colours, what changes time may effect in the new tints, and consequently prevent the discordance which would be the result of those changes.

"The art of restoring paintings likewise requires the most scrupulous nicety to cover no other than the damaged parts, and an extraordinary address to match the work of the restoration with that of the master, and, as it were, replace the first priming in all its integrity, concealing the work to such a degree that even an experienced eye cannot distinguish what comes from the hand of the artist from what belongs to that of the master.

" It is, above all, in a work of the importance of that of which we are speaking, that the friends of the arts have a right to require, in its restoration, all the care of prudence and the exertion of the first talents. We feel a real satisfaction in acquainting you with the happy result of the discriminating wisdom of the Administration of the CENTRAL MUSEUM OF THE ARTS; who, after having directed and superintended the first part of the restoration, employed in the second, that of the painting (which we call *pittoresque*) Citizen ROESER, whose abilities in this line were long known to them, and whose repeated success had justified their confidence."

After having assured the Institute that they consider the *pittoresque* part of the restoration of the *Madonna di Foligno* as pure as it was possible to be desired, the Commissioners proceed to call their attention to some discordance in the original design and colouring of this *chef d'œuvre*, and to make on it some critical observations. This they do in order to prevent any doubts which might arise in the mind of observers, and lead them to imagine that the restoration had, in any manner, impaired the work of RAPHAEL.

They next congratulate themselves on having at length seen this masterpiece of the immortal RAPHAEL restored to life, shining in all its lustre, and through such means, that there ought no longer to remain any fear respecting the recurrence of those accidents whose ravages threatened to snatch it for ever from general admiration.

They afterwards terminate their Report in the following words:

" The Administration of the CENTRAL MUSEUM OF THE ARTS, who have, by their knowledge, improved the art of restoration, will, no doubt, neglect nothing to preserve that art in all its integrity; and, notwithstanding repeated success, they will not permit the application of it but to pictures so injured, that there are more advantages in subjecting them to a few risks inseparable from delicate and numerous operations, than in abandoning them to the destruction by which they are threatened. The invitation which the Administration of the Museum gave to the National Institute to attend the restoration of the *Madonna di Foligno* by RAPHAEL, is to us a sure pledge that the enlightened men of whom it is composed, felt that they owed an account of their vigilance to all the connoisseurs in Europe.

LETTER XXXI.

Paris, December 10, 1801.

" OF all the bridges that were ever built," says Sterne, " the whole world, who have passed over " it, must own that the noblest - - - the grand- " est - - - the lightest - - - the longest - - - " the broadest that ever conjoined land and land " together upon the face of the terraqueous " globe, is the

" PONT NEUF."

The *Pont Neuf* is certainly the largest, and, on account of its situation*, the most conspicuous, and most frequented of any of the bridges in Paris; but, in the environs of the capital, is one which surpasses them all. This is the *Pont de Neuilly.*

The first stone of the *Pont Neuf* was laid by Henry III in 1578, and the foundation of the piles was begun to be formed on the opposite side, when the troubles of the League forced Du CERCEAU, the architect, to withdraw to fo-

---

* By the Plan of Paris, it will be seen that the *Pont Neuf* lies at the west point of the Island called *L'Ile du Palais*, and is, as it were, in the very centre of the capital.

reign countries. The work was not resumed till the reign of Henry IV, who ordered it to be continued under the direction of MARCHAND; but, owing to various causes, the *Pont Neuf* was not finished till 1674.

The length of this bridge is one thousand and twenty feet, and its breadth seventy-two; which is sufficient to admit of five carriages passing abreast. It is formed of twelve arches, seven of which are on the side of the *Louvre*, and five on the side of the *Quai des Augustins*, extending over the two channels of the river, which is wider in this place, from their junction.

In 1775, the parapets were repaired, and the foot-way lowered and narrowed. SOUFFLOT, the architect of the Pantheon, availed himself of this opportunity to build, on the twenty half-moons which stand immediately above each pile, as many rotundas, in stone, to serve as shops. On the outside, above the arches, is a double cornice, which attracts the eye of the connoisseur in architecture, notwithstanding its mouldering state, on account of the *fleurons* in the antique style, and the heads of Sylvans, Dryads, and Satyrs, which serve as supports to it, at the distance of two feet from each other.

As the mole that forms a projection on this bridge between the fifth and seventh arch, stands facing the *Place Dauphine*, which was built by

Henry IV, it was the spot chosen for erecting to him a statue. This was the first public monument of the kind that had been raised in honour of French kings. Under the first, second, and third race, till the reign of Lewis XIII, if the statue of a king was made, it was only for the purpose of being placed on his tomb, or else at the portal of some church, or royal residence which he had either built or repaired.

Parisians and strangers used to admire this equestrian statue of Henry IV., and before the revolution, all agreed in taking him for the model of goodness. In proof of his popularity, we are told, in the *Tableau de Paris*, that a beggar was one day following a passenger along the foot-way of the *Pont Neuf:* it was a festival. " In the " name of St. Peter," said the mendicant, " in " the name of St. Joseph, in the name of the " Virgin Mary, in the name of her divine Son, " in the name of God?" Being arrived before the statue of the conqueror of the League, " In " the name of *Henri quatre*," exclaimed he, " in the name of *Henri quatre?*"—" Here!" said the passenger, and he gave him a louis d'or.

Unquestionably, no monarch that ever sat on the throne of France was so popular as *Henri quatre*; and his popularity was never eclipsed by any of his successors. Even amidst the rage of the revolutionary storm, the military still held his memory in veneration. On opening the sepultures at St. Denis in 1793, the coffin of Henry IV was the first that was taken out of the vault of the Bourbons. Though he died in 1610, his body was found in such preservation that the features of his face were not altered. A soldier, who was present at the opening of the coffin, moved by a martial enthusiasm, threw himself on the body of this warlike prince, and, after a considerable pause of admiration, he drew his sabre, and cut off a long lock of Henry's beard, which was still fresh, at the same time exclaiming, in very energetic and truly-military terms: " And " I too am a French soldier! In future I will " have no other whiskers." Then placing this valuable lock on his upper lip, he withdrew, adding emphatically: " Now I am sure to conquer the " enemies of France, and I march to victory."

In Paris, all the statues of kings had fallen, while that of Henry IV still remained erect. It was for some time a matter of doubt whether it should be pulled down. " The poem " of the *Henriade* pleaded in its favour;" but, says Mercier, " he was an ancestor of the per-" jured king." Then, and not till then, this venerated statue underwent the same fate.

It has been generally believed that the deed of Ravaillac was dictated by fanaticism, or that he was the instrument employed by the Marchioness of Verneuil and the Duke of Epernon for assassinating that monarch. However, it stands recorded, I am told, in a manuscript found in the National Library, that Ravaillac killed Henry IV because he had seduced his sister, and abandoned her when pregnant. Thus time, that affords a clue to most mysteries, has also solved this historical enigma.

This statue of Henry IV was erected on the 23d of August, 1624. To have insulted it, would, not long since, have been considered as a sacrilege; but, after having been mutilated and trodden under foot, this once-revered image found its way to the mint or the cannon-foundry. On its site now stands an elegant coffeehouse, whence you may enjoy a fine view of the stately buildings which adorn the quays that skirt the river.

While admiring the magnificence of this *coup d'œil*, an Englishman cannot avoid being struck by the multitude of washerwomen, striving to expel the dirt from linen, by means of *battoirs*, or wooden battledores. On each side of the Seine are to be seen some hundreds hard at work, ranged in succession, along the sides of low barks, equal in length to our west-country barges. Such is the vigour of their arm that, for the circumference of half-a-mile, the air resounds with the noise of their incessant blows. After beating the linen for some time in this merciless manner, they scrub it with a hard brush, in lieu of soaping it, so that a shirt which has passed through their hands five or six times is fit only for making lint. No wonder then that Frenchmen, in general, wear coarse linen: a hop-sack could not long resist so severe a process. However, it must be confessed, that some good arises from this evil. These washerwomen insensibly contribute to the diffusion of knowledge; for, as they are continually reducing linen into rags, they cannot but considerably increase the supply of that article for the manufacture of paper.

Compared to the Thames, even above bridge, the Seine is far from exhibiting a busy scene; a few rafts of wood for fuel, and some barges occasionally in motion, now and then relieve the monotony of its rarely-ruffled surface. At this moment, its navigation is impeded from its stream being swollen by the late heavy rains. Hence much mischief is apprehended to the country lying contiguous to its banks. Many parts of Paris are overflowed: in some streets where carriages must pass, horses are up to their belly in water; while pedestrians are under the necessity of availing themselves of the temporary bridges, formed with tressels and planks, by the industrious Savoyards. The ill consequences of this inundation are already felt, I assure you; being engaged to dinner yesterday in the *Rue St. Florentin*, I was obliged to step into a punt in order to reach the bottom of the stair-case; and what was infinitely more mortifying to the master of the house, was, that, the cellar being rendered inaccessible, he was deprived of the satisfaction of regaling his guests with his best claret.

On the right hand side of the *Pont Neuf*, in crossing that bridge from the *Quai de l'École* to the *Quai de Conti*, is a building, three stories high, erected on piles, with its front standing between the first and second arches. It is called

LA SAMARITAINE.

Over the dial is a gilt group, representing Jesus Christ and the Samaritan woman near Jacob's well, pourtrayed by a basin into which falls a sheet of water issuing from a shell above. Under the basin is the following inscription:

Fons Hortorum
Puteus aquarum viventium.

These words of the Gospel are here not unaptly applied to the destination of this building, which is to furnish water to the garden of the *Tuileries*, whose basins were not, on that account, the less dry half the year. The water is raised by means of a pump, and afterwards distributed, by several conduits, to the *Louvre* and the *Palais du Tribunat*, as well as to the *Tuileries*.

In the middle, and above the arch, is a superstructure of timber-work faced with gilt lead, where are the bells of the clock and those of chimes, which ought to play every half-hour.

This tasteless edifice interrupts the view in every direction, and as it is far from being an ornament to the *Pont Neuf*, no one could now regret its entire removal. Under the old *régime*, however, it was nothing less than a government.

Among the functions of the governor, were included the care of the clock, which scarcely ever told the hour, and of the chimes, which were generally out of order. When these chimes used to delight Henry IV, it is to be presumed that they were kept in better tune. It was customary to make them play during all public ceremonies, and especially when the king passed.

" The *Pont Neuf* is in the city of Paris what the heart is in the human body, the centre of motion and circulation: the flux and reflux of inhabitants and strangers crowd this passage in such a manner, that, in order to meet persons one is looking for, it is sufficient to walk here for an hour every day. Here the *mou-*

chards, or spies of the police, take their station; and, when at the expiration of a few days, they see not their man, they positively affirm that he is not in Paris."

Such was the animated picture of the *Pont Neuf*, as drawn by Mercier in 1788, and such it really was before the revolution. At present, though this bridge is sometimes thronged with passengers, it presents not, according to my observation, that almost continual crowd and bustle for which it was formerly distinguished. No stoppage now from the press of carriages of any description, no difficulty in advancing quickly through the concourse of pedestrians. Fruit-women, hucksters, hawkers, pedlars, indeed, together with ambulating venders of lottery-tickets, and of *tisane*, crying " *à la fraiche! Qui veut boire?*" here take their stand as they used, though not in such numbers.

But the most sensible diminution is among the shoe-blacks, who stand in the carriage-way, and, with all their implements before them, range themselves along the edge of the very elevated *trottoir* or foot-pavement. The *décrotteurs* of the *Pont Neuf* were once reputed masters of the art: their foresight was equal to their dexterity and expedition. For the very moderate sum of two *liards*, they enabled an abbé or a poet to present himself in the gilded apartments of a dutchess. If it rained, or the rays of the sun were uncommonly ardent, they put into his hand an umbrella to protect the economy of his head-dress during the operation. Their great patrons have disappeared, and, in lieu of a constant succession of customers, the few *décrotteurs* who remain at their old-established station, are idle half the day for want of employment.

These Savoyards generally practise more than one trade, as is indicated by the *enseigne* which is affixed, on a short pole, above their tool-box.

> La France tond les
> chiens coupe les chats
> proprement et sa femme
> vat en ville et en campagne

Change the name only, and such is, line for line, letter for letter, the most ordinary style of their *annonce*. It is, however, to be presumed, that the republican belles have adopted other favourites instead of dogs and cats; for no longer is seen, as in the days of royalty, the aspiring or favoured lover carrying his mistress's lap-dog in the public promenades. In fact, the business of dog-shearing, &c. seems full as dead in this part of Paris as that of shoe-cleaning. The *artists* of the *Pont Neuf* are, consequently, chop-fallen; and hilarity which formerly shone on their countenance, is now succeeded by gloomy sadness.

At the foot of the *Pont Neuf*, on the *Quai de la Féraille*, recruiting-officers used to unfurl their inviting banners, and neglect nothing that art and cunning could devise to insnare the ignorant, the idle, and the unwary. The means which they sometimes employed were no less whimsical than various: the lover of wine was invited to a public-house, where he might intoxicate himself; the glutton was tempted by the sight of ready-dressed turkies, fowls, sausages, &c. suspended to a long pole; and the youth, inclined to libertinism, was seduced by the meretricious allurements of a well-tutored doxy. To second these manœuvres, the recruiter followed the object of his prey with a bag of money, which he chinked occasionally, crying out " *Qui en veut?*" and, in this manner, an army of heroes was completed. It is almost superfluous to add, that the necessity of such stratagems is obviated, by the present mode of raising soldiers by conscription.

Before we quit the *Pont Neuf*, I must relate to you an adventure which, in the year 1786, happened to our friend P———, who is now abroad, in a situation of considerable trust and emolument. He was, at that time, a half-pay subaltern in the British army, and visited Paris, as well from motives of economy as from a desire of acquiring the French language. Being a tall, fresh-coloured young man, as he was one day crossing the *Pont Neuf*, he caught the eye of a recruiting-officer, who followed him from the *Quai de la Féraille* to a coffee-house, in the *Rue St. Honoré*, which our Englishman frequented for the sake of reading the London newspapers. The recruiter, with all the art of a crimp combined with all the politeness of a courtier, made up to him under pretence of having relations in England, and endeavoured, by every means in his power, to insinuate himself into the good graces of his new acquaintance. P———, by way of sport, encouraged the eagerness of the recruiter, who lavished on him every sort of civility; peaches in brandy, together with the choicest refreshments that a Parisian coffee-house could afford, were offered to him and accepted: but not the smallest hint was dropped of the motive of all this more than friendly attention. At length, the recruiter, thinking that he might venture to break the ice, depicted, in the most glowing colours, the pleasures and advantages of a military life, and declared ingenuously that nothing would make him so happy as to have our countryman P——— for his comrade. Without absolutely accepting or rejecting his offer, P——— begged a little delay in order to consider of the matter, at the same time hinting that there was, at that moment, a small obstacle to his inclination. The recruiter, like a pioneer, promised to remove it, grasped his hand with joy and exultation, and departed, singing a song of the same import as that of Serjeant Kite:

> " Come brave boys, 'tis one to ten,
> " But we return all gentlemen."

In a few days, the recruiter again met Mr. P——— at his accustomed rendezvous; when, after treating him with coffee, liqueur, &c. he came directly to the point, but neglected not to introduce into his discourse every persuasive allurement. P———, finding himself pushed home, reminded the recruiter of the obstacle to which he had before alluded, and, to convince him of its existence, put into his hand His Britannic Majesty's commission. The astonishment and confusion of the French recruiter were so great that he was unable to make any reply; but instantly retired, venting a tremendous ejaculation.

LETTER XXXII.

Paris, December 13, 1801.

IN this gay capital, balls succeed to balls in an almost incredible variety. There are actually an immense number every evening; so that persons fond of the amusement of dancing have full scope for the exercise of their talents in Paris. It is no longer a matter of surprise to me that the French women dance so well, since I find that they take frequent lessons from their master, and, almost every night, they are at a dance of one kind or another. Added to this, the same set o dances lasts the whole season, and go where you will, you have a repetition of the same. However, this detracts not in the smallest degree from the merit of those Parisian belles who shine as first-rate dancers. The mechanical part of the business, as Mr. C――g would call it, they may thus acquire by constant practice; but the decorative part, if I may so term the fascinating grace which they display in all their movements, is that the result of study, or do they hold it from the bounteous hand of Nature?

While I am speaking of balls, I must inform you that, since the private ball of which I gave you so circumstantial an account, I have been at several others, also private, but of a different complexion; inasmuch as pleasure, not profit, was the motive for which they were given, and the company was more select; but, in point of general arrangement, I found them so like the former, that I did not think it worth while to make any one of them the subject of a distinct letter. In this line Madame Recamier takes the lead; but though her balls are more splendid, those of Madame Soubiran are more agreeable. On the 21st of Frimaire, which was yesterday, I was at a public ball of the most brilliant kind now known in Paris. It was the first of the subscription given this season, and, from the name of the apartment where it is held, it is styled the

BAL DU SALON DES ÉTRANGERS.

Midnight is the general hour for the commencement of such diversions; but, owing to the long train of carriages setting down company at this ball, it was near two o'clock before I could arrive at the scene of action, in the *Rue Grange Batelière*, near the Boulevards.

After I alighted and presented my ticket, some time elapsed before I could squeeze into the room where the dancing was going forward. The spectators were here so intermixed with the dancers, that they formed around them a border as complete as a frame to a picture.

It is astonishing that, under such circumstances, a Parisian Terpsichore, far from being embarrassed, lays fresh claim to your applause. With mathematical precision, she measures with her eye the space to which she is restricted by the curiosity of the by-standers. Rapid as lightning, she springs forward till the measure recalling her to the place she left, she traces her orbit, like a planet, at the same time revolving on her axis. Sometimes her " light, fantastic toe" will approach within half an inch of your foot; nay, you shall almost feel her breath on your cheek, and still she will not touch you, except, perhaps, with the skirt of her floating tunic.

Among the female part of the company, I observed several lovely women; some, who might have been taken for Asiatic sultanas, irradiating the space around them by the dazzling brilliancy of their ornaments; others, without jewels, but calling in every other aid of dress for the embellishment of their person; and a few, rich in their native charms alone, verifying the expression of the poet. Truth compels me to acknowledge that six or eight English ladies here were totally eclipsed. For the honour of my country, I could have wished for a better specimen of our excellence in female beauty. No women in the world, or at least none that ever I have met with in the different quarters I have visited, are handsomer than the English, in point of complexion and features. This is a fact which Frenchmen themselves admit; but for grace, say they, our countrywomen stand unrivalled. I am rather inclined to subscribe to this opinion. In a well-educated French woman, there is an ease, an affability, a desire to please and be pleased, which not only render her manners peculiarly engaging, but also influence her gait, her gestures, her whole deportment in short, and captivate admiration. Her natural cheerfulness and vivacity spread over her features an animation seldom to be found in our English fair, whose general characteristics are reserve and coldness. Hence that striking expression which exhibits the grace of the French belles to superior advantage.

Although my memory frequently disappoints me when I wish to retain names, I have contrived to recollect those of three of the most remarkable women in the ball-room. I shall therefore commit them to paper before I forget them. Madame la Princesse de Santa-Croce displayed more diamonds than any of her competitors; Mademoiselle Lescot was the best dancer among several ladies renowned for dancing; and Madame Tallien was, on the whole, the handsomest female that I saw in the room. There might possibly be women more beautiful than she at this ball, but they did not come under my observation.

I had previously seen Madame Tallien at the *Opera Buffa*, and was struck by her appearance before I knew who she was. On seeing her again at the *Salon des Étrangers*, I inquired of a French lady of my acquaintance, whose understanding and discernment are pre-eminent, if Madame T—— had nothing to recommend her but her personal attractions? The lady's answer is too remarkable for me not to repeat it, which I will do *verbatim*. " In Madame T——," said she, " beauty, wit, goodness of heart, grace, " talents, all are united. In a gay world, where " malice subsists in all its force, her inconsis- " tencies alone have been talked of, without any " mention being made of the numerous acts of " beneficence which have balanced, if they have " not effaced, her weakness. Would you be- " lieve," continued she, " that, in Paris, the " grand theatre of misconduct, where moral " obligations are so much disregarded, where " we daily commit actions which we condemn in " others; would you believe, that Madame T—— " experiences again and again the mortification of " being deprived of the society of this or that " woman who has nothing to boast of but her " depravity, and cannot plead one act of kind- " ness, or even indulgence? This picture is very " dark," added she, " but the colouring is true." —" What you tell me," observed I, " proves

"that, notwithstanding the irruption of immora-
"lity, attributed to the revolution, it is still ne-
"cessary for a woman to preserve appearances at
"least, in order to be received here in what is
"termed the best company."—" Yes, indeed,"
replied she; " if a woman neglects that main
"point in Paris, she will soon find herself low-
"ered in the opinion of the fashionable world,
"and be at last excluded from even the secondary
"circles. In London, your people of fashion are
"not quite so rigid."—" If a husband chooses
"to wink at his wife's incontinence," rejoined I,
"the world on our side of the water is sufficiently
"complaisant to follow his example. Now with
"you, character is made to depend more on the
"observance of etiquette; and, certainly, hypocrisy,
"when detected, is of more prejudice to society
"than barefaced profligacy."—The lady then resumed thus concerning the subject of my inquiry. " Were some people to hear me," said
she, " they might think that I had drawn you a
"flattering portrait of Madame T—— and say,
"by way of contrast, when the devil became old,
"he turned hermit; but I should answer that,
"for some years, no twenty-four hours have
"elapsed without persons, whom I could name
"on occasion, having begun their daily career by
"going to see her, who saved their life, when, to
"accomplish that object, she hazarded her own."

Here then is an additional instance of the noble energy manifested by women during the most calamitous periods of the revolution. Unappalled by the terrors of captivity or of death, their sensibility impelled them to brave the ferocity of sanguinary tyrants, in order to administer hope or comfort to a parent, a husband, a relation, or a friend. Some of these heroines, though in the bloom of youth, not content with sympathizing in the misfortunes of others, gave themselves up as a voluntary sacrifice, rather than survive those whose preservation they valued more than their own existence. Rome may vaunt her Porcia, or her Cornelia; but the page of her history can produce no such exaltation of the female character as has been exhibited within the last ten years by French women. Examples, like these, of generosity, fortitude, and greatness of soul, deserve to be recorded to the end of time, as they do honour to the sex, and to human nature.

If, according to the scale of Parisian enjoyment, a ball or rout is dull and insipid, *à moins qu'on ne manque d'y être étouffé*, how supreme must have been the satisfaction of the company at the *Salon des Étrangers!* The number present, estimated at seven or eight hundred, occasioned so great a crowd that it was by no means an easy enterprise to pass from one room to another.

Of course, there was no opportunity of viewing the apartments to advantage; however, I saw enough of them to remark that they formed a suite elegantly decorated. Some persons amused themselves with cards, though the great majority neither played nor danced, but were occupied in conversing with their acquaintance. There was no regular supper, but substantial refreshments of every kind were to be procured on paying; and other smaller ones, *gratis.*

From the tickets not being transferable, and the bearer's name being inserted in each of them, the company was far more select than it could have been without such a restriction. Most of the foreign ambassadors, envoys, &c. were present, and many of the most distinguished persons of both sexes in Paris. More regard was paid to the etiquette of dress at this ball than I have ever witnessed here on similar occasions. The ladies, as I have before said, were all *en grande toilette;* and the men with cocked hats, and in shoes and stockings, which is a novelty here, I assure you, as they mostly appear in boots. But what surprised me not a little, was to observe several inconsiderate French youths wear black cockades. Should they persist in such an absurdity, I shall be still more surprised, if they escape admonition from the police. This fashion seemed to be the *ignis fatuus* of the moment; it was never before exhibited in public, and probably will be but of ephemeral duration.

I cannot take leave of this ball without communicating to you a circumstance which occurred there, and which, from the extravagant credulity it exhibits in regard to the effects of sympathy, may possibly amuse you for a moment.

A widow, about twenty years of age, more to be admired for the symmetry of her person, than for the beauty of her features, had, according to the prevailing custom, intrusted her pocket-handkerchief to the care of a male friend, a gentlemanlike young Frenchman of my acquaintance. After dancing, the lady finding herself rather warm, applied for her handkerchief, with which she wiped her forehead, and returned it to the gentleman, who again put it into his pocket. He then danced, but not with her; and, being also heated, he, by mistake, took out the lady's handkerchief, which, when applied to his face, produced, as he fancied, such an effect on him, that, though he had previously regarded her with a sort of indifference, from that moment she engaged all his attention, and he was unable to direct his eyes, or even his thoughts, to any other object.

Some philosophers, as is well known, have maintained that from all bodies there is an emanation of corpuscles, which, coming into contact with our organs, make on the brain an impression, either more or less sympathetic, or of a directly-opposite nature. They tell you, for instance, that of two women whom you behold for the first time, the one the least handsome will sometimes please you most, because there exists a greater *sympathy* between you and her, than between you and the more beautiful woman. Without attempting to refute this absurd doctrine of corpuscles, I shall only observe that this young Frenchman is completely smitten, and declares that no woman in the world can be compared to the widow.

This circumstance reminds me of a still more remarkable effect, ascribed to a similar cause, experienced by Henry III of France. The marriage of the king of Navarre, afterwards Henry IV, with Marguerite de Valois, and that of the Prince de Condé with Marie de Cleves, was celebrated at the *Louvre* on the 10th of August, 1572. Marie de Cleves, then a most lovely creature only sixteen, after dancing much, finding herself incommoded by the heat of the ball-room, retired to a private apartment, where one of the waiting-women of the queen-dowager, seeing her in a profuse perspiration, persuaded her to make an entire change of dress. She had scarcely left the room when the Duke of Anjou, afterwards Henry III, who had also danced a great deal, entered it to adjust his hair, and, being overheated, wiped his face with the first thing that he found, which happened to be the shift she had just taken off. Returning to the ball, he fixed his eyes on her, and contemplated her with as much surprise as if he had never before beheld her. His emotion, his transports, and the attention which he began to pay her, were the more extraordinary, as during the preceding week, which she had passed at court, he appeared indifferent to those very charms which now made on his heart an impression so warm and so lasting. In short, he became insensible to every thing that did not relate to his passion.

His election to the crown of Poland, say historians, far from flattering him, appeared to him an exile, and when he was in that kingdom, absence, far from diminishing his love, seemed to increase it. Whenever he addressed the princess, he pricked his finger, and never wrote to her but with his blood. No sooner was he informed of the death of Charles IX, than he dispatched a courier to assure her that she should soon be queen of France; and, on his return, his thoughts were solely bent on dissolving her marriage with the Prince de Condé, which, on account of the latter being a protestant, he expected to accomplish. But this determination proved fatal to the princess; for, shortly after, she was attacked by a violent illness, attributed to poison, which carried her off in the flower of her age.

No words can paint Henry's despair at this event: he passed several days in tears and groans: and when he was at length obliged to shew himself in public, he appeared in deep mourning, and entirely covered with emblems of death, even to his very shoe-strings.

The Princess de Condé had been dead upwards of four months, and buried in the abbey-church of *St. Germain-des-Prés*, when Henry, on entering the abbey, whither he was invited to a grand entertainment given there by Cardinal de Bourbon, felt such violent tremblings at his heart, that not being able to endure their continuance, he was going away; but they ceased all at once, on the body of the princess being removed from its tomb, and conveyed elsewhere for that evening.

His mother, Catherine de Medicis, by prevailing on him to marry Louise de Vaudemont, one of the most beautiful women in Europe, hoped that she would make him forget her whom death had snatched from him, and he himsel perhaps indulged a similar hope; but the memoirs of those times concur in asserting that the image of the Princess de Condé was never effaced from his heart, and that, to the day of his assassination, which did not happen till seventeen years after, whatever efforts he made to subdue his passion, were wholly unavailing.

Sympathy is a sentiment to which few persons attach the same ideas. It may be classed in three distinct species. The first seems to have an immediate connexion with the senses; the second, with the heart; and the third, with the mind. Although it cannot be denied that the preference we bestow on this or that woman is the result of the one or the other of these, or even of all three together; yet the analysis of our attachments is, in some cases, so difficult as to defy the investigation of reason. For, as the old song says, some lovers

>Will " whimper and whine
>" For lilies and roses,
>" For eyes, lips, and noses,
>" Or a *tip of an ear*."

To cut the matter short, I think it fully proved, by the example of some of the wisest men, that the affections are often captivated by something indefinable, or, in the words of Corneille,

>" *Par un je ne sais quoi—qu'on ne peut exprimer.*"

LETTER XXXIII.

Paris, December 14, 1801.

I have already spoken to you of the *Pont Neuf*. To the east of it, as you will see by the Plan of Paris, the small islands in the middle of the Seine are connected to its banks by several bridges; while to the west, there are two only, though a third is projected, and, previously to the late rise of the river, workmen were employed in driving piles for the foundation. I shall now describe to you these two bridges, beginning with the

PONT NATIONAL.

Before the revolution, this bridge bore the appellation of *Pont Royal*, from its having been built by Lewis XIV, and the expenses defrayed out of his privy purse, to supply the place of one of wood, situated opposite to the *Louvre*, which was carried away by the ice in 1684. It is reckoned one of the most solid bridges in Paris; and, till the existence of the *Pont de la Concorde*, was the only one built across the river, without taking advantage of the islands above-mentioned. It stands on four piles, forming with the two abutments five elliptical arches of a handsome sweep. The span of the centre arch is seventy-two feet, that of the two adjoining sixty-six, and that of the two outer ones sixty. On each side is a raised pavement for foot-passengers, in the middle of which I should imagine that there is breadth sufficient to admit of four carriages passing abreast.

GABRIEL had undertaken this bridge from the designs of MANSARD. The work was already in a state of forwardness, when, at a pile on the side of the *Faubourg St. Germain*, the former could not succeed in excluding the water. A Jacobin, not a clubist, but a Jacobin friar, one FRANÇOIS ROMAIN, who had just finished the bridge of Strasburg, was sent for by the king to the assistance of the French architects, and had the honour of completing the rest of the work.

In the time of Henry IV, there was no bridge over this part of the river, which he used frequently to cross in the first boat that presented itself. Returning one day from the chace, in a plain hunting-dress, and having with him only two or three gentlemen, he stepped into a skiff to be carried over from the *Faubourg St. Germain* to the *Tuileries*. Perceiving that he was not known by the waterman, he asked him what people said of the peace, meaning the peace of Vervins, which was just concluded. "Faith! I " don't understand this sort of peace," answered the waterman; ". there are taxes on every thing,

" and even on this miserable boat, with which I
" have a hard matter to earn my bread."—" And
" does not the king," continued Henry, " in-
" tend to lighten these taxes?"—" The king
" is a good kind of man enough," replied the
waterman; " but he has a lady who must needs
" have so many fine gowns and gewgaws; and
" 'tis we who pay for all that. One would not
" think so much of it either, if she kept to him
" only; but, they say, she suffers herself to be
" kissed by many others."

Henry IV was so amused by this conversation,
that, the next morning, he sent for the waterman,
and made him repeat, word for word, before the
Dutchess of Beaufort, all that he had said the
preceding evening. The Dutchess, much irri-
tated, was for having him hanged. " You are a
" foolish woman," said Henry; " this is a poor
" devil whom poverty has put out of humour.
" In future, he shall pay no tax for his boat,
" and I am convinced that he will then sing
" every day, *Vive Henri! Vive Gabrielle!*"

The north end of the *Pont National* faces
the wing of the palace of the *Tuileries* distinguished by the name of the *Pavillon de Flore*.
From the middle of this bridge, you see the
city in a striking point of view. Here, the celebrated Marshal de Catinat used frequently to
make it part of his morning's amusement to

take his stand, and, while he enjoyed the beauty of the prospect, he opened his purse to the indigent as they passed. That philosophic warrior often declared that he never beheld any thing equal to the *coup d'œil* from this station. In fact, on the one side, you discover the superb gallery of the *Louvre*, extending from that palace to the *Tuileries*; and, on the other, the *Palais du Corps Législatif*, and a long range of other magnificent buildings, skirting the quays on each bank of the river.

These quays, nearly to the number of thirty, are faced with stone, and crowned with parapets breast high, which, in eighteen or twenty different spots, open to form watering-places. The Seine, being thus confined within its bed, the eye is never displeased here by the sight of muddy banks like those of the Thames, or the nose offended by the smell arising from the filth which the common sewers convey to the river.

The galiot of *St. Cloud* regularly takes its departure from the *Pont National*. Formerly, on Sundays and holidays, it used to be a very entertaining sight to contemplate the Paris cocknies crowding into this vessel. Those who arrived too late, jumped into the first empty boat, which frequently overset, either through the unskilfulness of the waterman, or from being overloaded. In consequence of such accidents, the boats of the Seine are prohibited from taking more than sixteen passengers.

Not many years ago, an excursion to *St. Cloud* by water, was an important voyage to some of the Parisians, as you may see by referring to the picture which has been drawn of it, under the title of " *Voyage de Paris à Saint Cloud par* " *mer, et le retour de Saint Cloud à Paris par* " *terre.*"

Following the banks of the Seine, towards the west, we next come to the

PONT DE LA CONCORDE.

This bridge, which had long been wished for and projected, was begun in 1787, and finished in 1790. Its southern extremity stands opposite to the *Palais du Corps Législatif*; while that of the north faces the *Place de la Concorde*, whence it not only derives its present appellation, but has always experienced every change of name to which the former has been subject.

The lightness of its apearance is less striking to those who have seen the *Pont de Neuilly*, in which PERRONET, Engineer of bridges and highways, has, by the construction of arches nearly flat, so eminently distinguished himself. He is likewise the architect of this bridge, which is four hundred and sixty-two feet in length by forty-eight in breadth. Like the *Pont National*, it consists of five elliptical arches. The span of the centre arch is ninety-six feet; that of the collateral ones, eighty-seven; and that of the two others near the abutments, sixty-eight. Under one of the latter is a tracking-path for the facility of navigation.

The piles, which are each nine feet in thickness, have, on their starlings, a species of pillars that support a cornice five feet and a half high. Perpendicularly to these pillars are to rise as many pyramids, which are to be crowned by a parapet with a balustrade: in all these, it is intended to display no less elegance of workmanship than the arches present boldness of design and correctness of execution.

On crossing these bridges, it has often occurred to me, how much the Parisians must envy us the situation of our metropolis. If the Seine, like the Thames, presented the advantage of braving the moderate winds, and of conveying, by regular tides, the productions of the four quarters of the globe to the quays which skirt its banks, what an acquisition would it not be to their puny commerce! What a gratification to their pride to see ships discharging their rich cargoes at the foot of the *Pont de la Concorde!* The project of the canal of

Languedoc must, at first, have apparently presented greater obstacles; yet, by talents and perseverance, these were overcome at a time when the science of machinery of every description was far less understood than it is at the present moment.

It appears from the account of Abbon, a monk of the abbey of St. Germain-des-Prés, that, in the year 885, the Swedes, Danes, and Normans, to the number of forty-five thousand men, came to lay siege to Paris, with seven hundred sail of ships, exclusively of the smaller craft, so that, according to this historian, who was an eye-witness of the fact, the river Seine was covered with their vessels for the space of two leagues.

Julius Cæsar tells us, in the third book of his Commentaries, that, at the time of his conquest of the Gauls, in the course of one winter, he constructed six hundred vessels of the wood which then grew in the environs of Paris; and that, in the following spring, he embarked his army, horse and foot, provisions and baggage, in these vessels, descended the Seine, reached Dieppe, and thence crossed over to England, of which, he says, he made a conquest.

About forty years ago, the scheme engaged much attention. In 1759, the Academy of Sciences, Belles-Lettres, and Arts of Rouen pro-

posed the following as a prize-question: " Was
" not the Seine formerly navigable for vessels
" of greater burden than those which are now
" employed on it; and are there not means
" to restore to it, or to procure it, that ad-
" vantage?" In 1760, the prize was adjourned;
the memoirs presented not being to the satisfaction of the Academy. In 1761, the new
candidates having no better success, the subject
was changed.

However, notwithstanding this discouragement,
we find that, on the 1st of August, 1766, Captain Berthelot actually reached the *Pont Royal*
in a vessel of one hundred and sixty tons burden. When, on the 22d of the same month, he
departed thence, loaded with merchandise, the
depth of the water in the Seine was twenty-five
feet, and it was nearly the same when he
ascended the river. This vessel was seven days
on her passage from Rouen to Paris: but a year
or two ago, four days only were employed in
performing the same voyage by another vessel,
named the *Saumon*.

Engineers have ever judged the scheme practicable, and the estimate of the necessary works,
signed by several skilful surveyors, was submitted
to the ministry of that day. The amount was
forty-six millions of livres (*circa* £1,916,600
sterling).

But what can compensate for the absence of the tide? This is an advantage, which, in a commercial point of view, must ever insure to London a decided superiority over Paris. Were the Seine to-morrow rendered navigable for vessels of large burden, they must, for a considerable distance, be tracked against the stream, or wait till a succession of favourable winds had enabled them to stem it through its various windings; whereas nothing can be more favourable to navigation than the position of London. It has every advantage of a sea-port without its dangers. Had it been placed lower down, that is, nearer to the mouth of the Thames, it would have been more exposed to the insults of a foreign enemy, and also to the insalubrious exhalations of the swampy marshes. Had it been situated higher up the river, it would have been inaccessible to ships of large burden.

Thus, by no effort of human invention or industry can Paris rival London in commerce, even on the supposition that France could produce as many men possessed of the capital and spirit of enterprise, for which our British merchants are at present unrivalled.

Yet, may not this pre-eminence in commercial prosperity lead to our destruction, as the gigantic conquests of France may also pave the way to her ruin? Alas! the experience of ages proves this melancholy truth, which has also been repeated by Raynal: " Commerce," says that celebrated writer, " in the end finds its ruin in the riches " which it accumulates, as every powerful state " lays the foundation of its own destruction in " extending its conquests."

LETTER XXXIV.

Paris, December 16, 1801.

No part of the engagement into which I have entered with you, so fully convinces me of my want of reflection, and shews that my zeal, at the time, got the better of my judgment, as my promising you some ideas on

FRENCH LITERATURE.

It would, I now perceive, be necessary to have inhabited France for several years past, with the determined intention of observing this great empire solely in that single point of view, to be able to keep my word in a manner worthy of you and of the subject. It would be necessary to write a large volume of rational things; and, in a letter, I ought to relate them with conciseness and truth; draw sketches with rapidity, but clearness; in short, express positive results, without deviating from abstractions and generalities, since you require from me, on this subject, no more than a letter, and not a book.

I come to the point. I shall consider literature in a double sense. First, the thing in itself; then, its connexions with the sciences, and the men who govern. In England, it has been thought, or at least insinuated in some of the papers and periodical publications, that literature had been totally annihilated in France within the last twelve years. This is a mistake: its aberrations have been taken for eclipses. It has followed the revolution through all its phases.

Under the Constituent Assembly, the literary genius of the French was turned towards politics and eloquence. There remain valuable monuments of the fleeting existence of that assembly. MIRABEAU, BARNAVE, CAZALÈS, MAURY, and thirty other capital writers, attest this truth. Nothing fell from their lips or their pen that did not bear at the same time the stamp of philosophy and literature.

Under the Legislative Assembly and the Convention, the establishments of the empire of letters were little respected. Literati themselves became victims of the political collisions of their country; but literature was constantly cultivated under several forms. Those who shewed themselves its oppressors, were obliged to assume the refined language which it alone can supply, and that, at the very time when they declared war against it.

Under the Directorial government, France, overwhelmed by the weight of her long misfortunes, first cast her eye on the construction of a new edifice, dedicated to human knowledge in general, under the name of *National Institute*. Literature there collected its remains, and those who cultivate it, as members of this establishment, are not unworthy of their office. Such as are not admitted into this society, notwithstanding all the claims the most generally acknowledged, owe this omission to moral or political causes only, on which I could not touch, without occupying myself about persons rather than the thing itself.

The French revolution, which has levelled so many gigantic fortunes, is said (by its advocates) to have really spread a degree of comfort among the inferior classes. Indeed, if there are in France, as may be supposed, much fewer persons rolling in riches, there are, I am informed, much fewer pining in indigence. This observation, admitting it to be strictly true, may, with great propriety, be applied to French literature. France no longer has a VOLTAIRE or a ROUSSEAU, to wield the sceptre of the literary world; but she has a number of literary degrees of public interest or simple amusement, which are perfectly well filled. Few literati are without employ, and still fewer are beneath their functions. The place of member of the Institute is a real public function remunerated by the State. It is to this cause, and to a few others, which will occur to you beforehand, that we must attribute the character of gravity which literature begins to assume in this country. The prudery of the school of DORAT would here be hissed. Here, people will not quarrel with the Graces; but they will no longer make any sacrifice to them at the expense of common sense.

In this literary republic still exist, as you may well conceive, the same passions, the same littleness, the same intrigues as formerly for arriving at celebrity, and keeping in that envied sphere; but all this makes much less noise at the present juncture. It is this which has induced the belief that literature had diminished its intensity, both in form and object: that is another mistake. The French literati are mostly a noisy class, who love to make themselves conspicuous, even by the clashing of their pretensions; but, to the great regret of several among them, people in this country now attach a rational importance only to their quarrels, which formerly attracted universal attention. The revolution has been so great an event; it has overthrown such great interests; that no one here can any longer flatter himself with exciting a personal interest, except by performing the greatest actions.

I must also make a decisive confession on this matter, and acknowledge that literature, which formerly held the first degree in the scale of the moral riches of this nation, is likely to decline in priority and influence. The sciences have claimed and obtained in the public mind a superiority resulting from the very nature of their object; I mean utility. The title of *savant* is not more brilliant than formerly; but it is more imposing; it leads to consequence, to superior employments, and, above all, to riches. The sciences have done so much for this people during their revolution, that, whether through instinct, or premeditated gratitude, they have declared their partiality towards the *savans*, or men of science, to the detriment of the mere literati. The sciences are nearly allied both to pride and national interest; while literature concerns only the vanity and interest of a few individuals. This difference must have been felt, and of itself alone have fixed the esteem of the public, and graduated their suffrages according to the merit of the objects. Regard being had to their specific importance, I foresee that this natural classification will be attended with happy consequences, both for the sciences and literature.

I have been enabled to observe that very few men of science are unacquainted with the literature of their country, whether for seeking in it pleasing relaxation, or for borrowing from it a magic style, a fluent elocution, a harmony, a pomp of expression, with which the most abstract meditations can no longer dispense to be received favourably by philosophers and men of taste. Very few literati, on the other hand, are unacquainted with philosophy and the sciences, and, above all, with natural knowledge; whether not to be too much in arrear with the age in which they live, and which evidently inclines to the study of Nature, or to give more colour and consistence to their thoughts, by multiplying their degrees of comparison with the eternal type of all that is great and fertile.

It has been so often repeated that HOMER, OSSIAN, and MILTON, knew every thing known in their times; that they were at once the greatest natural philosophers and the best moralists of their age, that this truth has made an impression on most of the adepts in literature; and as the impulse is given, and the education of the present day, by the retrenchment of several unnecessary pursuits, has left, in the mind of the rising generation, vacancies fit to be filled by a great variety of useful acquirements, it appears to me demonstrated, on following analogy, and the gradations of human improvement, that the sciences, philosophy, and literature will some day have in France but one common domain, as they there have at present, with the arts, only one central point of junction.

The French government has flattered the literati and artists, by calling them in great numbers round it and its ministers, either to give their advice in matters of taste, or to serve as a decoration to its power, and an additional lustre to the crown of glory with which it is endeavouring to encircle itself; but, in general, the palpable, substantial, and solid distinctions have been reserved for men of science, chymists, naturalists, and mathematicians: they have seats in the Senate, in the Tribunate, in the Council of State, and in all the Administrations; while Laharpe, the veteran of French literature, is not even a member of the Institute, and is reduced to give lessons, which are, undoubtedly, not only very interesting to the public, but also very profitable to himself, and produce him as much money, at least, as his knowledge has acquired him reputation.

It results from what I have said, that French literature has not experienced any apparent injury from the revolutionary storm: it has only changed its direction and means: it has still remaining talents which have served their time, talents in their maturity, and talents in a state of probation, and of much promise.

Persons of reflection entertain great hopes from the violent shock given to men's minds by the revolution; from that silent inquietude still working in their hearts; from that sap, full of life, circulating with rapidity through this body politic. "The factions are muzzled," say they; " but the factious spirit still ferments " under the curb of power; if means can be " found to force it to evaporate on objects " which belong to the domain of illusion and " sensibility, the result will prove a great blessing " to France, by carrying back to the arts and " to literature, and even to commerce, that exube- " rance of heat and activity which can no longer be " employed without danger on political subjects."

The same men, whom I have just pointed out, affirm that England herself will feel, in her literary and scientific system, a salutary concussion from the direction given here to the public mind. They expect with impatience that the British government will engage in some great measure of public utility, in order that the rivalship subsisting between the two nations on political and military points, which have no longer any object, may soon become, in France, the most active and most powerful vehicle for different parts of her interior improvement.

Of all kinds of literature, *Epic Poetry* is the only one in which France has not obtained such success as to place her on a level with TASSO and MILTON. To make amends, her poets have followed with advantage the steps of ARIOSTO, without being able to surpass him. From this school have issued two modern epic poems: *La guerre des dieux payens contre les dieux chretiens*, by PARNY; and *La conquête de Naples*, by GUDIN. The former is distinguished by an easy versification, and an imagination jocose and fertile, though, certainly, far too licentious. Educated in the school of DORAT, he possesses his redundance and grace, without his fatuity. His elegies are worthy of TIBULLUS; and his fugitive pieces are at once dictated by wit and sentiment: thus it was that CHAULIEU wrote, but with more negligence. The latter has thought to compensate for the energy and grace that should give life to his subject (which he considers only in a playful and satirical light), by a truly tiresome multitude of incidents. Conceive three huge volumes in octavo, for a poem which required but one of a moderate size, and, in them, a versification frequently negligent. These are two serious faults, which the French will not readily overlook. No where are critics more severe, on the one hand, against redundance that is steril, and on the other, respecting the essential composition of verse, which ought always to flow with grace, even when under restraint. Catholicism, however, has no more reason to be pleased with the loose scenes presented in this work, than christianity, in general, has with the licentious pictures of Parny; but Gudin is far less dangerous to Rome, because he will be less read.

Several authors have devoted their labours to *Tragedy*, during the course of the revolution. Chénier has produced a whole theatre, which will remain to posterity, notwithstanding his faults, as he has contrived to cover them with beauties. Arnault and Mercier of Compiegne are two young authors that seem to have been educated in the school of Ducis, who is at this day the father of all the present tragic writers. The pieces which they have produced have met with some success, and are of considerable promise.

Comedy lost a vigorous supporter under the tyranny of Robespierre. This was Fabre d'Eglantine. That poet seldom failed of success, drew none but bold characters, and placed himself, by his own merit, between Molière and Destouches. Colin d'Harleville and Legouvé produce agreeable pieces which succeed.

They paint, with an easy and graceful pencil, the absurdities and humours of society; but their pieces are deficient in plot and action. FABRE D'EGLANTINE pourtrayed, in striking colours, those frightful vices which are beyond the reach of the law. His pieces are strongly woven and easily unravelled. PICARD seems to have taken GOLDONI, the celebrated Venetian comic writer, for his model. Like him, an excellent painter, a writer by impulse, he produces, with wonderful fecundity, a number of interesting comedies, which make the audience laugh till they shed tears, and now and then give great lessons. PALISSOT, CAILHAVA, and MERCIER are still living; but no longer produce any thing striking.

I shall say little of French eloquence. Under the new form of government, orators have less opportunity and less scope for displaying transcendant talents than during the first years of the revolution. Two members of the government, CAMBACÉRÈS and LEBRUN, have distinguished themselves in this career by close, logical argument, bright conceptions, and discriminating genius. BENJAMIN CONSTANT and GUINGUÉNÉ, members of the Tribunate, shewed themselves to advantage last year, as I understand, in some productions full of energy and wisdom. DEMEUNIER and BOISSI D'ANGLAS are already, in the Tribunate, veterans of eloquence; but the man who unites, in this respect, all the approbation of that body, and even of France, is Daunou. In exterior means he is deficient; but his thoughts proceed at once from a warm heart and an open mind, guided by a superior genius; and his expressions manifest the source from which they flow.

Several capital works of the historic kind have made their appearance in France within the last ten years; but, with the exception of those of celebrated voyagers or travellers, such as La Pérouse, Baudin, Sonnini, Labillardière, Olivier, André Michaud, &c. those whose object has been to treat of the arts, sciences, and manners of Greece, such as the travels of Anacharsis, of Pythagoras, or of Antenor; those whose subject has not been confined to France, such as the *Précis de l'histoire générale*, by Anquetil; people ought to be on their guard against the merit even of productions written mediately or immediately on the revolution, its causes, and consequences. The passions are not yet sufficiently calmed for us not to suspect the spirit of party to interpose itself between men and truth. The most splendid talents are frequently in this line only the most faithless guide. It is affirmed, however, that there are a few works which recommend themselves, by the most philosophic impartiality; but none of these have as yet fallen under my observation. A striking production is expected from the pen of the celebrated VOLNEY. This is a *Tableau Physique des États Unis*; but it is with regret I hear that its appearance is delayed by the author's indisposition.

Novels are born and die here, as among us, with astonishing abundance. The rage for evocations and magic spectres begins to diminish. The French assert that they have borrowed it from us, and from the school of Mrs. RADCLIFF, &c. &c. They also assert, that the policy of the royalist-party was not unconnected with this propagation of cavernous, cadaverous adventures, ideas, and illusions, intended, they say, by the impression of a new moral terror to infatuate their countrymen again with the dull and soporific prestiges of popery. They see with joy that the taste for pleasure has assumed the ascendency, at least in Paris, and that novels in the English style no longer make any one tremble, at night by the fireside, but the old beldams of the provincial departments.

The less important kinds of literature, such as the *Apologue* or *Moral Fable*, which is not at this day much in fashion; the *Eclogue* or *Idyl*, whose culture particularly belongs to agrestical and picturesque regions; *Political Satire*, which is never more refined than under the influence of arbitrary power; these kinds, to which I might add the *Madrigal* and *Epigram*, without being altogether abandoned, are not generally enough cultivated here to obtain special mention. I shall make an exception only in favour of the pastoral poems of LECLERC (of Marne and Loire) of which I have heard a very favourable account.

At the end of a revolution which has had periods so ensanguined, *Romance,* (romantic poetry) must have been cultivated and held in request. It has been so, especially by sentimental minds, and not a little too through the spirit of party; this was likely to be the case, since its most affecting characteristic is to mourn over tombs.

Lyric poetry has been carried by LEBRUN, CHÉNIER, &c. to a height worthy of JEAN BAPTISTE ROUSSEAU. The former, above all, will stand his ground, by his own weight, to the latest posterity; while hitherto the lyric productions of CHÉNIER have not been able to dispense with the charm of musical harmony. FONTANES, CUBIÈRES, PONS DE VERDUN, BAOUR-LORNIAN, and DESPAZE are secondary geniuses, who do not make us forget that DELISLE and the Chevalier BERTIN are still living; but whose fugitive pieces sometimes display many charms.

When you shall be made acquainted that Paris, of all the cities in the world, is that where the rage for dancing is the most *nationalized;* where, from the gilded apartments of the most fashionable quarters to the smoky chambers of the most obscure suburbs, there are executed more capers in cadence, than in any other place on earth, you will not be surprised if I reserve a special article for one of the kinds of literature that bears the most affinity to this distinctive diversion of the Parisian belles, which has led MERCIER to say, that their city was the *guingette* of Europe; I mean *Song.* Perhaps, a subject new and curious to treat on, would be the influence of vocal music on the French revolution. Every one knows that this people marched to battle singing; but, independently of the subject being above my abilities, it would carry me too far beyond the limited plan which I have prescribed to myself.

Let it suffice for you to know, that there has existed in Paris a sort of lyric manufactory, which, under the name of " *Diners du vaudeville,*" scrupulously performed, for several years, an engagement to furnish, every month, a collection of songs very agreeable and very captivating. These productions are pretty often full of allusions, more or less veiled, to the political events of the moment; seldom, however, have they been handled as very offensive weapons against persons or institutions. The friends of mirth and wine are seldom dark and dangerous politicians. This country possesses a great number of them, who combine the talents required by the gravest magistracy with all the levity of the most witty and most cheerful *bon vivant.* I shall quote at random FRANÇOIS DE NEUFCHÂTEAU, the two SÉGURS, PIIS, &c. &c. Others, such as BARRÉ, DESFONTAINES, and RADET, confine themselves to their exclusive functions of professed song-makers, and write only for the little musical theatres, or for the leisure of their countrymen and their evening-amusements.

It is impossible to terminate a sketch of the literature of France, without saying a word of such of the *Journals* as I have yet perused, which are specially devoted to it. The *Mercure de France* is one of those held in most esteem; and habit, as well as the spirit of party, concurs in making the fortune of this journal. There exists another, conducted by a member of the Institute, named POUGENS, under the title of *Bibliothèque Française,* which is spoken of very favourably. But that which appears every ten days, under the name of *Décade Philosophique,* is the best production of the sort. A society of literary men, prudent, well-informed, and warmly attached to their country, are its authors, and deposit in it a well-digested analysis of every thing new that appears in the arts, sciences, or literature. Nevertheless, a labour so carefully performed, is perfectly disinterested. This is the only enterprise of the kind that does not afford a livelihood to its associates, and is supported by a zeal altogether gratuitous.

Without seeking to blame or approve the title of this last-mentioned journal, I shall only remark that the word *Décade*, coupled with the word *Philosophique*, becomes in the eyes of many persons a double cause of reprobation; and that, at this day, more than ever, those two words are, in the opinion the most in fashion, marked by a proscription that is reflected on every thing which belongs to the science of philosophy.

This would be the moment to inquire into the secret or ostensible causes which have led to the retrograde course that is to be remarked in France in the ideas which have been hitherto reckoned as conducive to the advancement of reason. This would be the moment to observe the new government of France endeavouring to balance, the one by the other, the opinions sprung from the Republic, and those daily conjured up from the Monarchy; holding in *equilibrio* two colours of doctrines so diametrically opposite, and consequently two parties equally dissatisfied at not being able to crush each other; *neutralizing* them, in short, by its immense influence in the employment of their strength, when they bewilder or exhaust themselves uselessly for its interests; but I could not touch on these matters, without travelling out of the domain of literature, which is the only one that is at present familiar to me, in order to enter into yours, where you have not leisure to direct me; and you may conceive with what an ill grace I should appear, in making before you, in politics, excursions, which, probably, would have for me the inconvenience of commanding great efforts, without leaving me the hope of adding any thing to your stock of information.

LETTER XXXV.

Paris, December 18, 1801.

DIVIDED as Paris is by the Seine, it seldom happens that one has not occasion to cross it more than once in the course of the day. I shall therefore make you acquainted with the bridges which connect to its banks the islands situated in that part of the river I have not yet described. Being out of my general track, I might otherwise forget to make any further mention of them, which would be a manifest omission, now you have before you the Plan of Paris,

We will also embrace the opportunity of visiting the *Palais de Justice* and the Cathedral of *Notre-Dame*. East of the *Pont-Neuf*, we first arrive at the

PONT AU CHANGE.

This bridge, which leads from the north bank of the Seine to the *Ile du Palais*, is one of the most ancient in Paris. Though, like all those of which I have now to speak, it crosses but one channel of the river, it was called the *Grand Pont*, till the year 1141, when it acquired its present name on Lewis VII establishing here all the money-changers of Paris.

It was also called *Pont aux Oiseaux*, because bird-sellers were permitted to carry on their business here, on condition of letting loose two hundred dozen of birds, at the moment when kings and queens passed, in their way to the cathedral, on the day of their public entry. By this custom, it was intended to signify that, if the people had been oppressed in the preceding reign, their rights, privileges, and liberties would be fully re-established under the new monarch.

On the public entry of Isabeau de Bavière, wife of Charles VI, a Genoese stretched a rope from the top of the towers of *Notre-Dame* to one of the houses on this bridge: he thence descended, dancing on this rope, with a lighted torch in each hand. Habited as an angel, he placed a crown on the head of the new queen, and reascending his rope, he appeared again in the air. The chronicle adds that, as it was already dark, he was seen by all Paris and the environs.

This bridge was then of wood, and covered with houses also of wood. Two fires, one of which happened in 1621, and the other in 1639, occasioned it to be rebuilt of stone in 1647.

The *Pont au Change* consists of seven arches. Previously to the demolition of the houses, which, till 1786, stood on each side of this bridge, the passage was sufficiently wide for three carriages.

Traversing the *Ile du Palais* from north to south, in order to proceed from the *Pont au Change* to the *Pont St. Michel*, we pass in front of the

PALAIS DE JUSTICE.

Towards the end of the ninth century, this palace was begun by Eudes. It was successively enlarged by Robert, son of Hugh Capet, by St. Lewis, and by Philip the Fair. Under Charles V, who abandoned it to occupy the *Hôtel St. Paul*, which he had built, it was nothing more than an assemblage of large towers, communicating with each other by galleries. In 1383, Charles VI made it his residence. In 1431, Charles VII relinquished it to the Parliament of Paris. However, Francis I. took up his abode here for some time.

It was in the great hall of this palace that the kings of France formerly received ambassadors, and gave public entertainments.

On Whitsunday, 1313, Philip the Fair here knighted his three sons, with all the ceremonies of ancient chivalry. The king of England, our unfortunate Edward II, and his abominable queen Isabella, who were invited, crossed the sea on purpose, and were present at this entertainment, together with a great number of English barons. It lasted eight days, and is spoken of, by historians, as a most sumptuous banquet.

This magnificent hall, as well as great part of the palace, being reduced to ashes in 1618, it was rebuilt, in its present state, under the direction of that skilful architect, JACQUES DE BROSSES. It is both spacious and majestic, and is the only hall of the kind in France: the arches and arcades which support it are of hewn stone.

Another fire, which happened in 1776, consumed all the part extending from the gallery of prisoners to the *Sainte Chapelle*, founded by St. Lewis, and where, before the revolution, were shewn a number of costly relics. The ravages occasioned by this fire, were repaired in 1787, and the space in front laid open by the erection of uniform buildings in the form of a crescent. To two gloomy gothic gates has been substituted an iron railing, of one hundred and twenty feet in extent, through which is seen a spacious court formed by two wings of new edifices, and a majestic façade that affords an entrance to the interior of the palace.

In this court Madame La Motte, who, in 1786, made so conspicuous a figure in the noted affair of the diamond necklace, was publicly whipped. I was in Paris at the time, though not present at the execution of the sentence.

In the railing, are three gates, the centre one of which is charged with garlands and other gilt ornaments. At the two ends are pavilions decorated with four Doric pillars. Towards the *Pont St. Michel* is a continuation of the building ornamented with a bas-relief, at present denominated *Le serment civique*.

At the top of a flight of steps, is an avant-corps, with four Doric columns, a balustrade above the entablature, four statues standing on a level with the base of the pillars, and behind, a square dome.

These steps lead you to the *Mercière* gallery, having on the one side, the *Sainte Chapelle*, and on the other, the great hall, called the *Salle des Procureurs*. In this extensive hall are shops, for the sale of eatables and pamphlets, which, since the suppression of the Parliament, seem to have little custom, as well as those of the milliners, &c. in the other galleries.

In what was formerly called the *grande chambre*, where the Parliament of Paris used to sit, the ill-fated Lewis XVI, in 1788, held the famous bed of justice, in which D'ESPRESMENIL, one of the members of that body, struck the first blow at royalty; a blow that was revenged by a *lettre de cachet*, which exiled him to the *Ile de St. Marguerite*, famous for being the place of confinement of the great personage who was always compelled to wear an *iron mask*. The courage of this counsellor, who was a noble and deputy of the *noblesse*, may be considered as the *primum mobile* of the revolution. Under the despotism of the court, he braved all its vengeance; but, in the sequel, he afforded a singular proof of the instability of the human mind. After having stirred up all the parliaments against the royal authority, he again became the humble servant of the crown.

After the revolution, the *Palais de Justice*

became the seat of the Revolutionary Tribunal, where the satellites of Robespierre, not content with sending to the scaffold sixty victims at a time, complained of the insufficiency of their means for bringing to trial all the enemies of liberty. Dumas, at one time president of this sanguinary tribunal, proposed to his colleagues to join to the hall, where the tribunal sat, part of the great hall of the palace, in order to assemble there five or six hundred victims at a time; and on its being observed to him that such a sight might in the end disgust the people; "Well," said he, " there's but one " method of accomplishing our object, without " any obstacle, that is to erect a guillotine in " the court-yard of every prison, and cause the " prisoners to be executed there during the night." Had not Robespierre's downfall involved that of all his blood-thirsty dependents, there seems no doubt that this plan would have been carried into speedy execution.

Nothing can paint the vicissitude of human events in colours more striking than the transitions of this critical period. Dumas who made this proposal, and had partially satisfied his merciless disposition by signing, a few hours before, the death-warrant of sixty victims, was the very next day brought before the same tribunal, composed of his accomplices, or rather his creatures, and by them condemned to die. Thus did experience confirm the general observation, that the multiplicity and enormity of punishments announces an approaching revolution. The torrents of blood which tyrants shed, are, in the end, swelled by their own.

In lieu of a tribunal of blood, the *Palais de Justice* is now appropriated to the sittings of the three tribunals, designated by the following titles: *Tribunal de cassation, Tribunal d'appel,* and *Tribunal de première instance.* The first of these, the *Tribunal de cassation*, occupies the audience-chambers of the late parliament; while the *grande chambre* is appointed for the meetings of its united Sections. The decoration of this spacious apartment is entirely changed: it is embellished in the antique style; and a person in contemplating it might fancy himself at Athens.

Adjoining to the *Palais de Justice,* is the famous prison, so dreaded in the early periods of the revolution, called

LA CONCIERGERIE.

From this fatal abode, neither talent, virtue, nor patriotism could, at one time, secure those who possessed such enviable qualities. Lavoisier, Malsherbes, Condorcet, &c. were here successively immured, previously to being sent to the guillotine. Here too the unfortunate Marie-Antoinette lived in a comfortless manner, from the 2nd of July, 1793, to the 13th of October following, the period of her condemnation.

On being reconducted to the prison, at four o'clock in the morning, after hearing her sentence read, the hapless queen displayed a fortitude worthy of the daughter of the high-minded Maria Theresa. She requested a few hours' respite, to compose her mind, and entreated to be left to herself in the room which she had till then occupied. The moment she was alone, she first cut off her hair, and then laying aside her widow's weeds, which she had always worn since the death of the king, put on a white dress, and threw herself on her bed, where she slept till eleven o'clock the same morning, when she was awakened, in order to be taken to the scaffold.

Continuing to cross the *Ile du Palais*, in a direction towards the south, we presently reach the

PONT ST. MICHEL.

This bridge stands in a direct line with the *Pont au Change*, and is situated on the south channel of the river. It was formerly of wood: but having been frequently destroyed, it was rebuilt with stone in 1618, and covered on both sides with houses. From the *Pont Neuf*, the back of these buildings has a most disagreeable and filthy appearance. It is said that they are to be taken down, as those have been which stood on the other bridges.

In severe winters, when there is much ice in the river, it is curious, on the breaking up of the frost, to behold families deserting their habitations, like so many rats, and carrying with them their valuables, from the apprehension that these crazy tenements might fall into the river. This wise precaution is suggested by the knowledge of these bridges, when built of wood, having been often swept away by ice or great inundations.

The *Pont St. Michel* consists of four arches. Its length is two hundred and sixty-eight feet, by sixty in breadth, including the houses, between which is a passage for three carriages.

If, to avoid being entangled in narrow, dirty streets, we return, by the same route, to the north bank of the Seine, and proceed to the westward, along the *Quai de Gêvres*, which is partly built on piles, driven into the bed of the river, we shall come to the

PONT NOTRE-DAME.

A wooden bridge, which previously existed here, having been frequently carried away by inundations, Lewis XII ordered the construction of the present one of stone, which was begun in 1499, and completed in 1507. It was built from the plan of one JOCONDE, a Cordelier, and native of Verona, and is generally admired for the solidity, as well as beauty of its architecture. It consists of six arches, and is two hundred and seventy-six feet in length. Formerly it was bordered by houses, which were taken down in 1786: this has rendered the quarter more airy, and consequently more salubrious.

It was on this bridge that the Pope's Legate reviewed the ecclesiastical infantry of the League, on the the 3d of June, 1590. Capuchins, Minimes, Cordeliers, Jacobins or Dominicans, Feuillans, &c. all with their robe tucked up, their cowl thrown behind, a helmet on their head, a coat of mail on their body, a sword by their side, and a musquet on their shoulder, marched four by four, headed by the reverend bishop of Senlis, bearing a spontoon. But some of this holy soldiery, forgetting that their pieces were loaded with ball, wished to salute the Legate, and killed by his side one of his chaplains. His Eminence finding that it began to grow hot at this review, hastened to give his benediction, and vanished.

December 18, in continuation.

Traversing once more two-thirds of the *Ile du Palais* in a direction from north to south, and then striking off to the east, up the *Rue de Callandre*, we reach the

CATHEDRAL OF NOTRE-DAME.

This church, the first ever built in Paris, was begun about the year 375, under the reign of the emperor Valentinian I. It was then called *St. Etienne* or *St. Stephen's*, and there was as yet no other within the walls of this city in 1522, when Childebert, son of Clovis, repaired and enlarged it, adding to it a new basilic, which was dedicated to *Notre Dame* or Our Lady.

More anciently, under Tiberius, there had been, on the same spot, an altar in the open air, dedicated to Jupiter and other pagan gods, part of which is still in being at the MUSEUM OF FRENCH MONUMENTS, in the *Rue des Petits Augustins*.

These two churches existed till about the year 1160, under the reign of Lewis the Young, when the construction of the present cathedral was begun partly on their foundations. It was not finished till 1185, during the reign of Philip Augustus.

This Gothic Church is one of the handsomest

and most spacious in France. It has a majestic and venerable appearance, and is supported by one hundred and twenty clustered columns. Its length is three hundred and ninety feet by one hundred and forty-four in breadth, and one hundred and two in height.

We must not expect to find standing here the twenty-six kings, benefactors of this church, from Childeric I to Philip Augustus, fourteen feet high, who figured on the same line, above the three doors of the principal façade. They have all fallen under the blows of the iconoclasts, and are now piled up behind the church. There lie round-bellied Charlemagne, with his pipe in his mouth, and Pepin the Short, with his sword in his hand, and a lion, the emblem of courage, under his feet. The latter, like Tydeus, mentioned in the Iliad, though small in stature, was stout in heart, as appears from the following anecdote related of him by the monk of St. Gal.

In former times, as is well known, kings took a delight in setting wild beasts and ferocious animals to fight against each other. At one of these fights, between a lion and a bull, in the abbey of Ferrières, Pepin the Short, who knew that some noblemen were daily exercising their pleasantry on his small stature, addressed to them this question: " Which of you feels

"himself bold enough to kill or separate those
"terrible animals?" Seeing that not one of
them stepped forward, and that the proposal
alone made them shudder: "Well," added he,
"'tis I then who will perform the feat." He
accordingly descended from his place, drew his
sword, killed the lion, at another stroke cut
off the head of the bull, and then looking
fiercely at the railers: "Know," said he to
them, "that stature adds nothing to courage,
"and that I shall find means to bring to the
"ground the proud persons who shall dare to
"despise me, as little David laid low the great
"giant Goliah." Hence the attribute given to
the statue of king Pepin, which not long since
adorned the façade of *Notre-Dame*.

The groups of angels, saints, and patriarchs,
which, no doubt, owe their present existence
only to their great number, still present to
the eye of the observer that burlesque mixture
of the profane and religious, so common in
the symbolical representations of the twelfth
century. These figures adorn the triple row
of indented borders of the arches of the three
doors.

Two enormous square towers, each two hundred and two feet in height, and terminated
by a platform, decorate each end of the cathedral.
The ascent to them is by a winding stair-case

of three hundred and eighty-nine steps, and their communication is by a gallery which has no support but Gothic pillars of a lightness that excites admiration.

Independently of the six bells, which have disappeared with the little belfry that contained them, in the two towers were ten, one of which weighed forty-four thousand pounds.

At the foot of the north tower is the rural calendar or zodiac, which has been described by M. Le Gentil, member of the Academy of Sciences. The Goths had borrowed from the Indians this custom of thus representing rustic labours at the entrance of their temples.

Another Gothic bas-relief, which is seen on the left, in entering by the great door, undoubtedly represents that condemned soul who, tradition says, rose from his bier, during divine service, in order to pronounce his own damnation.

None of the forty-five chapels have preserved the smallest vestige of their ornaments. Those which escaped the destructive rage of the modern Vandals, have been transported to the MUSEUM OF FRENCH MONUMENTS. The most remarkable are the statue of Pierre de Gondi, archbishop of Paris, the mausoleum of the Conte d'Harcourt, designed by his widow, the modern Artemisia, and executed by Pigalle, together with the group representing the vow of St. Lewis, by Costou the elder. Six angels in bronze, which were seen at the further end of the choir, have also been removed thither.

The stalls present, in square and oval compartments, bas-reliefs very delicately sculptured, representing subjects taken from the life of the Holy Virgin and from the New Testament. Of the two episcopal pulpits, which are at the further end, the one, that of the archbishop, represents the martyrdom of St. Denis; the other, opposite, the cure of king Childebert, by the intercession of St. Germain.

Some old tapestry, hung scantily round the choir, makes one regret the handsome iron railing, so richly wrought, by which it was inclosed, and some valuable pictures, which now figure in the grand Gallery of the CENTRAL MUSEUM OF THE ARTS.

The nave, quite as naked as the choir and the sanctuary, had been enriched, as far as the space would admit, with pictures, twelve feet high, given for a long time, on every first of May, by the Goldsmiths' company and the fraternity of St. Anne and St. Marcel.

On the last pillar of the nave, on the right, was the equestrian statue of Philip of Valois. That king was here represented on horseback, with his vizor down, sword in hand, and armed cap-à-pié, in the very manner in which he rode into the cathedral of *Notre-Dame,* in 1328, after the battle of Cassel. At the foot of the altar he left his horse, together with his armour, which he had worn in the battle, as an offering to the Holy Virgin, after having returned thanks to God and to her, say historians, for the victory he had obtained through her intercession.

Above the lateral alleys, as well of the choir as of the nave, are large galleries, separated by little pillars of a single piece, and bordered by iron balustrades. Here spectators place themselves to see grand ceremonies. From their balconies were formerly suspended the colours taken from the enemy: these are now displayed in the *Temple of Mars* at the Hôtel des Invalides.

The organ, which appears to have suffered no injury, is reckoned one of the loudest and most complete in France. It is related that Daquin, an incomparable organist, who died in 1781, once imitated the nightingale on it so perfectly, that the beadle was sent on the roof of the church, to endeavour to discover the musical bird.

Some of the stained glass is beautiful. Two roses, restored to their original state, the one on the side of the archiepiscopal palace, in 1726, and the other above the organ, in 1780, prove by their lustre, that the moderns are not so inferior to the ancients, in the art of painting on glass, as is commonly imagined.

Should your curiosity lead you to contemplate the house of Fulbert, the canon, the supposed uncle to the tender Héloïse, where that celebrated woman passed her youthful days, you must enter, by the cloister of *Notre-Dame*, into the street that leads to the *Pont Rouge*, since removed. It is the last house on the right under the arcade, and is easily distinguished by two medallions in stone, preserved on the façade, though it has been several times rebuilt during the space of six hundred years. All the authors who have written on the antiquities of Paris, speak of these medallions as being real portraits of Abélard and Héloïse. It is presumable that they were so originally; but, without being a connoisseur, any one may discover that the dresses of these figures are far more modern than those peculiar to the twelfth century; whence it may be concluded that the original portraits having been destroyed by time, or by the alterations which the house has undergone, these busts have been executed by some more modern sculptor of no great talents.

Leaving the cathedral, by the *Rue Notre-*

Dame, and turning to the left, on reaching the *Marché Palu,* we come to the

PETIT PONT.

Like the *Pont St. Michel,* this bridge is situated on the south channel of the river, and stands in a direct line with the *Pont Notre-Dame.* It originally owed its construction to the following circumstance.

Four Jews, accused of having killed one of their converted brethren, were condemned to be publicly whipped through all the streets of the city, on four successive Sundays. After having suffered the half, of their sentence, to redeem themselves from the other half, they paid 18,000 francs of gold. This sum was appropriated to the erection of the *Petit Pont,* the first stone of which was laid by Charles VI, in 1395.

In 1718, two barges, loaded with hay, caught fire, and being cut loose, drifted under the arches of this bridge, which, in the space of four hours, was consumed, together with the houses standing on it. The following year it was rebuilt, but without houses.

Proceeding to the east, along the quays of the *Ile du Palais,* you will find the

PONT AU DOUBLE.

This little bridge, situated behind the *Hôtel-Dieu*, of which I shall speak hereafter, is destined for foot-passengers only, as was the *Pont Rouge*. The latter was the point of communication between the *Cité* and the *Ile St. Louis*; but the frequent reparations which it required, occasioned it to be removed in 1791, though, by the Plan of Paris, it still appears to be in existence. However, it is in contemplation to replace it by another of stone.*

Supposing that you have regained the north bank of the Seine, by means of the *Pont Notre-Dame*, you follow the quays, which skirt that shore, till you reach the

PONT MARIE.

This bridge forms a communication between the *Port St. Paul* and the *Ile St. Louis*. The *Pont Marie* was named after the engineer who engaged with Henry IV to build it; but that prince having been assassinated, the young king, Lewis XIII, and the queen dowager, laid

* Workmen are, at this moment, employed in the construction of three new bridges. The first, already mentioned, will form a communication between the *ci-devant Collège des Quatre Nations* and the *Louvre*; the second, between the *Ile du Palais* and the *Ile St. Louis*; and the third, between the *Jardin des Plantes* and the Arsenal.

the first stone in 1614: it was finished, and bordered with houses, in 1635. It consists of five arches. Its length is three hundred feet by sixty-two in breadth. An inundation having carried away two of the arches, in 1658, they were repaired without the addition of houses, and in 1789, the others were removed.

Passing through the *Rue des Deux Ponts*, which lies in a direct line with the *Pont Marie*, we arrive at the

PONT DE LA TOURNELLE.

This bridge takes its name from the *Château de la Tournelle*, contiguous to the *Porte St. Bernard*, where the galley-slaves used formerly to be lodged, till they were sent off to the different public works. It consists of six arches of solid construction, and is bordered on each side by a foot-pavement.

You are now acquainted with all the bridges in Paris; but should you prefer crossing the Seine in a boat, there are several ferries between the bridges, and at other convenient places. Here, you may always meet with a waterman, who, for the sum of one *sou*, will carry you over, whether master or lackey. Like the old ferryman Charon, he makes no distinction of persons.

LETTER XXXVI.

Paris, December 20, 1801.

WHAT a charming abode is Paris, for a man who can afford to live at the rate of a thousand or fifteen hundred pounds a year! Pleasures wait not for him to go in quest of them; they come to him of their own accord; they spring up, in a manner, under his very feet, and form around him an officious retinue. Every moment of the day can present a new gratification to him who knows how to enjoy it; and, with prudent management, the longest life even would not easily exhaust so ample a stock.

Paris has long been termed an epitome of the world. But, perhaps, never could this denomination be applied to it with so much propriety as at the present moment. The chances of war have not only rendered it the centre of the fine arts, the museum of the most celebrated masterpieces in existence, the emporium where the luxury of Europe comes to procure its superfluities; but the taste for pleasure has also found means to assemble here all the enjoyments which Nature seemed to have exclusively appropriated to other climates.

Every country has its charms and advantages. Paris alone appears to combine them all. Every region, every corner of the globe seems to vie in hastening to forward hither the tribute of its productions. Are you an epicure? No delicacy of the table but may be eaten in Paris.—Are you a toper? No delicious wine but may be drunk, in Paris.—Are you fond of frequenting places of public entertainment? No sort of spectacle but may be seen in Paris.—Are you desirous of improving your mind? No kind of instruction but may be acquired in Paris.—Are you an admirer of the fair sex? No description of female beauty but may be obtained in Paris.—Are you partial to the society of men of extraordinary talents? No great genius but comes to display his knowledge in Paris.—Are you inclined to discuss military topics? No hero but brings his laurels to Paris.—In a word, every person, favoured by Nature or Fortune, flies to enjoy the gifts of either in Paris. Even every place celebrated in the annals of voluptuousness, is, as it were, reproduced in Paris, which, in some shape or another, presents its name or image.

Without going out of this capital, you may, in the season when Nature puts on her verdant livery, visit *Idalium*, present your incense to the Graces, and adore, in her temple, the queen of love; while at *Tivoli*, you may, perhaps, find as many beauties and charms as were formerly admired at the enchanting spot on the banks of the

Anio, which, under its ancient name of *Tibur*, was so extolled by the Latin poets; and close to the Boulevard, at *Frascati*, you may, in that gay season, eat ices as good as those with which Cardinal de Bernis used to regale his visiters, at his charming villa in the *Campagna di Roma*. Who therefore need travel farther than Paris to enjoy every gratification?

If then, towards the close of a war, the most frightful and destructive that ever was waged, the useful and agreeable seem to have proceeded here hand in hand in improvement, what may not be expected in the tranquillity of a few years' peace? Who knows but the emperor Julian's " *dear Lutetia*" may one day vie in splendour with Thebes and its hundred gates, or ancient Rome covering its seven mountains?

However, if *Tivoli* and *Frascati* throw open their delightful recesses to the votaries of pleasure only in spring and summer, even now, during the fogs of December, you may repair to

PAPHOS.

It might almost be said that you enter this place of amusement *gratis*, for, though a slight tribute of seventy-five *centimes* (*circa* seven-pence halfpenny sterling) is required for the admission of every person, yet you may take refreshment to the amount of that sum, without again putting your hand into your pocket; because the countermark, given at the door, is received at the bar as ready-money.

This speculation, the first of the kind in France, and one of the most specious, is, by all accounts, also one of the most productive. It would be too rigorous, no doubt, to compare the frequenters of the modern PAPHOS to the inhabitants of the ancient. Here, indeed, you must neither look for *élégantes*, nor *muscadins*; but you may view belles, less gifted by Fortune, indulging in innocent recreation, and for a while dispelling their cares, by dancing to the exhilarating music of an orchestra not ill composed. Here, the grisette banishes the *ennui* of six days' application to the labours of her industry, by footing it away on Sunday. Hither, in short, the less refined sons and daughters of mirth repair to see and be seen, and to partake of the general diversion.

PAPHOS is situated on that part of the Boulevard, called the *Boulevard du Temple*, whither I was led the other evening by that sort of curiosity, which can be satisfied only when the objects that afford it aliment are exhausted. I had just come out of another place of public amusement, at no great distance, called

LA PHANTASMAGORIE.

This is an exhibition in the *Cour des Capucines*, adjoining to the Boulevard, where Robertson, a skilful professor of physics, amuses or terrifies his audience by the appearance of spectres, phantoms, &c. In the piece which I saw, called *Le Tombeau de Robespierre*, he carries illusion to an extraordinary degree of refinement. His cabinet of physics is rich, and his effects of optics are managed in the true style of French gallantry. His experiments of galvanism excite admiration. He repeats the difficult ones of M. Volta, and clearly demonstrates the electrical phenomena presented by the metallic pile. A hundred disks of silver and a hundred pieces of zinc are sufficient for him to produce attractions, sparks, the divergency of the electrometer, and electric hail. He charges a hundred Leyden bottles by the simple contact of the metallic pile. Robertson, I understand, is the first who has made these experiments in Paris, and has succeeded in discharging Volta's pistol by the galvanic spark.

Fitzames, a famous ventriloquist, entertains and astonishes the company by a display of his powers, which are truly surprising.

You may, perhaps, be desirous to procure your family circle the satisfaction of enjoying the

Phantasmagoria, though not on the grand scale on which it is exhibited by Robertson. By the communication of a friend, I am happy in being enabled to make you master of the secret, as nothing can be more useful in the education of children than to banish from their mind the deceitful illusion of ghosts and hobgoblins, which they are so apt to imbibe from their nurses. But to the point—" You have," says my author, " only to call in the first itinerant foreigner, who perambulates the streets with a *galantee-show* (as it is commonly termed in London), and by imparting to him your wish, if he is not deficient in intelligence and skill, he will soon be able to give you a rehearsal of the apparition of phantoms: for, by approaching or withdrawing the stand of his show, and finding the focus of his glasses, you will see the objects diminish or enlarge either on the white wall, or the sheet that is extended.

" The illusion which leads us to imagine that an object which increases in all its parts, is advancing towards us, is the basis of the *Phantasmagoria*, and, in order to produce it with the *galantee-show*, you have only to withdraw slowly the lantern from the place on which the image is represented, by approaching the outer lens to that on which the object is traced: this is easily done, that glass being fixed in a moveable tube like that of an opera-glass. As for approaching the lantern gradually, it may be effected with the same facility, by placing it on a little table with castors, and, by means of a very simple mechanism, it is evident that both these movements may be executed together in suitable progression.

"The deception recurred to by phantasmagorists is further increased by the mystery that conceals, from the eyes of the public, their operations and optical instruments: but it is easy for the showman to snatch from them this superiority, and to strengthen the illusion for the children whom you choose to amuse with this sight. For that purpose, he has only to change the arrangement of the sheet, by requiring it to be suspended from the ceiling, between him and the spectators, much in the same manner as the curtain of a playhouse, which separates the stage from the public. The transparency of the cloth shews through it the coloured rays, and, provided it be not of too thick and too close a texture, the image presents itself as clear on the one side as on the other.

"If to these easy means you could unite those employed by ROBERTSON, such as the black hangings, which absorb the coloured rays, the little musical preparations, and others, you might transform all the *galantee-shows* into as many *phantasmagorias,* in spite of the priority of invention, which belongs, conscientiously, to Father KIRCHER, a German Jesuit, who first found means to apply his knowledge respecting light to the construction of the magic lantern.

" The coloured figures, exhibited by the phatasmagorists, have no relation to these effects of light: they are effigies covered with gold-beater's skin, or any other transparent substance, in which is placed a dark lantern. The light of this lantern is extinguished or concealed by pulling a string, or touching a spring, at the moment when any one wishes to seize on the figure, which, by this contrivance, seems to disappear.

" The proprietors of the grand exhibitions of *phantasmagoria* join to these simple means a combination of different effects, which they partly derive from the phenomena presented by the *camera obscura.* Some faint idea of that part of physics, called optics, which NEWTON illuminated, by his genius and experience, are sufficient for conceiving the manner in which these appearances are produced, though they require instruments and particular care to give them proper effect."

Such is the elucidation given of the *phantasmagoria* by an intelligent observer, whose friend favoured me with this communication.

LETTER XXXVII.

Paris, December 21, 1801.

IF Paris affords a thousand enjoyments to the man of fortune, it may truly be said that, without money, Paris is the most melancholy abode in the world. Privations are then the more painful, because desires and even wants are rendered more poignant by the ostentatious display of every object which might satisfy them. What more cruel for an unfortunate fellow, with an empty purse, than to pass by the kitchen of a *restaurateur*, when, pinched by hunger, he has not the means of procuring himself a dinner? His olfactory nerves being still more readily affected when his stomach is empty, far from affording him a pleasing sensation, then serve only to sharpen the torment which he suffers. It is worse than the punishment of Tantalus, who, dying with thirst, could not drink, though up to his chin in water.

Really, my dear friend, I would advise every rich epicure to fix his residence in this city. Without being plagued by the details of housekeeping, or even at the trouble of looking at a bill of fare, he might feast his eye, and his appetite too, on the inviting plumpness of a turkey, stuffed with truffles. A boar's head set before him, with a Seville orange between its tusks, might make him fancy that he was discussing the greatest interests of mankind at the table of an Austrian Prime Minister, or British Secretary of State; while *pâtés* of *Chartres* or of *Périgord* hold out to his discriminating palate all the refinements of French seasoning. These, and an endless variety of other dainties, no less tempting, might he contemplate here, in walking past a *magazin de comestibles* or provision-warehouse.

Among the changes introduced here, within these few years, I had heard much of the improvements in the culinary art, or rather in the manner of serving up its productions; but, on my first arrival in Paris, I was so constantly engaged in a succession of dinner-parties, that some time elapsed before I could avail myself of an opportunity of dining at the house of any of the fashionable

RESTAURATEURS.

This is a title of no very ancient date in Paris. *Traiteurs* have long existed here: independently of furnishing repasts at home, these

traiteurs, like Birch in Cornhill, or any other famous London cook, sent out dinners and suppers. But, in 1765, one BOULANGER conceived the idea of *restoring* the exhausted animal functions of the debilitated Parisians by rich soups of various denominations. Not being a *traiteur*, it appears that he was not authorized to serve ragouts; he therefore, in addition to his *restorative* soups, set before his customers new-laid eggs and boiled fowl with strong gravy sauce: those articles were served up without a cloth, on little marble tables. Over his door he placed the following inscription, borrowed from Scripture:
" *Venite ad me omnes qui stomacho laboratis, et*
" *ego restaurabo vos.*"

Such was the origin of the word and profession of *restaurateur*.

Other cooks, in imitation of BOULANGER, set up as *restorers*, on a similar plan, in all the places of public entertainment where such establishments were admissible. Novelty, fashion, and, above all, dearness, brought them into vogue. Many a person who would have been ashamed to be seen going into a *traiteur's*, made no hesitation of entering a *restaurateur's*, where he paid nearly double the price for a dinner of the same description. However, as, in all trades, it is the great number of customers that enrich the trader, rather than the select few, the *restaurateurs*, in order to make their business answer, were soon under the necessity of constituting themselves *traiteurs*; so that, in lieu of one title, they now possess two; and this is the grand result of the primitive establishment.

At the head of the most noted *restaurateurs* in Paris, previously to the revolution, was La Barrière, in the *ci-devant Palais Royal*; but, though his larder was always provided with choice food, his cellar furnished with good wines, his bill of fare long, and the number of his customers considerable, yet his profits, he said, were not sufficiently great to allow him to cover his tables with linen. This omission was supplied by green wax cloth; a piece of economy which, he declared, produced him a saving of near 10,000 livres (*circa* 400£ sterling) per annum in the single article of washing. Hence you may form an idea of the extent of such an undertaking. I have often dined at La Barrière's, and was always well served, at a moderate charge, and with remarkable expedition. Much about that time, Beauvilliers, who had opened, within the same precincts, a similar establishment, but on a more refined plan, proved a most formidable rival to La Barrière, and at length eclipsed him.

After a lapse of almost eleven years, I again find this identical Beauvilliers still in the full enjoyment of the greatest celebrity. Robert and NAUDET in the *Palais du Tribunat*, and VÉRY on the *Terrace des Feuillans*, dispute with him the palm in the art of Apicius. All these, it is true, furnish excellent repasts, and their wines are not inferior to their cooking: but, after more than one impartial trial, I think I am justified in giving the preference to BEAUVILLIERS. Let us then take a view of his arrangements: this, with a few variations in price or quality, will serve as a general picture of the *ars coquinaria* in Paris.

On the first floor of a large hotel, formerly occupied, perhaps, by a farmer-general, you enter a suite of apartments, decorated with arabesques, and mirrors of large dimensions, in a style no less elegant than splendid, where tables are completely arranged for large or small parties. In winter, these rooms are warmed by ornamental stoves, and lighted by *quinquets*, a species of Argand's lamps. They are capable of accommodating from two hundred and fifty to three hundred persons, and, at this time of the year, the average number that dine here daily is about two hundred; in summer, it is considerably decreased by the attractions of the country, and the parties of pleasure made, in consequence, to the environs of the capital.

On the left hand, as you pass into the first room, rises a sort of throne, not unlike the *estrado* in the grand audience-chamber of a Spanish viceroy. This throne is encircled by a barrier to keep intruders at a respectful distance. Here sits a lady, who, from her majestic gravity and dignified bulk, you might very naturally suppose to be an empress, revolving in her comprehensive mind the affairs of her vast dominions. This respectable personage is Madame BEAUVILLIERS, whose most interesting concern is to collect from the gentlemen in waiting the cash which they receive at the different tables. In this important branch, she has the assistance of a lady, somewhat younger than herself, who, seated by her side, in stately silence, has every appearance of a maid of honour. A person in waiting near the throne, from his vacant look and obsequious carriage, might, at first sight, be taken for a chamberlain; whereas his real office, by no means an unimportant one, is to distribute into deserts the fruit and other *et ceteras*, piled up within his reach in tempting profusion.

We will take our seats in this corner, whence, without laying down our knife and fork, we can enjoy a full view of the company as they enter. We are rather early: by the clock, I perceive that it is no more than five: at six, however, there will scarcely be a vacant seat at any of the tables. " *Garçon, la carte!*"—" *La voilà de-* " *vant vous, Monsieur.*"

Good heaven! the bill of fare is a printed

sheet of double *folio*, of the size of an English newspaper. It will require half an hour at least to con over this important catalogue. Let us see; Soups, thirteen sorts.—*Hors-d'œuvres*, twenty-two species.—Beef, dressed in eleven different ways.—Pastry, containing fish, flesh and fowl, in eleven shapes. Poultry and game, under thirty-two various forms.—Veal, amplified into twenty-two distinct articles.—Mutton, confined to seventeen only.—Fish, twenty-three varieties. —Roast meat, game, and poultry, of fifteen kinds. —Entremets, or side-dishes, to the number of forty-one articles.—Desert, thirty-nine.—Wines, including those of the liqueur kind, of fifty-two denominations, besides ale and porter.—Liqueurs, twelve species, together with coffee and ices.

Fudge! fudge! you cry—Pardon me, my good friend, 'tis no fudge. Take the tremendous bill of fare into your own hand. *Vide et lege.* As we are in no particular hurry, travel article by article through the whole enumeration. This will afford you the most complete notion of the expense of dining at a fashionable *restaurateur's* in Paris.

BEAUVILLIERS, RESTAURATEUR,

Anciennement à la grande Taverne de la République, Palais-Égalité,
No. 142, Présentement Rue de la LOI, No. 1243.

PRIX DES METS POUR UNE PERSONNE.—LES ARTICLES DONT LES PRIX NE SONT POINT FIXES, MANQUENT.

POTAGES.

	fr. s.
Potage aux laitues et petits pois	0 15
Potage aux croûtons à la purée	0 15
Potage aux choux	0 15
Potage au consommé	0 12
Potage au pain	0 12
Potage de santé	0 12
Potage au vermicel	0 12
Potage au ris	0 12
Potage à la julienne	0 12
Potage printanier	0 15
Potage à la purée	0 15
Potage au lait d'amandes	0 15
Potage en tortue	1 10

HORS-D'ŒUVRES.

Tranche de melon	1 0
Artichaud à la poivrade	0 15
Raves et Radis	0 6
Salade de concombres	1 10
Thon mariné	1 10
Anchois à l'huile	1 5
Olives	0 15
Pied de cochon à la Sainte-Ménéhould	0 12
Cornichons	0 8
Petit salé aux choux	1 5

	fr. s.
Saucisses aux choux......................	0 18
1 Petit Pain de Beurre...................	0 4
2 Œufs frais..........................	0 12
1 Citron.............................	0 8
Rissole à la Choisy.....................	1 0
Croquette de volaille....................	1 4
3 Rognons à la brochette.................	1 0
Tête de veau en tortue..................	2 5
Tête de veau au naturel.................	1 0
1 Côtelette de porc frais, sauce robert......	1 0
Chou-Croûte garni......................	1 10
Jambon de Mayence aux épinards.........	1 5

ENTRÉES DE BŒUF.

Bœuf au naturel ou à la sauce............	0 15
Bœuf aux choux ou aux légumes..........	0 18
Carnebif..............................	1 10
Rosbif................................	1 5
Filet de Bœuf sauté dans sa glace.........	1 5
Bifteck...............................	1 5
Entre-côte, sauce aux cornichons..........	1 5
Palais de Bœuf au gratin................	1 4
Palais de Bœuf à la poulette ou à l'Italienne.	1 0
Langue de Bœuf glacée aux épinards......	1 0
Jarrets de veau........................	0 15

ENTRÉES DE PATISSERIE.

Pâté chaud de légumes..................	1 5
2 petits Pâtés à la Béchamel.............	1 4
2 petits Pâtés au jus...................	0 16
1 Pâté chaud d'anguille.................	1 10
1 Pâté chaud de crêtes et de rognons de coqs.	2 0
Tourte de godiveau.....................	1 0
Tourte aux confitures...................	1 5
Vol-au-Vent de filets de volailles.........	2 0

	fr.	s.
Vol-au-Vent de Saumon frais	1	10
Vol-au-Vent de morue à la Béchamel	1	5
Vol-au-Vent de cervelle de veau à l'Allemande	1	5

ENTRÉES DE VOLAILLES.

(Toutes les entrées aux Truffes sont de 15 de plus).

	fr.	s.
Caille aux petits pois	2	10
Pigeon à la crapaudine	2	10
Chapon au riz, le quart	2	15
Chapon au gros sel, le quart	2	10
Demi-poulet aux Truffes ou aux Huitres	4	0
Fricassée de poulets garnie, la moitié	3	10
Fricassée de poulets, la moitié	3	0
Salade de volaille	3	0
Friteau de poulet, la moitié	3	0
Demi-poulet à la ravigotte ou à la tartare	3	0
Marinade de poulet, la moitié	3	0
Le quart d'un poulet à l'estragon ou à la crème ou aux laitues	1	10
Blanquette de poularde	2	10
1 cuisse de poulet aux petits pois	2	0
1 cuisse de volaille au jambon	2	0
2 côtelettes de poulet	3	0
1 cuisse ou aile de poulet en papillote	1	10
1 cuisse de poulet à la Provençale	1	10
Ragoût mêlé de crêtes et de rognons de coqs	3	0
Capilotade de volaille	3	0
Filet de poularde au suprême	3	0
Mayonaise de volaille	3	0
Cuisses de Dindon grillées, sauce robert	3	0
Le quart d'un Canard aux petits pois ou aux navets	1	10
Foie gras en caisses ou en matelote		
Perdrix aux choux, la moitié		
Salmi de perdreau au vin de Champagne		
Pigeons en compote ou aux petits pois	2	10

	fr.	s.
Béchamel de blanc de volaille	2	10
2 cuisses de poulet en hochepot	1	10
Ailerons de dinde aux navets	1	10
Blanc de volaille aux concombres	3	0

ENTRÉES DE VEAU.

Riz de veau piqué, à l'oseille ou à la chicorée	2	0
Riz de veau à la poulette	2	0
Fricandeau aux petits pois	1	5
Fricandeau à la chicorée	1	4
Fricandeau à la ravigotte	1	4
Fricandeau à l'oseille	1	4
Fricandeau à l'Espagnole	1	4
Côtelette de veau au jambon	1	4
Côtelette de veau aux petits pois	1	10
Côtelette de veau en papillotte	1	5
Côtelette de veau panée, sauce piquante	1	0
Côtelette de veau, sauce tomate	1	5
Blanquette de veau	1	0
Oreille de veau à la ravigotte	1	4
Oreille de veau farcie, frite	1	4
Oreille de veau frite ou en marinade	1	4
Cervelle de veau en matelote	1	4
Cervelle de veau à la purée	1	4
Tendons de veau panés, grillés, sauce piquante	1	4
Tendons de veau à la poulette	1	4
Tendons de veau en macédoine	1	5
Tendons de veau aux petits pois	1	5

ENTRÉES DE MOUTON.

Gigot de mouton braisé, aux légumes	1	0
Tendons de mouton grillés	0	18
Tendons de mouton aux petits pois	1	5
Hachi de mouton à la Portugaise	1	0
2 Côtelettes de mouton à la minute	1	5

	fr.	s.
2 Côtelettes de mouton aux racines..............	1	5
2 Côtelettes de mouton au naturel...............	0	18
2 Côtelettes de pré............................	1	0
Epigramme d'agneau...........................		
2 Côtelettes d'agneau au naturel................		
Tendons d'agneau aux pointes d'asperges........		
Tendons d'agneau aux petits pois...............		
Blanquette d'agneau...........................		
Filet de chevreuil.............................	1	5
Côtelette de chevreuil.........................		
Queue de mouton à la purée....................	1	5
Queue de mouton à l'oseille ou à la chicorée....	1	5

ENTRÉES DE POISSONS.

	fr.	s.
Merlan frit....................................		
Maquereau à la maître d'hôtel..................		
Saumon frais, sauce aux câpres..................	2	10
Raie, sauce aux câpres ou au beurre noir.........	1	10
Turbot, sauce aux câpres.......................	2	10
Cabillaud.....................................		
Morue fraîche au beurre fondu..................		
Morue d'Hol. à la maître-d'hôtel ou à la Provençale..	1	10
Sole frite.....................................		
Sole sur le plat...............................	5	0
Eperlans frits.................................		
Barbue.......................................		
Turbotin.....................................		
Matelote de carpe et d'anguille.................	2	0
Tronçon d'anguille à la tartare.................	1	10
Carpe frite, la moitié..........................	2	0
Perche du Rhin à la Vallesfiche.................		
Goujons frits.................................	1	5
Truite au bleu................................		
Laitance de carpe..............................		
Moules à la poulette..........................	1	5

	fr.	s.
Homard	3	0
Esturgeon	2	10

RÔTS.

	fr.	s.
Bécasse		
3 Mauviettes		
Poularde fine 9fr. la moitié	4	10
Poulet Normand, 7fr. la moitié	3	10
Poulet gras, 6fr. la moitié	3	0
1 Pigeon de volière	2	10
Perdreau rouge		
Perdreau gris	3	10
Caneton de Rouen		
Caille	2	0
Agneau		
Veau	1	0
Mouton		
Levreau		
Grive		
Obergine	1	10

ENTREMETS.

	fr.	s.
Gelée de citron	1	10
Concombres à la Béchamel	1	10
Laitues a jus	1	10
Petits pois à la Française ou à l'Anglaise	1	10
Haricots verts à la poulette ou à l'Anglaise	1	10
Haricots blancs à la maître-d'hôtel	0	18
Fèves de marais	1	10
Artichaud à la sauce	1	10
Artichaud à la barigoul	1	10
Artichaud frit	1	5
Truffes au vin de Champagne		
Truffes à l'Italienne		
Croûte aux truffes		
Navets	0	18

	fr.	s.
Carottes	0	18
Epinards au jus	0	18
Chicorée au jus	1	5
Céleri au jus		
Choux-fleurs à la sauce ou au parmesan	1	10
Macédoine de légumes	1	5
Pommes de terre à la maitre-d'hôtel	0	18
Champignons à la Bordelaise	1	4
Croûtes aux champignons	1	10
Œufs brouillés au jus	0	15
Œufs au beurre noir	1	0
Omelette aux fines herbes	0	15
Omelette aux rognons ou au jambon	1	0
Omelette au sucre ou aux confitures	1	5
Omelette soufflée	1	10
Beignets de pommes	1	10
Charlotte de pommes	1	10
Charlotte aux confitures	2	0
Riz soufflé	1	10
Soufflé aux pommes de terre	1	10
Le petit pôt de crême	0	10
Macaroni d'Italie au parmesan	1	5
Fondu	1	4
Plumpuding	1	10
Ecrevisses	2	0
Salade	1	0

DESSERT.

	fr.	s.		fr.	s.
Cerneaux	0	15	Pêche	0	12
Raisins	1	5	Prunes	0	3
Fraises			Figue	0	5
Cerises			Amandes	0	15
Groseilles			Noisettes	0	12
Framboises			Pommes à la Portugaise		
Abricot	0	8	Poires	0	8

	fr.	s.		fr.	s.
Pomme................			Marmelade d'abricots	1	10
Compote de verjus épépine.......			Gelée de groseilles..	1	4
			Biscuit à la crême...	1	8
Compote d'épine-vinette........			Fromage à la crême..	1	10
			Fromage de Roquefort	0	10
Compote de poires..	1	4	Fromage de Viry....	0	15
Compote de pommes			Fromage de Gruyère.	0	8
Compote de cerises..	1	4	——— de Neufchâtel.	0	5
Nix Vert........	0	10	Fromage de Clochestre ou Chester	0	10
Meringue..........	0	8			
Compote de groseilles	1	4	Cerises à l'eau-de-vie	0	12
Compote d'abricot...	1	4	Prunes à l'eau-de-vie	0	12
Compote de pêche..	1	4	Abricots à l'eau-de-vie		
Confitures..........	1	4	Pêches à l'eau-de-vie		
Cerises liquides.....	1	4			

VINS.

	fr.	s.		fr.	s.
Clarette...........	6	0	Vin de Silery blanc..	6	0
Vin de Bourgogne..	1	15	Vin de Pierri......	5	0
Vin de Chablis....	2	0	Vin d'Aï..........	5	0
Vin de Beaune....	2	5	Vin de Porto......	6	0
Vin de Mulsaux....	3	0	Latour............	6	0
Vin de Montrachet..	3	10	Vin de Côte-Rôtie..	5	0
Vin de Pomard....	3	10	Vin du Clos Vougeot de 88.........	7	4
Vin de Volnay......	3	10			
Vin de Nuits......	3	10	Clos St. Georges....	6	0
Vin de Grave......	5	0	Vin de Pomarel....	6	0
Vin de Soterne....	5	0	Vin du Rhin.......	8	0
Vin de Champagne mousseux	5	0	Vin de Chambertin..	5	0
			Vin de l'Hermitage rouge.........	5	0
Vin de champagne, mousseux......	4	0			
			Vin de l'Hermitage blanc.........	6	0
Tisane de Champagne	3	10			
Vin de Rosé........	5	0	Vin de la Romanée..	5	0
Vin de Silery rouge..	6	0	Romanée Conti.....	8	0

			fr.	s.				fr.	s.
Vin de Richebourg..			5	0	Vin de Bordeaux Lafite			5	0
Chevalier montrachet			6	0	Vin de Saint Emilion			5	0
Vin de Vône........			5	0	Bierre forte ou porter.			2	0
Vin de Bordeaux de Ségur.........			5	0	Bierre.............			0	10

VINS DE LIQUEURS.

				Vermoulth.........		
Vin de Chereste, demi-bouteille..	4	0		Chipre............		
Vin de Malvoisie, *idem*	4	0		Calabre...........		
Madère sec *id*.......	4	0		Paille.............		
Malaga............	3	0		Palme............		
Alicante *id*........	3	0		Constance........		
Muscat............	3	0		Tokai............		
Le petit verre......	0	10		Le petit verre......	1	0

LIQUEURS.

Anisette d'Hollande..	0	15		Liqueurs des Isles..	0	15
Anisette de Bordeaux	0	12		Marasquin.........	0	15
Eau-de-vie d'Andaye	0	10		Eau-de-vie de Dantzick..........	0	15
Fleur d'Orange......	0	10				
Cuirasseau.........	0	10		Eau-de-vie de Coignac	0	8
Rhum.............	0	10		Casé, la tasse 12s. la demie.........	0	8
Kirschewaser.......	0	10				
Eau Cordiale de Coradon..........	0	15		Glace............	0	15

One advantage, well deserving of notice, of this bill of fare with the price annexed to each article, is, that, when you have made up your mind as to what you wish to have for dinner, you have it in your power, before you give the order, to ascertain the expense. But, though you see the price of each dish, you see not the dish itself; and when it comes on the table, you may, perhaps, be astonished to find that a pompous, big-sounding name sometimes produces only a scrap of scarcely three mouthfuls. It is the mountain in labour delivered of a mouse.

However, if you are not a man of extraordinary appetite, you may, for the sum of nine or ten francs, appease your hunger, drink your bottle of Champagne or Burgundy, and, besides, assist digestion by a dish of coffee and a glass of liqueur. Should you like to partake of two different sorts of wine, you may order them, and drink at pleasure of both; if you do not reduce the contents below the moiety, you pay only for the half bottle. A necessary piece of advice to you as a stranger, is, that, while you are dispatching your first dish, you should take care to order your second, and so on in progression to the end of the chapter: otherwise, for want of this precaution, when the company is very numerous, you may, probably, have to wait some little time between the acts, before you are served.

This is no trifling consideration, if you purpose, after dinner, to visit one of the principal theatres: for, if a new or favourite piece be announced, the house is full, long before the raising of the curtain; and you not only find no room at the theatre to which you first repair; but, in all probability, this disappointment will follow you to every other for that evening.

Nevertheless, ten or fifteen minutes are sufficient for the most dainty or troublesome dish to undergo its final preparation, and in that time you will have it smoking on the table. Those which admit of being completely prepared beforehand, are in a constant state of readiness, and require only to be set over the fire to be warmed. Each cook has a distinct branch to attend to in the kitchen, and the call of a particular waiter to answer, as each waiter has a distinct number of tables, and the orders of particular guests to obey in the dining-rooms. In spite of the confused noise arising from the gabble of so many tongues, there being probably eighty or a hundred persons calling for different articles, many of whom are hasty and impatient, such is the habitual good order observed, that seldom does any mistake occur; the louder the vociferations of the hungry guests, the greater the diligence of the alert waiters. Should any article, when served, happen not to suit your taste, it is taken back and changed without the slightest murmur.

The difference between the establishments of the fashionable *restaurateurs* before the revolution, and those in vogue at the present day, is, that their profession presenting many candidates for public favour, they are under the continual necessity of employing every resource of art to attract customers, and secure a continuance of them. The commodiousness and elegance of their rooms, the savouriness of their cooking, the quality of their wines, the promptitude of their attendants, all are minutely criticized; and, if they study their own interest, they must neglect nothing to flatter the eyes and palate. In fact, how do they know that some of their epicurean guests may not have been of their own fraternity, and once figured in a great French family as *chef de cuisine?*

Of course, with all this increase of luxury, you must expect an increase of expense: but if you do not now dine here at so reasonable a rate as formerly, at least you are sumptuously served for your money. If you wish to dine frugally, there are numbers of *restaurateurs*, where you may be decently served with *potage, bouilli,* an *entrée,* an *entremet,* bread and desert, for the moderate sum of from twenty-six to thirty *sous.* The addresses of these cheap eating-houses, if they are not put into your hand in the street, will present themselves to your eye, at the corner of almost every wall in Paris. Indeed, all things considered, I am of opinion that the difference in the expense of a dinner at a *restaurateur's* at present, and what it was ten or eleven years ago, is not more than in the due proportion of the increased price of provisions, house-rent, and taxes.

The difference the most worthy of remark in these rendezvous of good cheer, unquestionably consists in the company who frequent them. In former times, the dining-rooms of the fashionable *restaurateurs* were chiefly resorted to by young men of good character and connexions, just entering into life, superannuated officers and batchelors in easy circumstances, foreigners on their travels, &c. At this day, these are, in a great measure, succeeded by stock-jobbers, contractors, fortunate speculators, and professed gamblers. In defiance of the old proverb, " *le ventre est le plus grand de tous nos ennemis,*" guttling and guzzling is the rage of these upstarts. It is by no means uncommon to see many of them begin their dinner by swallowing six or seven dozen of oysters and a bottle of white wine, by way of laying a foundation for a *potage en tortue* and eight or ten other rich dishes. Such are the modern parvenus, whose craving appetites, in eating and drinking, as in every thing else, are not easily satiated.

It would be almost superfluous to mention, that where rich rogues abound, luxurious courtesans are at no great distance, were it not for the sake of remarking that the former often regale the latter at the *restaurateurs*, especially at those houses which afford the convenience of snug, little rooms, called *cabinets particuliers*. Here, two persons, who have any secret affairs to settle, enjoy all possible privacy; for even the waiter never has the imprudence to enter without being called. In these asylums, Love arranges under his laws many individuals not suspected of sacrificing at the shrine of that wonder-working deity. Prudes, whose virtue is the universal boast, and whose austerity drives thousands of beaux to despair, sometimes make themselves amends for the reserve which they are obliged to affect in public, by indulging in a private *tête-à-tête* in these mysterious recesses. In them too, young lovers frequently interchange the first declarations of eternal affection; to them many a husband owes the happiness of paternity; and without them the gay wife might, perhaps, be at a loss to deceive her jealous Argus, and find an opportunity of lending an attentive ear to the rapturous addresses of her aspiring gallant.

What establishment then can be more convenient than that of a *restaurateur?* But you would be mistaken, were you to look for *cabinets particuliers* at every house of this denomination. Here, at BEAUVILLIERS', for instance, you will find no such accommodation, though if you dislike dining in public, you may have a private room proportioned to the number of a respectable party: or, should you be sitting at home, and just before the hour of dinner, two or three friends call in unexpectedly, if you wish to enjoy their company in a quiet, sociable manner, you have only to dispatch your *valet de place* to BEAUVILLIERS' or to the nearest *restaurateur* of repute, for the bill of fare, and at the same time desire him to bring table-linen, knives, silver forks, spoons, and all other necessary appurtenances. While he is laying the cloth, you fix on your dinner, and, in little more than a quarter of an hour, you have one or two elegant courses, dressed in a capital style, set out on the table. As for wine, if you find it cheaper, you can procure that article from some respectable wine-merchant in the neighbourhood. In order to save trouble, many single persons, and even small families now scarcely ever cook at home; but either dine at a *restaurateur's*, or have their dinners constantly furnished from one of these sources of culinary perfection.

But, while I am relating to you the advantages of these establishments, time flies apace: 'tis six o'clock.—If you are not disposed to drink more wine, let us have some coffee and our bill,

When you want to pay, you say: " *Garçon, la carte payante!*" The waiter instantly flies to a person, appointed for that purpose, to whom he dictates your reckoning. On consulting your stomach, should you doubt what you have consumed, you have only to call in the aid of your memory, and you will be perfectly satisfied that you have not been charged with a single article too much or too little.

Remark that portly man, so respectful in his demeanour. It is BEAUVILLIERS, the master of the house: this is his most busy hour, and he will now make a tour to inquire at the different tables, if his guests are all served according to their wishes. He will then, like an able general, take a central station, whence he can command a view of all his dispositions. The person, apparently next in consequence to himself, and who seems to have his mind absorbed in other objects, is the butler: his thoughts are, with the wine under his care, in the cellar.

Observe the cleanly attention of the waiters, neatly habited in close-bodied vests, with white aprons before them: watch the quickness of their motions, and you will be convinced that no scouts of a camp could be more *on the alert*. An establishment, so extremely well conducted, excites admiration. Every spring of the machine duly performs its office; and the regularity of the whole might serve as a model for the administration of an extensive State. Repair then, ye modern Machiavels, to N° 1243, *Rue de la Loi*; and, while you are gratifying your palate, imbibe instruction from BEAUVILLIERS.

END OF THE FIRST VOLUME.

C. and R. Baldwin, Printers,
New Bridge-street, London.

www.ingramcontent.com/pod-product-compliance
Lightning Source LLC
Chambersburg PA
CBHW051137230426
43670CB00007B/848